VALLEY OF GIANTS

VALLEY OF GIANTS

STORIES FROM WOMEN AT THE HEART OF YOSEMITE CLIMBING

edited by Lauren DeLaunay Miller

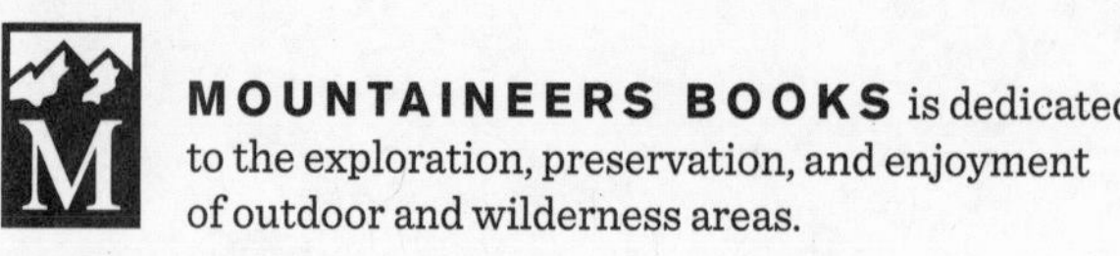

1001 SW Klickitat Way, Suite 201, Seattle, WA 98134
800-553-4453, www.mountaineersbooks.org

Printed in Canada
Distributed in the United Kingdom by Cordee, www.cordee.co.uk

25 24 23 22   1 2 3 4 5

Copyeditor: Lorraine Anderson
Design and layout: Jen Grable
Cartographer: Lohnes+Wright
Cover illustration: Rhiannon Klee Williams
Credits and permissions continued in Sources.

Library of Congress Cataloging-in-Publication Data is on file for this title at https://lccn.loc.gov/2021043131.

Mountaineers Books titles may be purchased for corporate, educational, or other promotional sales, and our authors are available for a wide range of events. For information on special discounts or booking an author, contact our customer service at 800-553-4453 or mbooks@mountaineersbooks.org.

Printed on 100% recycled and FSC-certified materials

ISBN (paperback): 978-1-68051-514-5

An independent nonprofit publisher since 1960

“It goes, boys.”

—Lynn Hill, after her first free
ascent of the *Nose* of El Capitan

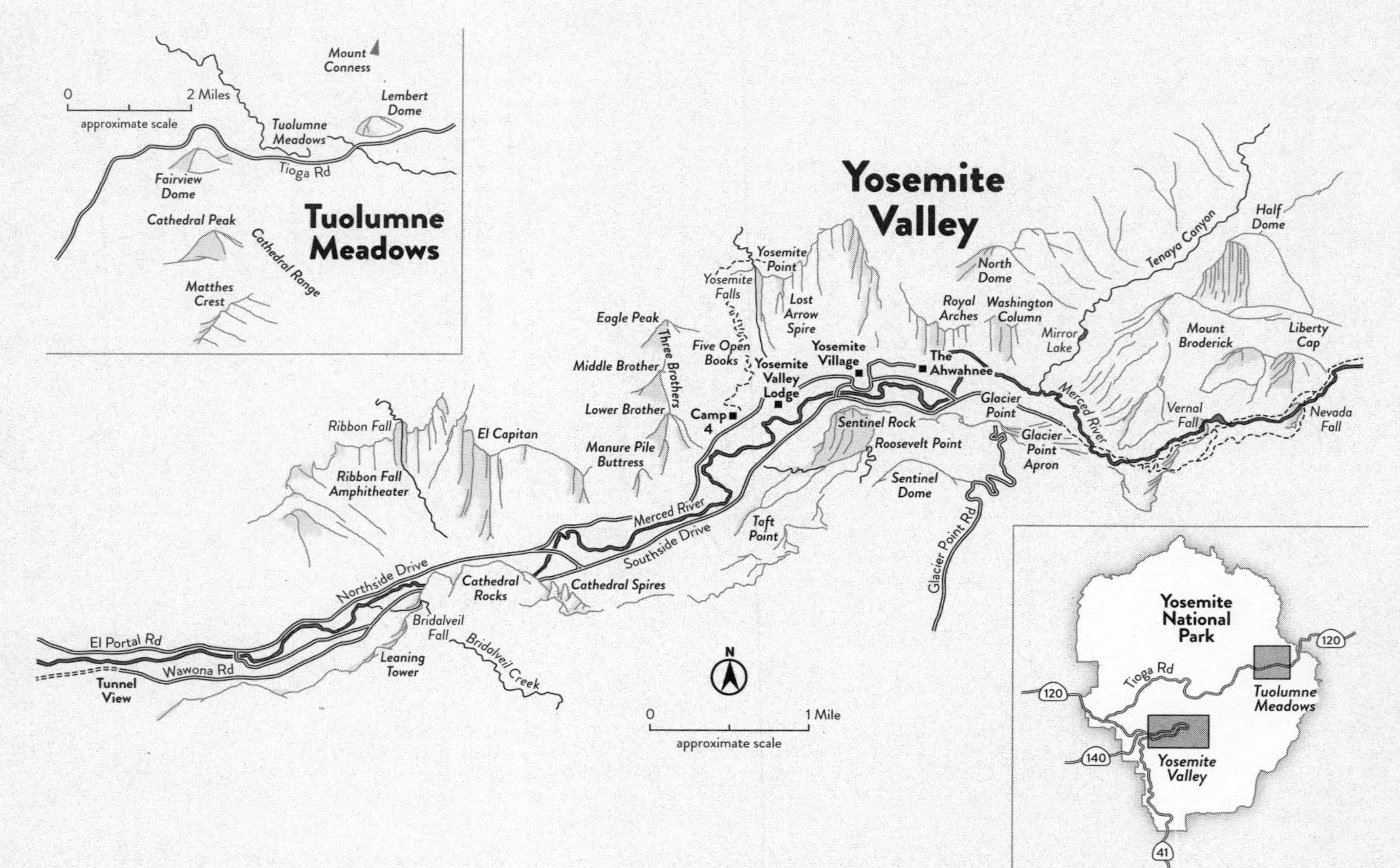
Tuolumne Meadows
0
2 Miles
approximate scale
Mount Conness
Lembert Dome
Tuolumne Meadows
Tioga Rd
Fairview Dome
Cathedral Peak
Cathedral Range
Matthes Crest
Yosemite Valley
Half Dome
Tenaya Canyon
North Dome
Yosemite Point
Yosemite Falls
Lost Arrow Spire
Royal Arches
Washington Column
Mirror Lake
Mount Broderick
Liberty Cap
Eagle Peak
Three Brothers
Middle Brother
Lower Brother
Manure Pile Buttress
Five Open Books
Yosemite Village
Yosemite Valley Lodge
Camp 4
The Ahwahnee
Glacier Point
Glacier Point Apron
Merced River
Vernal Fall
Nevada Fall
Sentinel Rock
Roosevelt Point
Sentinel Dome
Glacier Point Rd
Taft Point
Ribbon Fall
Ribbon Fall Amphitheater
El Capitan
Northside Drive
Southside Drive
Cathedral Rocks
Cathedral Spires
El Portal Rd
Wawona Rd
Tunnel View
Bridalveil Fall
Bridalveil Creek
Leaning Tower
N
0
1 Mile
approximate scale
Yosemite National Park
Tioga Rd
120
120
140
41
Tuolumne Meadows
Yosemite Valley

CONTENTS

DANCING IN THE SKY, 1990–2010

ON THE SHOULDERS OF GIANTS, 2011–PRESENT

FOREWORD

Mari Gingery

Yosemite Valley is one of the most iconic climbing areas in the rock universe, a granite crucible for aficionados of the steep for nearly a century. Notably, the volumes of stories that have been told around campfires and in climbing literature, of epics and adventures by uncountable numbers of aspirants scaling its walls, are almost all tales recounting the experiences of men.

While female climbers were relatively scarce in the Yosemite climbing population through most of the last century, women have been drawn to the Valley since technical rock climbing there began. Women have engaged with every genre of ascent the Valley offers, from bouldering to big walls. They have teamed up with men and with other women, and have climbed solo. Although their climbs were typically unsung, they were not unaccomplished. Starting with early forays on major rock formations, moving on to repeats of coveted Valley classics, and most recently doing pioneering modern free climbs, women in every generation have been drawn to Yosemite and absorbed into the climbing culture, and have lived keen adventures on the Valley cliffs.

In the new millennium, a burst of interest in climbing caused an unprecedented surge in the number of female climbers worldwide. Many women in this wave engaged with Yosemite's ageless vertical terrain and pulled off a plethora of climbing escapades. Some of these women found storytelling voices, but the diverse experiences of this entire succession of climbers are sparsely chronicled in climbing literature.

My own climbing experiences in Yosemite began in the late 1970s, an era when big-wall climbing techniques were being refined; strict, minimalist free-climbing ideals were beginning to be challenged by more lenient approaches; and new equipment (spring-loaded crack protection, portable sleeping platforms, and such) was being invented to accommodate the terrain. Bouldering was an esoteric specialty viewed mainly as training for "real" climbing. Women were a small but quite noticeable presence in the male-dominated climbing community and typically had unconventional, strong personalities. Climbing teams made up exclusively of women were rare and attracted attention as curiosities, due in part to an underlying sense that they were less capable of enduring the physical and mental demands of climbing and more likely to falter. Since then, the demographics of climbing have shifted seismically, and these days there are many skilled female climbers. Women have repeatedly and convincingly shown their prowess on rock, including establishing difficult climbs that remained unrepeated for many years. That women can climb proficiently is now evident, and any doubts have been put to rest.

Narratives by women offer fresh perspectives on the aspirations, situations, and resolutions encountered in rock climbing. While chasing the basic goal of ascent, they often differ in their motivations, their approaches to the climbing life, and their perceptions of the climbing experience. Climbing stories told by women illuminate climbing and the games climbers play in a different light, with a voice that is distinctly different from the typical tale of Valley exploits.

The accounts in this anthology trace an evolving spectrum of climbing styles over decades of experiences on Yosemite's rock faces, from the raw, exuberant recreation of Ruth Dyar Mendenhall on Washington Column in the 1930s to the polished skills and laser-focused determination of Babsi Zangerl on El Capitan more than eighty years later. The stories feature a medley of intrepid female characters from different generations, all of whom matriculated at the demanding School of Yosemite Granite. The tales of these women's exploits fill a gap in Yosemite climbing lore and add another layer to the richness of its climbing literature.

Mari Gingery was born on the East Coast, and her military family moved often before settling in the foothills near Los Angeles when Mari was six years old. She was introduced to climbing at the age of sixteen at Williamson Rock and continued to learn from the Stonemasters and other mentors at Tahquitz and Suicide Rocks, Joshua Tree, and Yosemite. She spent many summer vacations climbing walls in the Valley and Tuolumne, and was part of the first all-female ascent of the *Shield* on El Capitan with Lynn Hill (a story Lynn tells in her contribution to this book).

During her career as a university scientist and dedicated weekend climber, she climbed extensively in the Needles and on Clark Mountain in Southern California, with frequent trips to crags all over the country. In 1993, she wrote the first guidebook to bouldering in Joshua Tree. Mari is retired and lives in Joshua Tree with her longtime partner, Mike Lechlinski, and their cat, Cali.

PREFACE

The whispers of the natural world around me—the familiar caw of a raven, the knock-knock of a downy woodpecker, and, if I listened closely, the rustling of leaves caused by a buck sniffing for acorns—would no doubt delight me, if I could hear them over the tapping of my fingers on this keyboard. How fitting that I'm writing this reflection in the place that has, in so many ways, become the center of my universe. Camp 4, Yosemite National Park's campground for climbers, is quiet in the wake of a global pandemic, except for our eight-person search and rescue team nestled behind a number of empty campsites. For more than seventy years, this campground has hosted Yosemite's vertically minded, all of them inspired by the seas of granite that surround us.

I started climbing ten years ago in a small gym at the University of North Carolina. Chapel Hill is not exactly a mountain town. Waiting in the doctor's office one day, I picked up an issue of *National Geographic*, the cover displaying a lone climber on Half Dome. I didn't even know where Yosemite was, but my imagination soared.

The more I climbed, the more obsessed I became with Yosemite, and I fueled my interest through literature. I subscribed to all the climbing magazines and searched fanatically for memoirs about life as a big-wall climber. I felt so far away from my dreams, but reading those stories brought me closer. Reading books like Steph Davis's *High Infatuation* made big-wall climbing seem like not just a cool thing that *someone* could do but a cool thing that *I* could do. Gawking at the photos of my heroes way up on El Capitan, I imagined myself there and wondered what the ground would look like from 3,000 feet up.

Within days of graduating from college, I was on a plane heading north. The last frontier, Alaska, beckoned with its endless sources of adventure, and from there my life as a nomad began. I worked as a cruise ship guide, a ski lodge clerk, a barista, and a climbing instructor; I slept in shacks, parking lots, campgrounds, and parks. I ventured all around the great American

West, living a life that my parents, bound to the East Coast, could never quite wrap their heads around. But there was still one more place to go.

The first time I entered Yosemite it was dark. My climbing partner and I had driven all day from Colorado, where we'd been working that summer, to California and arrived in the Valley at three in the morning. We couldn't see a thing, but we could sense the walls' towering presence. We checked into Camp 4 after sleeping in line, waiting for one of a few coveted spots, then drove a few miles west, finally laying eyes on that rock that had been holding my imagination hostage for years: El Capitan. Most people cannot comprehend the scale of El Cap at first glance. They see Middle Cathedral Rock directly across the valley, and their unaccustomed eyes tell them that these rocks are equal in size. It is not until they spot a climber on one of the steep, smooth walls of El Cap—or, more realistically, a small speck that they are told is, indeed, a climber—that they step back in awe. The biggest granite monolith in the world, El Cap may not be as famous to tourists as the blank northwest face of Half Dome, but to climbers it is everything.

The Sierra Nevada, a mountain range that runs north–south throughout much of the eastern portion of California, has a long, storied history of mountain scrambling, but people didn't start climbing with ropes in Yosemite Valley until the 1930s. Members of outing groups like the Stanford Alpine Club and the Sierra Club adopted these European tactics to make quick work of Yosemite's walls. Popular climbs emerged on the Valley's obvious summits: the Cathedral Spires, Lost Brother, and Lost Arrow Spire among them. For two decades, no one even considered that El Cap would one day be climbed.

In fact, climbing El Cap was widely accepted as impossible. But by the time I first set foot in this hallowed park, women had climbed El Capitan in less than five hours. Women had established the Valley's hardest single-pitch route and had made the first free ascent of the *Nose,* El Cap's most popular route. I was surrounded by inspiring women and surprised that I hadn't heard more about them. The lore of Yosemite climbing history is plentiful, but its literature has been written largely by men. And while women usually make appearances in these texts, they are often a footnote, relegated to the roles of belayer or girlfriend. Steve Roper, in *Camp 4,* his widely read memoir of life in Yosemite first published in 1994, wrote: "Wives and girlfriends tried climbing of course, but they usually did it because their men were doing it—not for any particular love of the sport."

I eventually made my way onto the Yosemite Valley search and rescue team, where stories of the women who came before us abounded. Intrigued, I started to dig. The climbers around me shared legends they had heard, and my list of notable female climbers—the list that would eventually become this book's table of contents—grew and grew. The connecting threads became more apparent every day. Tracking down a climber for "the list," I always asked, "Who else should I talk to?" More names would be added, and on we went.

Now you hold in your hands the latest version of this list. I encourage you to think of this collection as *some* of the women at the center of Yosemite climbing, not a definitive tally. There are surely dozens of women who deserve inclusion in this text but who for one reason or another—be it deadlines, lack of interest, or death—are missing from these pages. Additionally, it is unfortunately obvious as you flip through these words and photos that this book is largely a white women's history of climbing. Rock climbing has long been an exclusive sport, and our country's national parks have not been as welcoming to people of color as they have been to white folks. Our sport's diversity issue has been at the forefront of discussion recently, but, my fellow climbers, we have a long way to go.

The stories in this book take place in Ahwahnee, the ancestral and present-day home of eight traditionally associated tribes: American Indian Council of Mariposa County, Southern Sierra Miwuk Nation, Bishop Paiute Tribe, Bridgeport Indian Colony, Mono Lake Kutzadika'a, North Fork Rancheria of Mono Indians of California, Picayune Rancheria of the Chukchansi Indians, and Tuolumne Band of Me-Wuk Indians. The many tribes that have called Yosemite home for millennia were systematically removed, creating a false sense of humanless wilderness. The California Gold Rush of 1849 first brought white miners to the Sierra Nevada, and a state-sponsored militia known as the Mariposa Battalion arrived in 1851 to expel Indigenous people from Yosemite. Though the militia was unsuccessful in driving all Native people onto a reservation, 90 percent of Indigenous inhabitants were dead or missing by 1910, and life was forever changed for those who remained.

So what, then, is the point of all this? Representation matters. Studies show that nearly two-thirds of American women cannot name a single outdoor female role model, and while I sit here as one of two women on an eight-person search and rescue team, I see how deeply this representation shapes our reality. Truthfully, I've always felt welcome in this wondrous valley and its surrounding high country. The mountains and walls do not care who we are, but they demand that we bring the very best of ourselves to our every interaction with them. That is why I began climbing, and that is what I hope to instill into the future generations of climbers, adventurers, and dreamers who may read the stories in this book.

These stories span the full range of human emotion, from heartbreaking losses to soaring joys and everything in between. If you've been to Yosemite and been lucky enough to swim, even momentarily, in its seas of granite, you may recognize the names and places described in these pages. If you haven't yet set foot in this sliver of the mighty Sierra Nevada, may these stories inspire and tantalize you. Most of all, may they demonstrate that women have always been at the center of Yosemite climbing. Women have been scaling these walls since modern climbing began, crafting their own equipment, establishing new routes, and dancing with grace in the harshest of earthly environments. This book is not a re-creation of history but merely a reflection. Our foremothers have much to teach us, if only we stop and listen.

Lauren DeLaunay Miller
Yosemite Valley

LEARNING TO RISE

1930–1959

Deciding where to begin is always the first hurdle. The Sierra Nevada, including the area now known as Yosemite National Park, has a long and storied history of mountain exploration and what many today call scrambling, or climbing that is difficult enough to require the use of your hands and feet but typically done without any equipment to protect you in the event of a fall. The Indigenous peoples of California, in addition to generations of settlers, built a legacy of "peak bagging" that is still strong in the Sierra Nevada. But our story begins with what we now refer to as rock climbing, propelled by the introduction of ropes and pitons.

In the 1930s, American climbers began returning from European travels equipped with new knowledge and the gear to expand their climbing objectives. California climbers honed their skills in smaller areas like Indian Rock in Berkeley and Tahquitz and Suicide Rocks in Idyllwild before venturing to the cliffs of Yosemite. For many years, the biggest walls were deemed impossible, but there were many others with attainable heights. In this era, climbers were largely focused on establishing new routes on features that had yet to be climbed. Climbing clubs were gaining in popularity, and the Stanford Alpine Club and Sierra Club grew their memberships by hosting organized climbs and offering classes.

Women's involvement in climbing during this era started strong; early records of a number of climbing clubs indicate equal participation by male and female climbers. Historians have documented the rise in women's employment during World War II, a trend we see paralleled in climbing club participation. But, interestingly, the proportion of women on club rosters appears to have declined in the years following World War II. Perhaps the cultural shift toward domestication and family life is to blame.

But the women who did break through the cultural barriers were not content to sit on the sidelines of the sport. They participated in a number of early ascents and even contributed to the advancement of the sport by forging pitons, as you'll read about in the interview with Bea Vogel. These women no doubt paved the way for the countercultural movement that would embolden women of the subsequent period. And though they may have never met each other, they left a strong legacy of "manless" climbing that would continue to inspire women for generations to come.

PIONEER

Marjory Bridge Farquhar

This story is an excerpt from an interview conducted by Ann Lage in 1977 as part of the Sierra Club Oral History Project. It is printed here with considerable help from the Sierra Club's William E. Colby Library and the Bancroft Library at the University of California, Berkeley.

I'm a second-generation Californian. . . . My family always loved wilderness and country and the outdoors, and they became so fond of Marin County in California that my mother and father finally settled in Mill Valley. . . . But my father . . . liked the bay. He and my mother had a rowing club even before they were married, with these beautiful shell boats that they kept over by Tiburon, and a small group of people back in the nineties had this little rowing club. Then later on my father had a sailboat, and as my sister got older she would provide her friends as the crew, and my father always had beautiful weekend trips out on the bay. . . . It was during that process that I learned to climb the mast—shinny up the mast—because the river was such that we had these levees, and from a boat on the water you couldn't see over the levees to see what was growing. But if I got up the mast or climbed up on the sail rungs or rigging, I could look over, and if there was a big cornfield or a good fig orchard I'd let them know. Then we'd tie up to the bank and go ashore and make a deal with the farmer. So I started my climbing young, and apparently wasn't bothered by heights. . . .

You see, I was the youngest of four girls, and my father took the second girl and treated her more like a boy, and then he treated me more like a boy. I was a constant companion of my father's, and living in Mill Valley and loving the country as much as we did, I was with him constantly in and around nature and the country. Growing up in the country like that, why, we'd go swimming in the creek, and we would play around in the wilderness and climb the trees, so that I was used to the outdoors far more than I was accustomed to the city. . . . Mother might have objected, but Dad wouldn't listen to her. I remember she used to get quite provoked when he would have us help him move the furniture, and we always had to carry heavy bags, and we always had to help him do things. She didn't think it was particularly ladylike, but he said it was good for us, and I think he was quite right. It was. My mother did believe in having her daughters independent and individuals. We were never after a pattern at all; we were always allowed to develop our own initiative and our own resources, so that I think the combination of her giving us the freedom and my father's guidance, why, we just came along. . . .

In those days the Sierra Club had a four-week trip, and you could go for two or four. I went the first time for four and was just elated and thrilled with every experience that I had, so I think I went just as much as I could every year after. Harriet Parsons was going to go with me in 1929, and this other friend that had been at girls' camp too in 1918. But the friend got married, and Harriet wasn't well that summer and the doctor wouldn't let her go into the mountains at all. But she was awfully nice; she took me down to the railroad station—the Mole—and introduced me to everybody she could think of to give me a good start. That trip of course was in the days when you took the train at the Southern Pacific Mole and went down the San Joaquin Valley. We got off at Fresno. Then we got buses and went over and around and up to Florence Lake and then went across through Blaney Meadows. We started off on the trip from there and ended up at Tuolumne Meadows.

By that time I had become very good friends of Ansel's and Virginia's [Adams] and Cedric's and Rhea's [Wright] and that whole group on the trip. I never will forget having been out for a whole month—in those days Dan Tachet was a marvelous cook, but just the same you did get canned string beans and all kinds of canned things, and no milk. When a group of nine of us left Tuolumne Meadows to go down to the Valley, we stopped—I think it was at Little Yosemite—and Virginia phoned her father and figured out about what time we'd be back down, and she said, "Be sure and meet us with lots and lots of fresh milk!" It wasn't the ride from Happy Isles that was so appreciated as it was the fresh milk that we got from her father! . . .

I had never really climbed much in mountains until I went on the Sierra Club trip in 1929. That was my first experience of climbing mountains. I had taken a fishing rod along and thought I would fish, but the only time we used it was to get a pin or something that had fallen down between two rocks, and I undid the fishing rod and swept that out from Lake Ediza. Mountain climbing was so wonderful to me, and it was such an exhilarating sport that I was just thrilled to death when I was able to climb both Mount Ritter and Banner all in one day. Then Francis led a trip up Seven Gables, and that was the first. They announced at the campfire that anyone who wished to go the next morning could meet Francis at seven o'clock and go. I went, and that was the start of it. I just loved the climbing, and it was thrilling to go to the top and to see the beautiful views of the Sierra.

That was in 1929, and then I went on the High Trip in 1930, but that was right after the Depression and my recollection is that there were very few men on the trip. Now I don't know if I was looking for men or not, but there were very few, and so there were a group of us girls that got together and did a fair amount of climbing together. Carolyn Coleman was one of them, and I've forgotten now who the others were, but in 1930 I did climb Mount Hilgard and Mount Abbot, and I did climb Turret Peak with Jules Eichorn and Glen Dawson, and I did Darwin, and I know that I did Goddard with a hen party. I remember on the climb of Goddard a group of us women went off and knapsacked up out of Colby Meadow and stayed all night. Then we went over and climbed the north face of Goddard. We went over an awful lot of snow, and one of the girls on the trip just couldn't take it very well. Every step she made we sort of had to hold her feet so she wouldn't slip back, so it was quite a workout, but anyhow, we did it. Then I think that I had to go out at the end of three weeks; I had to be a bridesmaid at a friend's wedding, so I left when we got down to LeConte Meadow.

In 1930 Francis had gone up to Canada with the Harvard Mountaineering Club and climbed, and that was where he really got in on the technique of rope work properly. So when I went up on the Sierra Club trip in 1931, Jules Eichorn came and said that Francis Farquhar had just come back, and he was going to take a group up and show them how to use a rope—would I like to go? So of course I did! That was the time there were, I think, five boys and myself, the only girl, and Francis, and we climbed up the north face of Unicorn and had the rope lessons....

Back in 1931, when Francis taught them all, Bob Underhill came down for the last week or the last two weeks of the Sierra Club outing. Then they went down and made the first ascent of the east face of Mount Whitney, but they didn't invite me to go. My feelings were a little hurt, but anyway I wasn't invited. I don't know that I could have gone, but it would have been nice to say no. I didn't have a chance. I think it was after that that Dick [Leonard] got started with the Cragmont Climbing Club. We used to go out to Cragmont Park up here in Berkeley, and on the east side there's some marvelous—well, call them cliffs if you want—and we could practice climbing there. Then after we got organized with the Cragmont Climbing Club we petitioned the Sierra Club to become a Sierra Club section and became the Rock Climbing Section in 1932. We would schedule climbs every single Sunday. We had lots of fun scouting out places to climb; there was Cragmont Park, and there was the Pinnacle Rock, and there was Grizzly Rock—that wasn't too good—and Indian Rock, and then we would find other rocks all over wherever we could. I remember one time we went up to Napa and found some rocks up there to climb on, on Mount St. Helena. Of course we liked to do the rocks along the coast, but they're awfully bad rotten stuff, so you had to be very careful for that. Then sometimes we would go down to the Pinnacles and have a weekend, but usually we scheduled these rock climbs in San Francisco or around Berkeley and met every Sunday....

It started out where the club would accept no responsibility, but people had to follow the rules. The whole point was to teach people how to belay and how to catch a falling climber, and then the other person would practice climbs. We had all kinds of climbs there, and they were all numbered, and you would do one climb after another....

In looking over the records [of the Rock Climbing Section] today, I notice that there were a lot of [women involved].... I was the first woman up Higher Cathedral Spire, but Virginia Greever was the first woman up Lower Spire, and she was a very good climber. As you look through the records now, I see that there were a lot of women that went up. Of course Helen LeConte did a lot of climbing, and Harriet Parsons did a lot of climbing....

Francis brought in the rope, and then we had development with the pitons, and then a great discussion would come up—would you use pitons only for safety, or should you use them as direct aid? And then of course you'd hear, "Well, the British school doesn't believe in anything like that—you should have a natural climb." I believed in them for safety, but to tell you the honest truth, the last 12 feet of Higher Cathedral Spire was done by direct aid for a long time for everybody, and then finally they did get another route. Of course, part of the difficulty, I think, was that on the first number of climbs that were done—later it became called an easy day for a lady—but at first it was longer to do and harder to do because it was new, and there was the emotional thing, and there wasn't the time to work it out. Then when it became an easier climb, and more people were used to doing it, they got going earlier and they managed to find another route without the direct aid. I guess maybe that's more or less the only time that I've used direct aid, although I approve of the pitons for safety. Then of course, you're having trouble now when too many people's pitons get drilled in, you're defacing the cliffs, and even if you take them out, there's still to a certain extent the hole in the crack. Now the pendulum is swinging so they're beginning to try to do their climbing without the aids now—so, that's another phase of it. But, all the time that I was climbing, on the whole, it was for the sport of it and to see if you could master the proposition. . . .

Francis obviously met me in 1931, although I met him in 1929, and we were married in December of 1934. It was in October of 1934 that I climbed Higher Cathedral Spire, and lots of people said that Francis said he wouldn't marry me if I couldn't make it! Anyhow, I *did* make it, and we *were* married, so it was all right. . . .

I will admit that my active rock climbing days disappeared, really perhaps for two reasons: one because I went into the baby production business, and the other because of the war. Our first child, Peter, was born in 1938, and Suzanne came in 1940. . . . I always still climbed, but I didn't go back to rock climbing because if you're not in condition, the agility's gone, as far as I was concerned. We took the children on camping trips and always took them with the Sierra Club. We went back on the High Trips; each time a child was nine it was allowed to go on a High Trip, as far as our own were concerned. . . . I have climbed, but there's no rock climbing for me any more, unless I'm teaching a grandchild. I still do that. . . . Rock climbing is awfully good, in some respects—the physical exercise and the mental challenge—as long as it doesn't get to the point of trying to beat someone or show off. But if you get true enjoyment out of proving to yourself that you can do a thing and do it well and do it safely, I think it's very creditable.

Marjory Bridge Farquhar was born in 1903 in San Francisco, and after graduating from the University of California, Berkeley, in 1925, she began climbing with the Sierra Club. Marjory was part of a small group of Sierra Club climbers pioneering new technical routes in Yosemite and the Sierra Nevada after her soon-to-be husband, Francis Farquhar, brought Robert Underhill to California to teach new climbing techniques. In 1934, she became the first woman to climb Yosemite's Higher Cathedral Spire and soon after made the first female ascent of the east face of Mount Whitney.

A passionate photographer, Marjory remained active in the Sierra Club and the American Alpine Club most of her life, though her climbing career faded with the birth of her three children. She was known for her fierce wit along with her energetic contributions to American climbing and dedication to California conservation. Marjory died in 1999 at the age of ninety-five.

WASHINGTON COLUMN

Ruth Dyar Mendenhall

This letter from Ruth to her parents is from the collection *Woman on the Rocks: The Mountaineering Letters of Ruth Dyar Mendenhall.*

June 3, 1938
Dear Ma and Fa,

I guess I'd better start to write about our Yosemite trip. We did have so much fun. It should be recorded before I forget everything we did.

Art's car was a weird little ancient Ford with a rumble seat, a huge gas tank holding thirty-three gallons which he had installed in addition to the other tank, and a system of lighting like a General Electric model home. Art himself was as Art Johnson-ish as one could hope for. He wasn't much bigger than Marg—a little on the ape-like side, with hair sticking up in every direction through a green eye shade. He alternated between long silences and strange bursts of humor. We liked him in an impersonal sort of way. When Jim demanded a pun on "isthmus," Art replied, "If you wait long enough, Chr-isthmus will come." We became much more fond of Jim than we had been before. He was awfully nice to camp with, and his character seemed to take a turn for the better. He really loves the woods, is a competent woodsman, and frightfully cute.

Art and Jim took turns driving and riding in the rumble seat, so we took a long time getting anywhere. Had dinner in Fresno at a joint that gave very poor service. We were grumbling that they probably had to send out for all the food, and then found out that they really did send clear around the block for everything we ordered!

We went in the back road from Fresno, which is not only the shortest but the best way now, since the floods demolished the year-round highway. Got into the Valley around midnight, wandering around looking for the Sierra Club campground, number 12, found it, kicked pine needles into piles for mattresses, and went promptly to bed.

Quantities of people kept arriving all day Saturday. There were about five hundred Sierra Club people, a hundred and eighty from the south and the rest from around San Francisco. A lot of them ate in the central commissary, run by three cooks. We were glad we had our own grub. A lot of very funny looking people swaggered about in odd outing costumes with cups on their hips, who were the older Sierra Club people. However, they didn't hurt us any.

It rained a little that afternoon, and we found Art in camp with all our gear, under the tarp. Art was in a bad condition, as he had just got bitten by a rattlesnake! He said he had reached up and didn't see it; but we found out later (from strangers) that he was fooling around with it and trying to pick it up.

I had never seen a snake bite victim before, so found it quite interesting. It was a baby snake and got him in the finger with only one fang, or it might have been far more serious. As it was, his arm swelled all up clear to the shoulder, and he felt utterly lousy the rest of the trip. He refused to go and get a shot for it, as he claimed it would cost $10 and do no good. He spent most of the time lying in a stupor in his sleeping bag wearing an old dark red stocking cap. The first night he moaned and groaned for hours.

Sunday was my best day, and my first big rock-climb. I had been told by any number of good kindly souls that there wouldn't be any rock-climbing I could do, so when Glen Dawson himself appeared prepared to take some of us beginners up Washington Column to Lunch Ledge, quite a difficult climb, I was quite eager to go. Jim disapproved to the utmost, and even offered to take me on an easier climb, I guess so I wouldn't feel I couldn't go climbing anywhere. But I resolved to myself that if Mary Van Velzer and Sophie Rice could go, I certainly could. We started out at 8:00, I having hastily gathered together a foul little lunch of buttered pumpernickel, rye-crisp, and candy bars.

It was rather a weird expedition, totally different from anything I'd ever done before, and yet it came perfectly natural. There were eight of us going up in all. Washington Column is a huge perpendicular projection of cliff about 1,200 feet high. Lunch Ledge was about halfway up. We drove up to the woods at the foot of the cliff; climbed over granite talus for a few minutes through underbrush and swarms of nasty little mosquitoes; and finally roped together for the climb.

Homer Fuller and Sophie Rice went up on one rope. Sophie is a tall, very nice looking girl—one of the few girls who really look well, and at home, in outdoor clothes. Her brother Bill Rice is one of the outstanding rock-climbers. She doesn't know much about it and was rather scared, and I don't think she should have been allowed to go. Some guys, led by little Muir Dawson, went up on the second rope. And Glen, who is a very excellent rock climber, and very matter of fact and nice, led our rope. I was in the middle of the rope, and Mary Van, a little wench of whom I am very fond, on the end. I think there is about 40 feet of rope between each person. It is a very highly developed technique, and with a good leader, there is hardly any danger of getting hurt, as he gives you an "upper belay" and if you fall, you just fall on the rope and go your way. However, for myself, I didn't fall.

I could readily see where experience would help—at first the rope seems to get in the way so, for one thing; the theory of progression is that the leader climbs up first, belays the second man up, who belays the third man up, and on you go. Each stretch which you climb without stopping is a "pitch." The places we went! It is just as well that you can't see them. Never had I been in such places, and it was so weird to keep on climbing up and up, hour after hour. Of course it took us much longer than necessary, as we had so many people to wait for. While I was belaying Mary, Glen would usually give me an "anchor" from above, so we couldn't possibly have gotten hurt.

We climbed for about 3½ hours, going up and up; up perpendicular cracks with no handholds, that one mounted merely by sticking the toes of your tennis shoes in the crevice; up one weird place where one toe went in one crack and the other in another; up a sort of "chimney" climbed with back on one wall and knees on the other. I simply loved it! I think I ought to become a good rock climber in my time (said she modestly), if I could do that well with only two practice climbs at Eagle Rock to my credit. Of course, my whole life has been devoted more or less to that sort of thing. It was so wonderful to be way way up on the remote granite cliffs where almost no one ever gets—so far above the valley; it was a marvelous day, neither hot nor cold, sunny, breezy; little shrubs and trees and ferns and succulents grew way up on the cliff. It seemed so peaceful and far away.

About 12:30 we got to Lunch Ledge, and the great Glen Dawson shook my hand and said, "Congratulations on a good climb!" My, I felt so proud. He congratulated Mary and Sophie but did not tell them it was a good climb. And when we roped down, they had to be belayed down, they were so tired, and I did not. We stayed up there quite a while, eating our lunch and drinking water out of the thimble-sized cap on Glen's canteen. My candy bars were rather in poor condition, as water leaked on them, the pitons cut them up, and they got rather mashed in the knapsack going up the chimney. I forgot to say that in rock climbing etiquette, the leader doesn't have to carry anything, so Mary Van and I hauled up the knapsacks full of rope, jackets, carabiners, pitons, lunch, water, etc.

Then we roped down. It is the most wonderfully easy way of descending. It is so fine to know you don't have to climb down, as climbing down is harder than going up, as anyone knows. We came down in six or seven long rope-downs, most of them about 100 feet long. One is supposed to have a leather patch on his pants—and you certainly need it! However, those of us who didn't stuffed our jackets or sweaters into our pants and tied a knapsack over our shoulder for protection. The theory is that with the rope twined just so around your hips and shoulders, the friction lets you down gradually. The rope is fastened double through a piton or a "sling" of rope tied around a tree and can be pulled down after the last man.

And at the end of the next-to-last rope-down we had the most pleasant surprise! We found a body! All my life I have hankered after finding a corpse, and finally I helped find one. One of the fellows suddenly said, as we were sitting about on a sloping ledge drinking from the brook, "Here is an old shoe with some bones in it!" First we hardly believed it. Yet we looked—and it was: a weathered man's shoe, lying upside down, filled with human bones. For some reason, we were all immensely pleased. It didn't seem horrible, as it was so old and mossy and impersonal. We decided we ought not to disturb it, but go and report to the ranger. We felt sure there were more bones under the pile of gravel. Later the head ranger and some of the boys went and dug up the remains. They found more bones, though not the whole body, a camera case, a watch case, and various odds and ends. They do not know who it is, but figure it must be six or seven years since the person died. Probably he was carelessly climbing on the cliff, alone, in the wrong kind of shoes, and fell down. He could have easily remained unfound forever. We thought that was a sprightly close to a rock-climb, and maybe it was as well that we didn't find it before we started.

Monday morning we took a long time for breakfast. About 11:00, we got all the crud lashed in a scientific fashion on half the rumble seat and over the running boards. It was a hot day. In Bakersfield we had dinner. Then I took a turn at the rumble seat going over the ridge. It was windy, and nice and remote, and the sky was full of stars. Finally about 11:00 we got home, felt an earthquake (the first I ever felt) and went to bed.

I have been gosh-awful busy all week. I get busier instead of less so. It is fiendish. Today I have washed clothes and hair. Now I have to wash the dinner dishes.

Please write soon, and much love.
Ruth

Born in 1912 and raised in Spokane, Washington, Ruth Dyar Mendenhall developed the skills and courage from an early age that would contribute to her fifty-year climbing career. After moving to California in 1937 following her graduation from the University of Washington, she joined the Sierra Club and was soon introduced to climbing. Yosemite was to her, as it was to many, the perfect place to prepare and train on technical rock for subsequent adventures in the high peaks.

In the following years, Ruth climbed all twelve of California's 14,000-foot peaks and established numerous first ascents in the High Sierra. She served on the board of directors of the American Alpine Club, and with her husband, John, she traveled to the Canadian Rockies and across the American West, all while they raised two daughters. Ruth combined her love of journalism with that of the outdoors as the editor of *The Mugelnoos*, the Sierra

Club's Ski Mountaineers and Rock Climbing Sections newsletter, as well as numerous books. Letters to her family narrating her climbing adventures are collected in *Woman on the Rocks: The Mountaineering Letters of Ruth Dyar Mendenhall*, edited by her daughter Valerie Mendenhall Cohen and published in 2007. Ruth died in 1989 at the age of seventy-six.

"THAT SHOULD BE CHALLENGING ENOUGH"

Bea Vogel

This excerpt is from an interview John Rawlings conducted in 1997 as part of the Stanford Oral History Project.

John Rawlings: *Bea, you were a junior transfer?*

Bea Vogel: Yes, that's right, class of '52. I was only at Stanford four quarters. I grew up in Billings, Montana, and I had gone to prep school in Michigan, for the last two years of high school. That used up a lot of the family finances. Billings had a couple of colleges; one was Eastern Montana College, so I was there for two years and decided to go to Stanford but they couldn't accept me until the third quarter of the junior year. So I worked for one quarter and then took some more classes at Eastern the second quarter, then transferred out to Stanford in the spring. My parents placed a high value on education, and they felt Stanford was a better school than any of the state colleges, maybe some snob appeal too. I was interested in science and decided to study math at Stanford. . . .

JR: *Did you climb before coming to Stanford?*

BV: Yes, I was born climbing. I did a lot of tree climbing. I didn't know anything about rock climbing. Billings is in a valley that has a wonderful sandstone cliff running along the north side of it, with huge talus boulders. That was often the Sunday afternoon hike when we were very small, and we scrambled all over the house-sized boulders. I did a lot of bouldering when I was a child. They were sandstone and I learned a lot of friction climbing before I knew what friction climbing was. My father did a lot of unroped mountaineering in the Beartooths; I went along on a couple of those trips. He did most of his climbing before he got married, and then didn't do so much afterwards.

JR: *Once at Stanford, how did you get hooked up with the Alpine Club?*

BV: Well, at prep school (Kingswood School-Cranbrook), they encouraged women's sports and I was on the basketball team, and field-hockey was compulsory because it was a "lady-like" game; I thought it was pretty fierce myself. Kingswood School-Cranbrook (in Bloomfield Hills, north of Detroit) at that time had both a girls' and boys' school, quite separated, and they had a grade school, science institute, and a famous art institute. And I got out to Stanford and I was all excited because I was going to a big university and I'd always enjoyed running; I wanted to go out for track. I liked distance running. So I approached the woman who was head of the PE department and was told, "We don't have a track program for women because it's too hard on your bodies and might affect your child-bearing abilities." This was 1951. No basketball either; there was swimming but just between dorms—no between-school competitions. Even if there was golf it wouldn't have interested me. Well this wasn't any fun, I thought. And I somewhere had heard of the Alpine Club, and thought that should be challenging enough, so I went out right away with them.

In the club there was no prohibition of women becoming rope leaders; they just hadn't so far. I was an assertive person, and I just assumed that I could become a leader and demonstrated that I was capable of it. I started out as a novice and did a lot of climbing. I was strong but I wasn't reckless. I felt strongly about the teamwork, that I was responsible to the other members of the rope; didn't matter if I was a second or leader, every person is responsible for everybody else. And I suppose that attitude showed. It seems to me I was certified fall quarter 1952. In Yosemite I remember leading *Royal Arches* (seconded by Marian Steineke), *Arrowhead Spire*, and the *West Face* on Lower Brother, and there were some others. Dave Harrah was somewhat annoyed with the latter climb. It was with Marian, a strong second climber, and Mary Kay Pottinger. I led the whole climb barefoot, and fourth class (using just one fixed piton), and we did it in three and a half hours, which was a very fast time for a rope of three. There was one particularly long pitch where I had to ask Marian to go off belay so I would have enough rope to reach the belay spot. We rappelled down the south side.

JR: *It was that you climbed barefoot and didn't place protection that irked Harrah?*

BV: That, and we did it very fast. I think it was a matter of competition. We didn't set out to beat any records; it just worked out that way. If you don't put in pitons you can climb faster.

JR: *Betsy Crowder doubted your contention that women could climb on an equal basis with men.*

BV: Women have different skills; it's not a matter of strength (of course nowadays I don't know what it's a matter of given the incredible level of climbing both men and women do). Though I remember Virginia Stevens, a very slim woman, weighed about one hundred and fifteen pounds, and she could do more chin-ups than any of the guys. She was a very good climber too, particularly good in chimneys and stemming. I think a lot of it is a matter of attitude. Women are socialized differently. I grew up kind of wild. I climbed trees as young as three or four years old. It's something I always enjoyed doing, and my parents didn't get upset by it.

JR: *You broke the ice and other women were then certified as leaders too?*

BV: I don't recall now. I often climbed with other women as seconds. I did some all-woman climbs in the Tetons including the *CMC Route* on Mount Moran and the *Southwest Ridge* on Symmetry Spire. I did a day climb of the Grand [Teton] from Jenny Lake with George and John Mowat. We met Leigh Ortenburgher on the Lower Saddle waking up about 9:00 a.m. He loaned me a sweater because I hadn't brought enough clothing. We were on the summit by 1:00 p.m., and then down by sunset.

JR: *What about your time in Yosemite Valley?*

BV: I claim responsibility for starting Warren Harding up El Capitan in June '57. Warren was complaining about Royal Robbins finishing the *Regular Northwest Face* of Half Dome without him. He was pouting and moaning because he had been left out. Well I told him, "Oh Hell! There are lots of other walls. Why don't you do El Capitan," and standing in El Cap Meadow and pointing at a line, I said, "You can climb right up the South Buttress" (the *Nose*). And he looked at it and said, "Well, OK, maybe we can." But you know, he didn't give me credit for the inspiration in anything he wrote.

I lived in San Francisco after Stanford. I got married in '53 to Alex Horak and divorced in '56, and took up with rock climbers again. I climbed in Yosemite Valley with Bob Swift and Warren Harding. I met Harding through Swift. My first husband wasn't a climber but I met him through John Mowat. The swimmers all lived in the boathouse on Lake Lag. Horak came along to one of the Pinnacles climbs; that's where I met him.

JR: *What role did the club play in your life?*

BV: It was extremely important. It was a very interesting experience. It was eventually the kind of experience that people developed into Outward Bound–type programs. We were encouraged by other members to try things that often seemed beyond our limits and capabilities. We weren't told that there were limits on our ability or you can't do such-and-such, because you aren't strong enough, because you're a woman. There was a wonderful spirit of camaraderie and cooperation. We were told, "You can do it, you can do it," "Try this, try that." People learned skills even if they started off timid.

There was a wonderful spirit of camaraderie and cooperation. Novices were encouraged to do all kinds of physical things that also required mental strength, and it struck me how different all this was from normal expectations where the males would do their physical activities and there would be all this male-bonding rigmarole. I felt what there was in the Alpine Club was group bonding: shared experiences of perhaps a dangerous nature. Club members still get together for our sporadic reunions and pick up conversation started years ago as though it had been yesterday.

It was a revelation for both boys and girls that they could interact on the kind of footing that occurred in the club. And it was more than climbing. It was a close group. We would meet in the Old Union daily for lunch, we had a study table in the library, and after the library closed we would drink tea together in the Student Union. And when dorm food was inedible, we'd all go out to some local place and have dinner together. I don't know if this type of situation developed in other clubs; I didn't hang around with people outside of the club. There was still a kind of sorority mentality at Stanford even though there weren't sororities. I mean in the dorm there was the pressure to dress up, date, make an impression, play a role. In the club we were comfortable being ourselves.

JR: *What about the piton story?*

BV: I had always been interested in making things. I had a course in jewelry at Eastern and had always been interested in metal-working, and I had always used tools. And Maxine Steineke, who was studying physics, told me about the wonderful machine shop in the Engineering Department. I also knew Salathé [John Salathé, a pioneer of rock climbing in Yosemite] forged pitons, so I just signed up for metal shop, learned the procedures from the Scottish shop instructor, and went at it. I did well and after a while a lot of the engineering students would ask me how to perform some operation or the other because they knew I was paying attention all the time in class....

Bea Vogel was born in Billings, Montana, in 1930. Her lifelong affection for bugs drew her to the Stanford University biology program, where she quickly discovered a love for rock climbing as a member of the Stanford Alpine Club. She learned to forge her own pitons and was admired by her climbing partners as a strong, talented climber, integral to many early Yosemite ascents.

Bea later earned a master's in science from the University of Colorado and a PhD in biology from Yale University, specializing in spider science and amassing a large collection. She was a passionate artist and activist. In 1950, she helped build her family's cabin on East Rosebud Lake, Montana, where she enjoyed every summer until her passing in 2018 at the age of eighty-eight.

SEEING FARTHER

1960–1974

The Golden Age. And why shouldn't it be? The 1960s were revolutionary for American women. In a span of four years, the timeline of women's rights sped up dramatically. In 1960, the Food and Drug Administration approved the first commercially available birth control pill, and in 1963, President Kennedy signed the Equal Pay Act into law. Equipped with a pathway toward financial independence and the freedom to control reproduction, women were being enlightened by the ideals of second-wave feminism and the writings of women like Betty Friedan and Gloria Steinem.

At the same time, women were proving their independence in the world of Yosemite climbing. More than anything else, the Golden Age was the era of the big walls. After the first ascent of the *Nose* in 1958, which climbers worked on for years, half a dozen new routes went up on El Cap's most intimidating faces in the 1960s, and climbing gear was developed rapidly to keep up with the demands of Yosemite granite. Climbing disciplines began to merge as this generation of climbers found innovative ways to approach routes. Women as well as men were free climbing what they could, but before the introduction of modern climbing shoes and camming devices, climbers were still aid climbing many of Yosemite's largest walls. Clean climbing was starting to make its mark, with climbers encouraging one another to avoid damaging the rock by moving away from pitons and toward removable forms of protection as much as possible.

In the 1960s, the presence of women became more and more apparent in the Valley, but the early 1970s were really the pinnacle of women's own Golden Age. Liz Robbins became the first woman to climb the steep northwest face of Half Dome in 1967, and by 1971, women were taking on Yosemite's biggest wall: El Capitan. From that moment, there was no turning back.

TALES OF AN ORDINARY WOMAN

Chela Varrentzoff Kunasz

In 1959, I met George Atkinson, a math genius who at only sixteen was already studying at the University of California at Berkeley. He later ended up flunking out after discovering all that Berkeley had to offer, especially rock climbing and the hiking club, home at the time to Chuck Pratt, Charlie Raymond, Janie Taylor (then Royal Robbins's girlfriend), and many other pioneering climbers and cavers. George invited me, while I was still in high school in San Francisco, on a four-day Thanksgiving trip to Tahquitz Rock in Southern California. He helped me buy climbing shoes and taught me some knots, and we rappelled off the roof of my home for practice. When we actually arrived at Tahquitz, I was shocked and very scared to see the enormous size and verticality we were to climb, but a few days later, in the midst of the *Fingertip Traverse,* hundreds of feet up the face, I fell completely in love with climbing just as George had.

I had been a serious ballet student and a member of a young people's ballet troupe, Ballet Celeste, that performed in the San Francisco Bay Area. When I was fifteen I studied ballet with Kyra Nijinsky, daughter of the famous Vaslav Nijinsky. Vaslav taught Kyra, who taught me, specialized methods for attaining unusual balancing skills by activating the small muscles and connective tissue around one's spine. Because of her, I was primed to be interested in a sport that valued balance. With the addition of exposure, climbing felt like dancing in the sky. Shortly after the Tahquitz trip, I began practicing at Cragmont Rock in Berkeley with two high school friends, Diane and Sharon, and their new friend at San Francisco State, Frank Sacherer.

I also went to Indian Rock in Berkeley and met Sierra pioneers like Carl Weisner and Ed Roper (Steve Roper's father), who had me prusiking up ropes, rappelling, and catching falls. Carl, not a little guy, tested me once after I set up a belay for him, by jumping, unannounced, off the cliff on which I was sitting, having said I was "all set." I thought he would climb down and test me with an easy tug on the rope. Fortunately, I had gloves on and caught him, but my nylon parka fused where the rope ran over it. We had no nice belay hardware then. Soon after that, in the summer of 1961, I began running San Francisco hills to get in better shape at the suggestion of Bill Amborn and Chuck Pratt. Chuck had become a friend after he "borrowed" the first rope I bought and used it for his climb of the *Salathé Wall* on El Cap with Royal Robbins and Tom Frost. After the climb, he returned my extremely beat-up rope and recommended I trash it. Wanting to see Yosemite for myself, I got a ride on a Vespa all the way from Berkeley to the fabled Valley with grad student climber Howard Sturgis to begin my own Yosemite adventures. The wheel fell off just as we neared Camp 4.

Chuck Pratt had been feeling that the Sierra Club, with its aging (but long useful) structure of "Members of the Rock Climbing Section," or RCS, and "Certified Leaders," or CLs, was behind the times. So when he saw my application for the RCS, he suggested I go to Yosemite to climb with Bill Amborn and himself and get practice by setting up all the belays and rappels. Then, he said, "*We* will sign your forms even though we are *not* CLs." He was pretty famous by that time and commented, "We will see if they are sticking to their own rules or not. If they accept my signature certifying all your skills, we'll have blown their cover." So we did that, the three of us; the climb was probably Higher Spire, or maybe Middle Cathedral Rock. Chuck and Bill basked in the sunshine laughing while I put in anchors and set up belays and rappels. Chuck did sign my application. On the back side, he offered the Sierra Club officials an alternate "application form" for the "Yosemite Climbing Club," requiring first ascents of various exotic and challenging routes. And yes, my application was accepted, and I got into the

RCS in spite of their rule. Chuck and Bill enjoyed themselves. I was eighteen by then.

After enrolling as a student at UC Berkeley, I began climbing a lot with members of the hiking club there. Interest was growing as to who would first free climb the short pendulum section on *Coonyard Pinnacle,* a thinner slab 550 feet above Monday Morning Slab on Glacier Point Apron. Others had climbed the route, but none had done it *completely* free. It was a popular climb that attracted many of the best climbers of the day. Steve Roper's book *A Climber's Guide to Yosemite Valley* said that Frank Sacherer and Chuck Ostin did the first free ascent of *Coonyard,* but this could not be verified until, much later, registers in bad shape were recovered from the summit. The copied register indicated Sacherer and Howard Sturgis had done the first free ascent. But I, too, was on that climb in 1961, as was a fourth person. I clearly remember that after many tries, Howard Sturgis was the first to free climb the pendulum section. It is possible that the fourth person and I were not named in the register because we did not lead, or perhaps the entry was simply illegible.

During the period of great interest in *Coonyard,* I hiked up the approach with friends who planned to climb it. I had a worsening cold and decided not to climb that day. Enjoying the scenery near the base of Monday Morning Slab, I fell asleep in my sleeping bag but was rudely awakened and annoyed, as I thought one of my climbing buddies was teasing me by hauling me, deep down in my sleeping bag, through the brush. After shouting complaints to no avail, I pulled my head out and was shocked to see an equally shocked large black bear face within a paw swipe of mine. After we stared at each other a long, frozen minute, he/she finally lumbered off. I kept that sleeping bag for years as it had a lovely large set of teeth marks in the fabric, and I felt lucky that my feet had not been under them.

One day in the early '60s, Layton Kor rounded up anyone handy in Camp 4, especially relative beginners like me, for a fun and relaxing climbing "jaunt." Scrounged food was available, too, and I joined a motley crew as we roped up and rapidly climbed the first pitches of the *Royal Arches* climb, with Layton scurrying around us, giving climbing advice with a smile to any and all, himself completely unroped and off route, fooling around. That got me interested in doing the complete *Royal Arches* route. Howard Sturgis, my frequent climbing pal, was up for it. I was pretty young then and thought that since Howard was a much better and more experienced climber than I (and a male!), he would take care of me. Ha!

We started the climb with enthusiasm and speed. All went well until we came to the fabled Rotten Log, now long gone but in the day the scariest part of the climb, as it spanned a deep gap that had steep walls one would crash into should that log (which one could see daylight through) finally break apart. For years, however, climbers had successfully shinnied up the slanted tree trunk across the gap to the other side and finished the many remaining pitches. But Howard freaked out when he saw that log. I tried to encourage him, to no avail. I offered to lead it myself, but he was afraid that if the log broke when he was following, he would bash into the other wall. So we took three hours to complete our extremely uncool nailed aid route to get around the dreaded log, and we were way behind schedule, reaching the rim as the sun was getting low.

We hiked along the rim and started to climb and rappel down. But we did this too soon, missing the correct rappel route, and we ended up in the dark on the cliff with only some very small footholds and ledges and no clear next rappel. We were out of food and, more important, water. Howard was even more scared than I was. Then it got cold. We made a very small fire on an eight-inch ledge at shoulder level. When it was out, I tried to remove the remains and burnt my hand picking up a rock I didn't think would be warm. This would not be good for the next day's rappels. It was impossible to sleep; our future was totally uncertain. I was so thirsty that I kept reciting a new mantra: "Two lemon Cokes, a root beer, and an iced tea."

Next morning, we saw some ledges below us and did a few rappels off small trees and granite nubbins. After that, a next rappel seemed impossible. I saw a small ledge below, way off to one side, but it seemed likely that if one slipped attempting that rappel, the result would be a huge pendulum and a tiring, frightening prusik. Howard then curled up into a fetal position on our tiny ledge and said, "We're going to die here." I argued and said I would do the rappel first and try to secure the rope ends to the small tree on our goal ledge. He didn't like that idea. Then he said, "And besides, I don't want to do that rappel, secured rope or not, with my pack." I offered to do the rappel carrying both packs, and placed prusik loops on the rope in case I needed them. He said he would think about it. I began that angled rappel, moving slowly, and made it to the tree. It took me a half hour to persuade

Howard, now packless and with the ends of the rappel secure, to come on down, which he finally did. We were very lucky to find reasonable rappels to complete our retreat.

On the valley floor, some friends had gathered and were looking for us and considering a rescue but were happy to see us as we made our way down. Howard never climbed again after that day. And I made a huge leap for a girl born in the '40s not to ever again think that I could count on anyone to "take care of me" or "take me up a climb"—so *not* an issue for today's female climbers and pioneers of new routes.

But my confidence would soon get me into some trouble of my own. During a mid-1960s winter Yosemite climbing trip with Paul Kunasz and Tony Qamar, I took a 60-foot leader fall, getting off route on one of the new climbs near *Moby Dick* at the base of El Cap. The climb was hard for me, with a strenuous layback requiring hammering in nested bong pitons for protection. Smaller cracks didn't seem to exist. I really was off route. As that layback went on and on, I became too eager for it to end, and I stretched out, reaching for the top of the slab just enough to lose my counterforce. I popped off and immediately pulled my nested pitons. A one-inch Chouinard piton resisted at first, slowing my fall, but then it pulled out too. That day was the first time I had used a "swami cord" instead of just tying directly into the rope, and my fall seemed to take so long that I thought I had come untied and was going all the way down to the pine trees hundreds of feet below. Surprisingly, I felt very calm. Although I bounced off some ledges with the pitons on my slings making quite a clatter, I mostly fell free of any obstacles. My husband-to-be, Paul Kunasz, caught me, letting the rope run generously as I suddenly stopped. As I had climbed, I had traversed a ledge, trailing my rope behind a large pine tree. I fell on the other side of that, and the rope dug a deep groove in the tree's bark that greatly eased the final halt as I hung against a vertical wall. I had sprained my ankle, but we rappelled down under our own steam. I was lucky that although I'd grazed my head, I was okay, with no serious injury but with an unforgettable experience still commemorated by a scar on my hand.

In addition to not having harnesses in those days, we also did not have good climbing shoes with sticky rubber, jumars, helmets, or protection other than pitons and bolts. We went through soft iron Austrian pitons that would bend easily but not break, RURPs, and Ed Leeper's useful wavy pins. I realize that today many climbers have far more exciting experiences on much more significant climbs than I had, but I enjoy memories of my adventures that happened on the way to the achievements of today's women climbers.

In fact, when I began to climb in 1959, I heard tales of women who were well known and much more accomplished than I would ever be. A bit later, as the '70s arrived, I heard a *lot* about Bev Johnson, about whom much has been written. She was only four years younger than me and one of the most incredible climbers, pilots, skiers, adventurers, and filmmakers on the planet. My memories of her remind me how much things have changed since the '50s. As I was finishing a lead of *Mechanic's Route* at Tahquitz Rock in California, some guy shouted up that he thought I was the first female to lead that. I shouted back that Bev Johnson had just led the route the week before. Another male rejoined, "She's not a female." And, of course, that was because she was fantastic and that man couldn't accept that for a woman climber.

I left California for Colorado in 1969, and though I stopped climbing by 2006, I still feel like a climber. My hands sweat watching today's climbers, and I treasure all my memories while celebrating the inspiring history of women who climb.

Chela Varrentzoff Kunasz was born and raised in San Francisco, California. Her father, who had escaped the Soviet Union in 1933, took Chela mushroom foraging and hiking around Marin County, instilling in her a love of nature. When Chela enrolled at the University of California, Berkeley, she joined the hiking club and learned to climb, drawing on her experience in ballet to master the intricate balance the sport requires. Climbing in Yosemite in the 1960s, Chela was one of few women leading alongside her male counterparts.

Meanwhile, she earned both an undergraduate and a master's degree in mathematics and worked as an astrodynamics engineer and then as a computer specialist, eventually settling in Boulder, Colorado, with her husband, Paul. In retirement, Chela founded and now directs Friends of Tibetan Settlements in India after her heart was captured by the plight of Tibetan refugees in Asia and those she met in her community.

CRACKDOWN IN CAMP 4

Meredith Little

Someday in August 1963
Yosemite Valley

Dear Penny,

No one knows how decisive they are about it, but the rangers are at it again. Frank S. received a citation for "overdue camping" last Monday, and after pleading in vain with a commissioner of something and the park superintendent, he was still as firmly told, LEAVE. He said that they told him they didn't want climbers around here all year round anymore, because they are noisy, dirty, keep a messy camp, steal, clutter up the Lodge, etc. Frank replied that he and most of the others were not like this at all, and the good superintendent replied that he knew it was only 5% of all the climbers, but just the same, the rest will have to suffer. Frank seemed to think that they are very serious about enforcing the 10-day limit from now on, as the man kept referring to a large book, patting it gently, and saying, "it's in this book—a law, passed by the US Congress, and my duty is to enforce it." So Frank and the others left. It ought to be most interesting in the fall, to see if they really intend to enforce the rule, or if they will be lax. Perhaps the climbers will just keep coming and coming. Many sidelights to the story (I was an on-the-spot witness, in between trying to get my stuff out of Camp 4 before they confiscated it).

Too late—Kay and I had to retrieve it from the Ranger's Office, who with great formality (they love ceremony, I think) called in from his patrol the ranger who had picked it up, and who then led us to the rescue cache, a room up in the maintenance section behind the museum, and had me itemize everything I took, sign my name and residence. Since I am sort of in Camp 6 now, I told him I was an employee living in Camp 6. "Where do you work?" "I teach piano." "For the Curry Co?" "No, I am independently employed." He didn't question that—perhaps he liked the official sound of the words "independently employed"—but I didn't seem to remember the number of my tent in Camp 6, for some reason. Anyway, they still have a couple more boxes, but it seems they were picked up by another ranger, who put them in yet a different place, so I have to go back. Perhaps this is a late enactment of the Summerhillian cops-and-robbers stage, except that I think it's all very funny. Kay rather got a kick out of it, too.

Another sidelight is that just the night they were closing in (the Rangers on the Climbers), John, our John, arrived. Knowing nothing of all this, he sacked out in the Bear's Lair. Next night, of course, he found all his equipment gone. Upon retrieving it, he was asked roughly, "Are you a climber?" and answered, "Oh, no, I just arrived last night from the East Coast." "Well," the Rangers said, "You can't stay in Camp 4 unless you have a pet." "Oh," said John. In talking about it later, we were thinking of starting a pet rental service for those who happened to come up without a pet. Or we imagined the various pets which might be brought along for the weekend—goldfish, lizards, fleas, white rats. We imagined climbers going to various friends in the City in order to check out a pet for the weekend. Just like you borrow skis, or a rack for your car. Anyway, Frank was told not to come back until next year, when he will have 10 more days. I think he went to Tuolumne.

Love,
H. M. Ellis

Meredith Ellis Little was born in Stockton, California, in 1934. In the mid-1950s she spent a summer working in Yosemite, where a friend introduced her to the world of rock climbing. Soon after, she transferred to Stanford and became involved in the school's well-known Alpine Club. She made ascents of Yosemite's most popular formations, including Higher and Lower Cathedral Spires, *Royal Arches*, the Water Cracks on Lembert Dome, and Washington Column.

Meredith had a deep love of music, and in 1967 she received her PhD in musicology from Stanford. After a long career as a harpsichordist and musicologist, she switched careers and graduated from the University of Arizona College of Law in 1990. She practiced law in Tucson for seventeen years. Meredith passed away in 2020 at the age of eighty-six.

WE WERE THE JEWELS

Hope Morehouse Meek

YOSEMITE'S CAMP 4 IN THE SIXTIES

We were the jewels on the walls of the valley,
The young and the beautiful, rebellion on granite.
Climbing our passion, our family Camp 4
We loved and we trusted our lives to each other
On the end of a rope. A sexual high,
As is flying, rappelling with tinkling hardware,
Pitons and beeners chiming on stone,
Breathtaking slow motion, our music drifts down,
Ignoring Viet Nam, final exams, anxious mothers,
And more. We were poor, but we ate and we drank
Like the royalty we were.
The tourists in campers were our quarry for food.
Together we foraged our family's meals
From their blanketed compounds complete with RVs
And TVs ignoring the glory around them.
Their steaks and wine were fine with us,
Just so long as they didn't dine with us.

As a child, Hope Morehouse Meek, descended from Dutch settlers of Manhattan and raised in a prominent New York society family, was expelled from several elite boarding schools for her risk-taking antics. She moved to California as a single mother and took up rock climbing with the Sierra Club, where she was introduced to Jim Baldwin. They became weekend climbing companions for the next two years, doing all the Yosemite classics of the time. In 1963, they did the first ascent of *Great White Book* on Tuolumne Meadows' Stately Pleasure Dome, accompanied by Jeff Foote.

Jim was content to continue his dirtbag existence indefinitely, and Hope married someone else. Jim was later killed in a climbing accident, and afterward Hope wrote many poems about their carefree days together, including the one printed here. She stayed in touch with her climbing community throughout her life and died in 2014 at the age of eighty-six.

GIRLS CAN BE DIRTBAGS TOO

Jan Sacherer

I was a freshman at the University of Colorado in 1963 when I signed up with their hiking club and went on an introductory hike. One of the men asked me if I would like to learn to rock climb. I jumped at the opportunity, and after a few brief instructions, Joe O'Laughlin and I were ready to do the Third Flatiron. I leaned in too far on my first rappel and fell, scraping my knuckles, but learned a very valuable lesson: the belay rope holds. After that I was not afraid to fall, enabling my rapid progress. Shortly after, I met Layton Kor, and by my fourth weekend in Boulder, he and I were climbing in Eldorado Canyon. In those days it was possible to climb there on a weekend and be the only two people on the rock! Usually, though, we climbed with Pat Ament or Larry Dalke as a third.

During 1964, two Yosemite climbers named Chris Fredericks and Chuck Pratt spent the winter in Boulder, tantalizing us with their tales of the best rock climbing on earth. As a result, summer vacation of 1965 saw a car jammed with six Coloradoans headed for the Valley. The other five were going for a few weeks, but I was making a permanent move. Wages in California were double those of Colorado and tuition fees almost nil. Everything I brought with me fit into two garbage bags. As far as I know, I was the first woman climber to go to Yosemite intending to spend the whole summer climbing unaccompanied by a husband or boyfriend.

Alas, fate had other ideas. First was the problem of the hostility toward outsiders. Layton had already warned us of this with a funny story. Royal had told him, "Come to the Valley. If you can climb as well as my girl, Janie Taylor, I will buy you a beer." Then Layton told us with a chuckle, "I never got that beer." More alarming was being told by several prospective rope mates in Camp 4, "I never climb with a girl because they can't hold a leader fall." I had never encountered a problem finding partners in Colorado.

There was also the sandbagging that sent Rodger Raubach and me to Koko Ledge, an aid testpiece just west of Rixon's Pinnacle. Rodger placed three postage-stamp-sized RURPs in a row before the top one pulled and he took a 40-foot zipper. There were no belay devices then, so I was doing a hip belay in nylon stirrups. Rodger was not a small man, so his weight pulled me up and jammed my left wrist into the haul bag. There we both were, hanging from one large bong piton, him with broken ribs and me with a broken left wrist. Nevertheless, I held him, and no one after that could ever use not catching a leader fall as an excuse not to climb with me. My summer plans, however, were in ruins. All I managed that summer was *Church Bowl Chimney*, where the noise of my cast scraping on the walls drove my climbing partners crazy.

I was told that I was the first woman to spend the summer alone in Camp 4. Pratt, Fredericks, Tom Gerughty, Sheridan Anderson, and I were the Camp 4 Five, while Jim Bridwell, Frank Sacherer, and Chuck Ostin came and went. Pratt slept in his van while the rest of us slept out on tarps since none of us owned a tent. Bears wandered through our campsites nightly on their way to the more lucrative tourist camps farther down the hill. In the fall when it rained, we moved under overhanging rocks.

I did at least get some climbing in that fall once my wrist healed. The hardest climb I ever did in the Valley was *Coonyard Pinnacle*, a friction route on the Apron rated 5.9. I believe I was probably the second woman to free climb it after Chela Kunasz. This was no small feat given we were still climbing in klettershoes, long before sticky rubber. Mostly though, I did easier classics like *Royal Arches*—when the Rotten Log was still there—and the chimney route on Washington Column. The latter was finished off by a treacherous multihour night descent of the infamous North Dome Gully. No one had thought to bring headlamps for the difficult routefinding. Jokingly I was told that epic was what made me a real Valley climber.

Later that fall I married Frank Sacherer, and he set out to make climbing so unpleasant for me that I would quit. Known for being hard on his climbing partners, he shouted things like "Do you think Roper would fumble a piton like that?" and "Do you think Beck would tangle a rope like that?" I persevered until finally on Middle Cathedral Rock I got so frustrated that I untied the belay rope and soloed down a full pitch of 5.6, leaving him alone and aghast. It was the last time I ever climbed with him or any man in Yosemite.

Later we moved to Switzerland after Frank was hired to work as a physicist at CERN. When he wanted to climb near Geneva with a group of coworkers and needed a partner, he was surprised to see I could free climb anything they could, and unlike some of them, I never hung on a fixed piton. It was those fixed pitons that made all the difference. Instead of using up precious arm strength beating out hardware, I could concentrate on climbing. Looking back, I believe the turning point for women rock climbers in the United States that enabled them to really forge ahead was getting rid of pitons so they could concentrate on climbing instead.

That revolution had already begun when I returned as a single woman to climb in the Valley in 1973. By that time, I had had experience on the Matterhorn, Mont Blanc, Grand Teton, and Mount Rainier and had spent a summer teaching for Colorado Outward Bound. Unlike during my high school days when I lived nearby in Marble, Colorado Outward Bound had finally begun hiring women, and I spent a summer teaching for them. Molly Higgins and Barb Eastman were fellow instructors who joined me in Yosemite, where we did the *Iota* together, a classic Yosemite chimney, trying out our new hexes and stoppers. Years later when they climbed the *Nose* on El Cap, the first all-woman team to do so, they sent me their iconic summit photo, which I still treasure.

My own life took a different path as I went to Nepal to study the remote valley of Rolwaling for a doctorate in anthropology. Unbeknownst to my French thesis supervisor, I chose the research site from an adventure travel brochure so that I could combine research with climbing. As the valley was eight days' walk from the nearest road, electricity, running water, post office, and medical care, my summer in Camp 4 stood me in good stead. My Colorado background did as well, since I managed to climb a number of 19,000-foot passes and one 20,200-foot mountain. Most of these were done with Sherpa women porters in Sherpa style. We camped out with no tents at altitudes of 18,000 feet, cooking our salted butter tea over wood fires and eating balls of precooked tsampa and butter, singing and laughing in the Sherpa language far into the night. Nowadays the granddaughters of the Rolwaling women I knew are making mountaineering history. In 2018, Nima Jangmu from Rolwaling climbed Everest, Lhotse, and Kanchenjunga within a twenty-five-day period. The year before, Dawa Yangzum became only the second woman in Asia to be certified as an international mountain guide.

Today I can no longer rock climb because of arthritis and neuropathy in my well-worn feet (one of my research projects in Nepal involved trekking five hundred miles from west to east, surveying Sherpa villages). I'm happy instead just to get up a Colorado fourteener. I will always count myself incredibly lucky to have been in Yosemite during the Golden Age, Berkeley in the 1960s, and Nepal in the 1970s during its golden age for anthropologists. Retired back in Boulder after thirty years of teaching in Japan, I have become reacquainted with my old climbing pals Joe and Rodger, met many old Yosemite friends at various Yosemite reunions, and enjoy the company of the Rolwaling Sherpa families settled in Boulder. Technical feats in climbing are short-lived, but the memories and friendships endure forever.

Jan Sacherer grew up in western Colorado skiing in Aspen and hiking in the Maroon Bells–Snowmass Wilderness. She spent her summers in the ghost town of Marble, site of the first American Outward Bound school, which at the time did not employ women. After attending college in Colorado and California, she received her doctorate in anthropology from the Sorbonne in Paris and then taught anthropology and Asian studies for the University of Maryland for thirty years on the tropical island of Okinawa.

Jan sees rock climbing and her time in Yosemite as foundational to much of her later life. Interested in preserving the history of Yosemite climbing, she has contributed extensively to biographies of all the climbing personalities she knew during the 1960s. Now retired near Boulder, with two rescue dogs she brought from Japan and a cat, she still teaches online and hikes.

FIRST ASCENT

Liz Robbins

This excerpt is from a story that first appeared in *Alpinist* in 2008.

NUTCRACKER
MANURE PILE BUTTRESS
YOSEMITE NATIONAL PARK
SIERRA NEVADA RANGE
CALIFORNIA

Sometimes things that make no sense on the surface make perfect sense inside. In 1960 I arrived in Yosemite on break from UC Berkeley, where I'd been doing what was expected of a conventional, middle-class girl: join a sorority, go to classes, find direction and maybe even fall in love with an up-'n'-comer. But the beer bashes at frat houses after football games had left me uninspired, and the boys who looked pretty cool in class looked pretty stupid at night.

At first Camp 4 was just a dusty landscape: cluttered tables, dirty tents, people coming and going. Yet something there seemed to hum with a raw, unselfconscious honesty. As the climbers gathered at dusk, this sensation became almost tangible. Whatever the energy was, I wanted some of it. Here, individuals were what they were, like it or not. When someone asked me if I wanted to go on a little climb, I said yes . . .

Initially Royal Robbins reminded me of a Berkeley professor. After climbing with him on Cathedral Peak, I realized this aloof, quiet, contemplative demeanor concealed intensity and passion. Royal required unproven feats of his imagination, spiritual and physical tests not yet dreamed of—a need that would drive him to make ascents other people couldn't comprehend. Climbing was new to me, but the integrity underlying Royal's pursuits was something I knew I could rely upon in any circumstance. To the bewilderment of my family and friends back home, I adopted his eccentric-seeming way of life.

In the spring of 1967, after seven years of climbing and five years of marriage, Royal and I were sitting at the top of Yvon Chouinard's *After Six*, on Manure Pile Buttress, speaking with gratitude about the fun route and the perfect weather. Then Royal, in a way that had become familiar, left me and the moment. His eyes went from soft to serious as he turned to gaze at an undiscovered line about 200 feet east.

On a recent trip to England Royal had learned about using nuts for protection. If he could prove that they worked on American rock as well as on British, then maybe American climbers would adopt this method, preventing the piton scars that had been damaging the walls. Here was a chance to try out this new style.

We started up one early April morning, scrambling the first twenty feet. Then a squeeze chimney . . . not hard, but enough to squeeze out an "ugh" or two. Here Royal placed a couple of his new gadgets. Following, I tugged hard on them. They would have held a fall.

Along the top of a flake, he traversed right, threading what runners he could on the odd spike. He wedged a small nut in a tiny crack (psychological, I thought), then crossed a thin, touchy traverse to a dihedral with a fluid grace. Maybe it's easier than it looks, I thought . . . Or maybe he just makes it look easy. Well, now it was my turn!

The rope came down at a diagonal. Ahead the rock seemed completely smooth. If I fell I'd pendulum. When my eyes adjusted a little, microflakes began to appear. It reminded me of bird-watching: at first a warbler looks like a drab little gray bird, but after a shift in focus, it turns white, yellow and green—the bird is full of color! More and more tiny features materialized for my fingertips and toes. The thrill of this exposure, the hammering of my heartbeat and the knowledge that I was sharing this experience with the man I trusted and loved brought a quiet mind and a soul-felt gratitude. This is why I climb, I thought. With a breath of satisfaction, I stepped across into the trough.

On the next pitch, after Royal laced a pair of vertical cracks with chocks, it became clear that placing nuts was only half the trick. The fingers of my left hand stuck insecurely in one of the cracks, while my right hand toyed with an uncooperative little chunk of metal. The nut would wiggle around and I'd think, "I've got it!"—only to have it stick and wiggle and stick again. My fingers and feet would need a change, so with my right hand jammed, my feet tapped for baby flakes again, and my sweaty, fatigued left hand took its turn.

"Is everything OK?" Royal asked, without impatience, simply wanting me to know he was there with me. Sometimes I questioned that forbearance; his silence would become eerie when I was taking forever to make some move. "Let me give you some tension."

"I'm fine," I yelled back. I was beginning to like this method. Unlike pitons, which took the force of a hammer, these chocks demanded a delicate and analytic approach. At last I found the right combination to crack the nut. Royal shared my pride.

"Be ready," he called out on the third pitch, sounding composed as usual. After traversing another seemingly blank face, he'd disappeared around a corner. "I've found a crack, but the next moves look tough."

"Go for it," I said, double-checking my stance and tightening my grip on the rope. Royal's inflection never let me know just how perilous a move might be. I still didn't completely trust those chocks. The rope snaked on; after a while, the tranquil voice called down, "Come on up." I felt a warm rush of relief, like the first sip of Teton Tea on a cold night.

Once again the rope angled toward me. Breath and pulse quickened—it could be a bouncing, scraping, swinging fall—but there was no choice, so I kept going. It felt good to know that under pressure I could think clearly and do whatever was necessary. Soon I was directly below Royal. He looked down at me from the ledge and said, "The hard move is just above you. After that it gets easier." He rarely gave me more specific tips; he knew my strengths and his were different and that I had to climb in my own manner.

I took out the two protecting nuts and studied the short, steep step split by a crack. Finally some pushing-pulling combinations and a bit of jamming got me to the ledge. Royal greeted me as if I'd just arrived from the moon. To avoid the headwall, we now moved left and easily reached the top over broken rock. We'd done it: 600 feet long and no pitons!

Royal would make the second ascent with Yvon Chouinard, adding the direct finish over the headwall. This final pitch, now standard, contains the most difficult part of the climb: a mantelshelf onto a big, flat ledge. Soon after, Royal and I made the third ascent so I could try the move. After several scrambling failures, I had to admit that I didn't have the arm strength for the crux, so I focused on finding my own way. Once more, the rock was like the drab little warbler. On the wall to the left, I picked out some tiny flakes. I tiptoed up, thrilled and proud.

At times, over the years, at the base of some climb, I'd feel a clutching anxiety, and I wasn't sure why; maybe it was a fear that the route might demand more than I could dig out of myself. And yet, the greatest nonsense was: once committed to an uncertain move or an adventurous life, I always found that hidden, inner world contained everything I needed.

I'd only just begun the excavation.

Liz Robbins was born and raised in Modesto, California, near Yosemite, but it wasn't until she moved there in 1959 to work at the Ahwahnee Hotel that she discovered the adventure that mountains could provide. Through her job editing the winter newspaper, she was introduced to people from all different walks of life, and eventually to her future husband, Royal. With Royal, every day was an adventure, and they soon began pioneering new routes, fueled by a free-spirited love of climbing. In 1967, Liz made the first female ascent of the *Regular Northwest Face* of Half Dome, and the couple also established the climb mentioned in this story. The *Nutcracker Suite* started a clean climbing revolution, pushing climbers away from placing protection that damaged the rock. This route would go on to become one of Yosemite's most popular climbs, but at the time, it felt to Liz like just another day of adventure.

Today, Liz splits her time between the home in Modesto (the same one she was raised in) and her mountain home in Pinecrest, California, affectionately named the Robbins' Nest.

JUST KEEP CLIMBING

Elaine Matthews

What was that? Something made the carabiners shift on the bolt anchor. I was hauling up the big bag and it was taking all my concentration, and then *Pop! Shift! Bump! What the hell happened?* Then I saw that the day pack with all our raingear and warm clothes had fallen. *Shit! Too bad, just keep hauling.*

When my partner, Chuck Ostin, arrived on the ledge, he told me he had snuck a chicken dinner and a camera into the pack to surprise me on our first bivy. Too bad, just keep climbing. Chuck Ostin was the sweetest, most generous person I have ever known, but he was mysterious; he didn't camp with us dirtbags in Camp 4, and one never really knew his plans. Anyway, it was June, so it was pretty warm on that first night and the next. No chicken dinner, but heck, we had lots of sardines!

THE CLIMBING WENT WELL, AND WE WERE REALLY IN A GROOVE. BUT ON the Great Roof pitch, it began to rain. Chuck was lucky: he had on a long-sleeved shirt and pants, but I was in a lightweight tee and short shorts. All the warm stuff had fallen. Too bad, just keep climbing.

At the Camp VI ledge, shivering, we spread out our haul bags and climbed into dry down sleeping bags. There was only half a day of climbing to the top tomorrow. But it kept raining and blowing. We tried to eat, but the shivering was pretty bad and had taken our appetites away. The down bags were sodden.

In the morning, Chuck tried to climb in the rain but was too cold and retreated after a bit. It kept raining and blowing. During the day, I still couldn't make myself eat, and the shivering continued. But we were certain we could outlast the storm and finish the climb. So when people started calling to us from below to see how we were, we insisted we were fine. But they had found the day pack with our raingear and made their own decision. A troop of our friends gathered warm clothes and thermoses of hot coffee, hiked to the top of El Cap, and proceeded to set up fixed ropes.

Tom Bauman rappelled down. However much we thought we could still do this on our own, Tom was a welcome sight. He had wool pants and hot coffee! Wonders of the world!

But then there was the question from Tom: Are you going to jug the ropes out or stay to finish the climb? We jugged out. Why? Because only a year and a half before, Jim Madsen had fallen to his death trying to reach his friends in a storm, and we were terrified Tom might do the same now. Chuck was a man of the utmost compassion and respect for others. He thought we had to do it for Tom because he had risked his life for us. I agreed.

Chuck and I thought we would come back in the fall and do the *Triple Direct*. We never did. Life, as it is wont to do, got in the way.

Elaine Matthews was introduced to rock climbing in Minnesota in 1965 and quickly made a name for herself as one of few women tying into the sharp end. She traveled west in search of big adventure, which she found in Yosemite, the Tetons, and the Wind River Range. Her ascent of the *Nose* described in this story is considered by many to be the first female ascent of El Capitan, but because she jumared out the final pitches, her climb is often overlooked.

She eventually moved to the Gunks (the Shawangunk Mountains of New York), where she opened a climbing gym and continued pushing her limits. Elaine continues to climb with the same enthusiasm she's felt for more than five decades. She lives in New Paltz, New York, with her partner and two cats.

WALLS WITHOUT BALLS

Sibylle Hechtel

This story first appeared in the *American Alpine Journal* in 1974. The journal's editors rejected Sibylle's title on the basis of vulgarity and suggested "Keeping Abreast of El Cap" instead. Frustrated that naming women's body parts was acceptable but naming men's was not, Sibylle insisted it run untitled. Her title was finally used when the story was reprinted in *Ordeal by Piton*, edited by Steve Roper and published in 2003.

El Capitan. I wanted to approach but then I didn't. Like David tackling Goliath. It would be the fulfillment of a dream, but fear was my predominant emotion now that it was really happening. Somehow I could never quite believe it was real: we were actually going up to climb El Capitan. I was afraid Bev would tell me she'd changed her mind and didn't want to do the climb after all, or that she thought we'd be too slow, or that we wouldn't be able to haul the sack.

I'd climbed for two years in the Valley and somehow never been interested in El Capitan. The original impetus for doing a wall was that I wanted to sleep in the sky. At that time Half Dome seemed the ultimate one could desire, replete with waterfalls on the left sweeping down into a variously colored rope coiling along the base of the Apron toward the Sentinel at the valley exit; Mirror Lake sitting on the right like the seventh level of the Inferno, the waters receding whenever parched climbers stoop to sip. From this vantage one wakes to mist crawling along the valley floor and curling up the sides while the crescent moon scurries behind Middle Cathedral Rock to hide from the advancing sun. El Capitan, the Cathedral Rocks, and North Dome become dwarfed misshapen lumps with only the stark smooth face containing reality. When asked when I would climb El Cap, I'd laugh, shrug a "Don't want to, there's no view, nothing to see from there."

True. The view looking out from the wall is not particularly inspiring, but nothing can surpass the enormity seen when waking on the face. The wall that confronts one when carrying up the haul sack has no relation to the rock one sees when hiking up to climb the pinnacles at the base. The former is incredibly huge, formidable, a surrealistic scene more part of the sky than born of earth.

It first occurred to me to climb the Captain when Annie and I were coming down off the Column after a three-day epic. That morn we were destitute and parched. The night had been one of trial by thirst. We had been through thunder and lightning and baked onto the rock. Our second night, a storm front advanced; we spoke of giving up climbing. Ominous black clouds were joined by lightning sufficiently accurate to make us wonder why we were the target.

"Have you ever thought there might be a God after all?" Annie asked. We huddled in cagoules [rain jackets], precariously perched in belay seats. "When I get back to the city, I'm going to grow fingernails and buy a dress." Annie appealed to the gods, offering sacrifices in return for safe deliverance. We solemnly promised not to mention climbing once back in Berkeley.

But Chris and the sun met us on top. Chris brought a quart apiece of orange juice and milk plus a half gallon of water. As we walked down North Dome Gully, Annie and I talked of climbing El Capitan.

This vague interest did not become a passion until I went up on *Pacific Ocean Wall* with Jim Bridwell. Going up the first seven pitches of this not yet completed route, I knew I must spend some time climbing to the sky. Bev mentioned she might be interested. Several men either offered to "take me up it" or asked if I'd like to do the climb with them, but I wasn't particularly interested in being "taken up it." Doing an all-female ascent, the first all-female ascent in fact, was not a significant consideration: I simply knew Bev much better than any of the men interested. Being up there with another woman can be incredibly comfortable, relaxed, and hilariously funny, but, with men, even close friends, there is always a certain pressure to prove that women can do things, as well as the tendency to whimper when things get tough and to let them do it for us.

THE CLIMB. WE DECIDED TO FIX FOUR PITCHES AND WITH THIS START, hopefully to reach a ledge our first night. The first three pitches went well, the hauling still fairly easy since not all gear was packed yet, but our afternoon start prevented us from fixing the fourth that same day. Our next trip, halfway up the fourth pitch, the hammer smashed my finger in preference to the pin. Was this fear subconsciously influencing materials to give occasion for retreat? Or were these genuine omens warning us to desist in our challenge? X-ray plates pronounced the suspectedly broken finger unharmed; thus the borrowed alarm was to insure our predawn departure the following day.

Dinner was a final indulgence in orange milkshakes and hot apple pie, neither of which succeeded in driving away the fear creeping in. I ate with three friends but was not really there at all, finally fleeing for the phone to call a man unseen in four months. There being little left in the way of procrastination after taking four days to fix as many pitches, I reluctantly headed for the tent to quake in terror of the coming day. But I ran into a friend just back from the city who wanted to talk and hear the news. "Come stay with me tonight," I begged. "I'm so afraid."

Fortunately walls are too active to permit terror to share the mind with action: if not leading, belaying while keeping two ropes running smoothly, unpacking the camera from the haul sack to take a picture, digging out extra pins, and attempting to grab some food keeps one occupied. The first day was to be our most difficult climbing: the dread Half Dollar (a flaring 5.9 chimney), a steep, difficult face pitch that can also be hooked (either alternative equally undesirable), and the "5.9, A3" pitch were waiting for us. Except for the face pitch they were not as bad as their reputations. That one; I stood on a grinding wiggling hook, looked at the next placement, and gave it to Bev. She strategically placed a hook behind a large nubbin which broke off and hit her in the head. Grumbling about the inferiority of the alternative placement, she kept on hooking.

Hauling was our biggest problem in this section: the bag was the heaviest and the rock had the lowest angle. In doing walls, this is no doubt the factor that places women at the greatest disadvantage: a fast male team can get away with 80 pounds, about half their weight; but on our slow journey the sack rivaled my 120 pounds. At first, we were forced to wait until one of us had cleaned the pitch and we would then haul together. Ferrying the sack across Mammoth Terraces was a major obstacle: just barely able to lift it between us, we'd stagger a few feet, drop it, and get ready for the next lap.

Upon reaching the ledge that night, we promptly passed out. Pitches blend together, but the nights stand apart, each unique in the position we had to assume: gingerly on one's side on a long narrow ledge, or a night-long battle to regain territory on the sloping variety.

The next few days were routine, one much like the other, the pounding in of pins succeeded by their extraction. Once as I cleaned a pitch, cursing to the best of my ability, Bev burst out laughing. "It sounds so funny to hear another chick swear," she sputtered. Thereafter I tried to exercise more creativity in my cursing, a difficult feat in tense situations.

As it was, the Fates spun their threads favorably. The storm that had struck earlier, delaying our departure, never returned to take advantage of us now that we had fewer avenues of escape. The heat was oppressive on our second and third days, so much so that one midday we pitched our rain-fly and retreated beneath its shade. Our water dwindled. The winds battering the brow of the Captain—gusts that blow the rope out horizontally and stuff its end into distant cracks—were not entirely unwelcome.

Traversing gray bands to reach the *Nose*, we got thoroughly lost. Without a topo and with no idea how far we had to traverse, we tried a crack straight up, one to the left and then climbed right as far as possible to examine possibilities there. At least there was a ledge for the night of restless sleep, filled with strange dreams. I woke to find myself on a narrow ledge 2,000 feet off the ground. I turned to tell Bev my dreams. She had dreamt of traversing over to the *Salathé* to get a route description.

Fortified with our dreams, we picked a likely crack and started on the last leg of our journey. After sleeping at Camp V that night, we reached Camp VI early the next day to find a quart of water awaiting us. Exhausted, we collapsed for an extensive lunch and debated the wisdom of fixing two pitches and spending the night there. The gray clouds floating in from

Tenaya Canyon made us wonder who would reach the top first: the storm or us. Shouts from the summit clinched the decision: we would go for it.

Three pitches later I flailed about, trying to clean a flaring crack/ chimney in the dark by headlamp. With a pack on my back, could I squirm up high enough to unclip from the next nut? I finally struggled onto a 10 x 24-inch stance to be told that it was my bed. "And don't you dare complain," Bev said. "Mine's even smaller." Having never bivouacked in slings, I didn't really know what to do. Bev was extremely helpful. "Figure it out yourself." After standing there long enough, I did.

This remains one of the most memorable and beautiful nights of my life. Despite any physical discomforts of my position, I was glad to be there. Serene in the knowledge that we were only three pitches below the top and would reach it early the next morning, I settled back to munch gorp and read Asimov. The rock swelled into a roof up to the right, a beautifully sculptured curve that I could just perceive in the beam of the headlamp. Cars twinkled by, 3,000 feet down, threading their way along the flowing moonlight below me where the river had been earlier that day. I leaned back to await my last sunrise here and, perchance, to sleep.

Born in Germany, Sibylle Hechtel followed her father, a well-known alpinist and scientist, up limestone cliffs starting at age three. She continued to climb everything she could find after her family moved to Southern California when she was eight. Trips to Yosemite naturally followed, and 1973 saw three of the most important ascents of her life: the first ascent of *Degringolade* in the Bugaboos, an all-female ascent of Yosemite's Washington Column with Anne-Marie Rizzi, and the first all-female ascent of El Capitan with Beverly Johnson via *Triple Direct*.

Sibylle later completed her PhD in biology and worked as a science writer while traveling to the greater ranges of the world. She lives in Silverthorne, Colorado, where she teaches skiing at Beaver Creek and climbs and cross-country skis as often as she can.

AFICIONADOS OF THE STEEP

1975–1989

Perhaps no group is more venerable in Yosemite than that of the Stonemasters, a loosely organized crew of young climbers based in Southern California. In the mid-1970s, climbing in Yosemite turned sharply toward athleticism above all else. The activity that had long been regarded as a hobby became a sport, and its participants treated it as such. They trained, using bouldering, slacklining, and weight lifting to increase their physical fitness. Aid climbing, of course, was still required to scale many of Yosemite's big walls, but climbers focused heavily on free climbing whatever they could. The year 1975 ushered in this new era, as leading Stonemasters established testpiece free climbs like *Astroman* and completed the first *Nose*-in-a-day.

Not everyone climbing in the age of the Stonemasters was, himself or herself, a Stonemaster. The original tribe of Stonemasters had a test: *Valhalla*, a 5.11 route at Southern California's Suicide Rock. The first woman to climb it? Maria Boone Cranor. While Maria stayed largely out of the public eye, better-known climbers of this generation, including Lynn Hill and Mari Gingery, credit her with inspiring them.

The women climbing during the late 1970s and 1980s benefited greatly from both their predecessors and women's advancements in American society. Many of the leading climbers of this generation also had careers that afforded them financial independence. In the 1980s, American women forged ahead into roles that not long before had been the exclusive domain of men: space travel, vice presidential nominations, and the Supreme Court. It wasn't until 1984 that Mississippi finally ratified the Nineteenth Amendment (though women in every state had been able to vote since 1920).

While early Yosemite climbers hailed largely from California, over time the Valley began to draw adventurers from all over the country and around the world, a generation of the world's top athletes—men and women alike—who advanced the sport.

RUNNING IT OUT

Sally Moser

THE FIRST TIME IT CAME INTO VIEW, YOSEMITE VALLEY WAS BEYOND COMprehension. It was 1975, and the gigantic gray rocks, swaths of trees, and remnants of snow on the valley rim jutted out from the landscape. Riding shotgun in a borrowed Ford Pinto driven by a friend, I clutched a job requisition paper for a position as a salad maker at the Lodge. With my last fifty dollars, I had bought a pair of hiking boots at the Berkeley REI. As Charlie dropped me and my backpack off at the dorms, he had said, "If you don't like it, you can come back to Berkeley, give plasma, and collect food stamps again." *Uh, no.* With that, the next chapter began.

In the morning, a visit to the lodge kitchen sent me back to the personnel office as the position had already been filled. The hiring manager said, "You're going to be a bus person at the Ahwahnee." "OK. I just need a job." I checked in at the hotel to get my uniform and ended up gaping at Glacier Point through the dining room windows. Little did I know I had won the Yosemite lottery. My roommate in L Dorm was a maid who earned in one week what I made in one night in tips. Expenses were minimal. The company deducted six dollars per week for a dorm room and twenty cents an hour for food.

After a few months, I graduated to waitressing, and a couple of Ahwahnee waiters offered to take me climbing. Before work, Tom, Randy, and I went to Church Bowl, and I watched them stroll up the 5.6 pitch of *Bishop's Balcony*. Then they tied me in. My new hiking boots were no match for the slippery granite. Pulling on the rope didn't get me off the ground either, not surprising for an overweight, out-of-shape, cigarette-smoking girl from Wisconsin. After that, I focused on hiking, working, and kicking my tobacco habit. I wheezed and gulped as my treks took me to the valley rim and the high country. I made it to the summits of Mount Dana, Mount Lyell, Mount Conness, and more. On Mount Conness, we had planned to camp close to the summit, but an unexpected snowstorm meant we found a flat spot and pitched the tent. My hiking partner, Joan, was on a special diet, and all she brought were Triscuits, cheese, and a couple heads of raw garlic. We noshed merrily away and exuded garlic for a week.

I made friends with folks who hiked, but surprisingly many people just wanted to hang out and drink, smoke, or pop pills all day long. When drug dealers came up from the Bay Area, the news spread like wildfire. "Benny is in Tecoya E14 from noon until three. Get there early for the good stuff." While I can't say I never imbibed, I didn't go to work high. I do remember snorting some white powder one Thanksgiving shift, but it only made me more efficient. Carol, one of my hiking partners, worked as a nurse at the Valley clinic. The nurses floated easily among the social classes in the park, maybe because no one knew when they would have to go to the clinic and be cared for. National Park Service folks, Curry Company employees, and climbers generally did not intermingle. Law enforcement officers avoided everyone, as they never knew who they would be called on to arrest or subdue.

One day I visited Carol, and she said, "We need another person. There are three climbers who want to climb Cathedral Peak and we could use one more to even out the pairs. Come with us!"

"I've tried climbing and I can't do it. You should go," I said.

"No, they said it is easy and even I can do it. We need another person, c'mon!" Her confidence rubbed off on me. *If she could do it, maybe I could too.* I borrowed a swami belt and Sticht plate, and we drove to the Meadows. The hike and climb passed in a blur. All of us squeezed onto the summit. I reveled in the panorama of the High Sierra, marveling at the fact that I had actually made it up this rock. *I can do it!* I wanted to do it again.

The transition from civilian to climber was difficult. As a woman who didn't know what was safe or unsafe, I felt scared going into Camp 4 to find partners. I met one traveling climber and we spent a naked evening in Stoneman Meadow. "I want to go climbing," I said.

"Oh yeah. Let's go at 8:00 a.m." The next morning the clock said 8:00, then 8:15, then 8:30. I learned an important lesson the hard way: never put out until after they take you climbing . . . and probably not even then.

Living in the dorms, while cheap, was not easy. A "ghost" roommate, someone who had a boyfriend with a private room, was hard to find. One weekend, my newly assigned roommate had her boyfriend up from the Bay Area. That night I woke up to the bottom bunk rocking. Camp 4 climbers were on the hunt for Curry girls, and they weren't going to catch me. Often when I got back from work at midnight, climbers were taking showers and using the dorm bathroom. I ranked dirtbags as the lowest form of life on the food chain.

Eventually I found Sue, another Curry employee, who could lead. I latched onto her and tried to be the best second I could be. I learned to belay, coil the rope, take out gear, and be supportive and flexible. Sue worked at the Four Seasons and stared down runouts with a steely gaze. I didn't want that gaze directed at me. Sometimes we'd ride our bicycles up out of the valley to Chinquapin or Crane Flat and come screaming down the highway, passing cars. We'd climb sporadically whenever our work schedule allowed, sticking to easy routes I could do. Once we went up the Apron to climb the *Cow*. In the late morning heat we came upon two other women, who were climbing topless. Ah, California!

Sue wanted to practice routefinding, so one day we motored up to Cathedral Peak. We were halfway up the route when we spied a party on our left. An older guy and a girl were heading to the summit. He looked over at us and said, "Hey, a couple of girls up here, that's pretty good!" I wanted to say, "Hey, an old guy up here, that's pretty good," but I didn't. As they were smooching on every belay, we let them have a moment together on the summit. When we joined them at the top, Fred Beckey invited us to his campsite in the Meadows. Inconveniently, we had to get to the Valley to work the dinner shift, so we kept moving.

The demanding nature of Yosemite climbing necessitated arm strength. I watched Sue do ten pull-ups on the rails of the tent we lived in at the Ahwahnee Dorms while I couldn't do one. I realized that in order to reach my potential, I had to work on building up my arms. Carrying heavy trays and treading the cement floors at the hotel left little energy or time to devote to training. I wanted to climb, but I also wanted to get my college degree. The wad of Ahwahnee tips in my bank account allowed me to go anywhere. I picked the University of Colorado. My first semester in Boulder, my bible was a weight-training book for women on how to develop arm strength. I lifted weights. I swam in the pool with hand paddles, thereby increasing resistance. Progress was slow. After that semester and establishing residence in Colorado for the in-state tuition, I bicycled across the Canadian Rockies and down Highway 1 on the West Coast, ending up back at the Ahwahnee to replenish my coffers. I still thought of myself as a biker, not a climber.

At some point I realized I enjoyed the culture and amenities of an urban area more than living in a small town where everyone knew where you were, who you were with, what you were doing, and how long you were doing it for. To see a movie or live music or go shopping involved driving two hours to Fresno or Merced. The only source of entertainment was the *San Francisco Chronicle* Sunday edition. My waitress job, though lucrative, literally weighed on me, and I didn't qualify for National Park Service jobs. Doing anything else meant working more and making less money. Friends and boyfriends turned over in the spring and the fall. Finding a compatible roommate who did not come with a dirtbag boyfriend was always a challenge.

Back in Boulder, I had two semesters left. Just as important as getting a degree was gaining arm strength. During my final semester, a gymnastics course allowed me to set a goal of ten pull-ups. To succeed, I fine-tuned my strategies. I did as many lower-downs as I could with a ten-pound weight around my waist. I aced my final exam by completing ten pull-ups, plus one more because I could. I buildered at the Mackey pit, a subterranean stairwell on campus. The goal was to traverse the full length of the pit, out and back. I eventually sent the traverse, and that's what gave me the chops to climb harder. Climbing in Boulder had many of the same challenges as climbing in Yosemite. I didn't lead, and I was never in Boulder long enough to develop trusted climbing partners. Weather rained out three of the four climbing classes I signed up for at CU. A friend set me up with an Australian climber, and we climbed the *Bastille Crack,* a 5.7. It scared the bejesus out of me. *Steep and tricky, that was 5.7?*

After I earned my degree in spring 1981, my goal was to lead 5.10. It seemed like a logical career move at the time. I pilgrimaged back to Yosemite, where the climbing and the eventual job awaited. But I knew this would be my final Yosemite hurrah. On the first day I followed a couple of hard

5.10s without falling. I hoped that following 5.10 would translate into leading 5.8 without too many problems. My testpiece was the *Surprise*, a recommended 5.8, one of the Five Open Books near the base of Yosemite Falls. To up the commitment, I recruited Dianne, also an aspiring leader.

The day began auspiciously enough, with Dianne backing off the 5.6 lead. I motored through, then embarked on the crux. A challenge, yes, but not beyond my honed abilities. After bringing her up, I only had to decipher the last pitch. Confident by this time, I moved upward with no protection between me and the belay. I had cruised the crux pitch, and the topo said 5.7. But where was the exit? This should be easy. I went up, then traversed right; no, that wasn't the way. I returned left . . . *eeyah!*

A mini-boulder I had used as a handhold liberated itself from the munge and moss, and became airborne. It flew, and so did I. Time extended as I bounced down the rock for 30 feet before landing in a large manzanita on a ledge. Stunned, I wrestled with the bush, cursing and not appreciating the fact that it had saved me from several broken bones. I threw in a piece, belayed Dianne up, and tossed the rack at her.

"Get us out of here. Go left. I went right and that's not the way."

Eyeing my bleeding knees and elbows, she had no choice but to suck it up and tough it out. Placing gear every few feet, she hesitantly led the final section and set a belay. I followed, feeling a ripping pain in my side every time I tried to pull myself up.

After limping down the descent, I headed immediately for a shower. Blood and dirt mingled with soap and water as Dianne, a registered nurse, inspected and sponged off my cuts and scrapes.

"I think you'll be okay," she said. "Do you want to go to the clinic?"

My lack of health insurance as well as my plan to live in Camp 4 and Tuolumne for the summer precluded me from paying any expensive medical bills. I slunk into the Mountain Room Bar and proceeded to order all the white wine I could drink. One of the guides entered.

"Surprised on *Surprise*, Sal? Well, you aren't the first."

I barely looked up from my glass of liquid anesthetic to acknowledge that comment. Friends who had heard of my humbling stopped by, and at midnight I left the bar and stumbled to my tent.

The next day dawned harsh and clear. A pitbull hangover conspired with my injuries to make leaving the tent the hardest move I'd ever contemplated. Eventually, the necessity of relieving myself compelled me to commit. I contorted my stiffened body through the tent door, then lurched the 50 yards to the Camp 4 bathroom.

For the next few days, I rued my existence. My right leg ballooned to elephantine proportions; wearing shoes or socks was impossible. It hurt to breathe, laugh, or sneeze. Each morning I had to peel the sleeping bag off my oozing wounds. I finally received some medical attention when a third-year med student in camp practiced his diagnostic skills on me.

"Your leg? A subdermal hematoma that will recover in time. Watch those lacerations for signs of infection—the one on your elbow is deep and could have used a couple of stitches. Your ribs are bruised and not cracked, otherwise you'd have black-and-blue marks where the blood seeped out."

"Hey, Jeremy," he called to his friend, "come over here and see what rock climbing will do for you!"

I contemplated what climbing had done for me as I watched my campmates climb the *Steck-Salathé* on Sentinel from my lawn chair in Camp 4. Would I climb again? Of course, everyone said, yes, you have to climb. Inwardly, I recoiled at the thought. All the pull-ups and lower-downs I had done had prepared me for success but not for this. What went wrong? Did I overestimate my skills, was I too cocky, or was I just inexperienced? Probably all three.

Mike, one of my climbing partners, came by my tent and offhandedly said, "This is good for you. What doesn't kill you keeps you alive."

My dander rose immediately. "Bullshit. There's nothing good about this, my climbing summer is ruined, I'll never lead 5.10."

But after he left, the second part of what he said stuck in my head. Although I was hurting, the part of me that had trained relentlessly toward my goals wanted to climb again. I hadn't died. I had paid a price and now I understood the high stakes of the game I played. In the future I would be more cautious, put in more pro, test the holds for looseness. Fear of falling was now impressed upon my brain cells, my ribs, my leg, my elbows. This experience was a gift that presented, on some level, what I needed to know.

As summer heat commenced at full force in the Valley, four of us moved to Tuolumne. I knew Mike and Pete from working at the hotel. Bill, their buddy from the Gunks, joined us. Bill wore his dark sunglasses around the nightly campfire as well as all day. I never saw his eyes and didn't trust him. Seemed to me he was the quintessential dirtbag, although he had money. A site in Loop F, the backpackers' campground, became our home for the next two and a half months. Our only car was Mike's beat-up orange "Mazdarati," and he moved it strategically as necessary. We didn't pay and no one noticed. We became experts in hanging food, avoiding rangers, and climbing Tuolumne knobs. Various friends, including my partner Sue, worked at the Lodge. Still healing from the fall, I gingerly followed easy climbs.

One of the first routes we climbed was *Great Pumpkin.* Maybe it's only 5.8, but the bolts are few and far apart, even by Tuolumne standards. While Pete was no slouch in the slab-climbing department, Mike was our unquestioned face ace. Mike led the way with Bill and waited as Pete and I followed. Near the top I could hear Pete squawking and mumbling on the lead. "Michael, where's the next bolt?" "You're at the bolt?" "Yeah." "Well, there aren't any more." Pete dug deep and kept it together. I watched him climb out of sight with bated breath.

Digging deep, that's what Tuolumne climbing is all about. There's no alternative. The Tuolumne cast of characters included refugees looking to escape the Valley heat and regulars from other parts of the world who came to caress the golden edges and look for bolts that were always elusive. The perfect weather, impeccable stone, incomparable views, and free camping equaled paradise for our little tribe. Our job was to climb.

Social activities and partner finding centered around the store parking lot. Mike went climbing with Louise, an Australian gal he tried mightily to impress without succeeding. One of Australia's leading climbers, she led him up *Blues Riff*, a 5.11 finger crack. I met an English climber with whom I went climbing on my birthday. That night when Sue and Leslie walked over to our campsite with a carrot cake from the Lodge, I was a no-show. Pete attempted to dissuade them from taking the cake home, saying, "You know, bears *loovve* carrot cake." But they knew that climbers did as well. They took their chances with the bears and kept the cake, which I claimed the next day.

Finally my mind healed from the fall and my confidence returned. Pete and I went up to the *Great Circle,* where I led the first pitch and proceeded to attempt the 10a second pitch. Pete—"Coach" we called him because he would tell you what to do and how to do it although he hadn't been there—yelled up encouragement and beta. I stalled out at the second bolt and looked around. "Put your right foot up, put your right foot up. That's how to do it," he said. I tried a couple times but it didn't work, so I retreated to the belay. Pete edged up the glacier polish to the second bolt, assessed the move, and said, "Ohhh, it's the left foot!" Damn. That was the first and last time I paid attention to his or anyone else's beta. I went back a few days later and led my first 10a.

Paradise wasn't free. Money was running out. Bill bought food, and Pete and Mike supplemented rations by shoplifting from the store. My cash supply dwindled. Eventually, one by one, we drifted back to the Valley and the Ahwahnee gold mine, while Bill remanded to the Gunks. My face climbing skills honed by months of knob climbing kept me in the game, but I had a lot to learn.

Fortunately, Sue acquired Phil, a non-dirtbag climbing boyfriend. Phil and I had cruised around the Meadows many days listening to Little Feat as we scoped the routes. A big-wall veteran, he did carpentry in the Bay Area in the winter to afford his time off. Phil's wiry build and technique allowed him to shinny up squeeze chimneys where others feared to tread. Phil and I climbed a lot as Sue worked day shifts. Phil never hesitated to take me on routes he wanted to do. He loved all sizes of cracks and knew he could get me up one way or another. A day after doing the *Rostrum,* he wanted to lead the first four pitches from the rap-in anchors.

"Sure, I'll go," I said. "Do I need to tape?"

"No," he said.

We did the first two pitches and arrived at the 10c cupped-hands pitch. I hadn't come across this size before and struggled mightily. My dinner shift started at 4:30, so I had to get up. With copious amounts of tension, I finally made it. My hands looked like raw hamburger.

I went to work in the dining room with oozing gobies. I kept the backs of my hands down and deposited the plates in front of the diners as surreptitiously as possible. That was the last time I let someone tell me whether to tape or not to tape.

The *Center of the Cookie,* another memorable Phil route, introduced me to squeeze chimneys. Phil slithered up and I seconded. Once I inhaled, I was stuck. I couldn't move my head and went upward an inch at a time if I was lucky. An eternity later, I arrived at the belay. Our third, Dianne, who had been with me on the *Surprise,* laybacked the whole thing. Cheating! After a year of crack wrestling and stashing the free-flowing tips, I quit the Ahwahnee for good. My back spasmed, and I went to Joshua Tree for a month to recover before moving back to Colorado. Living in JT ranks right up there with my summer in Tuolumne.

Since then I've visited Yosemite many times, and after forty years I still know folks who work at the Ahwahnee. I marvel at the twist of fate that took me to the Valley. Yosemite made me and is a part of who I am. Every time I hear Little Feat, I am transported to the Meadows, cruising for routes in Phil's green VW van: *Sweet Jesus, Hemispheres, Guardians of the Galaxy, Big Boys Don't Cry, American Wet Dream, Table of Contents, Golden Bars, OZ*—the climbs go on and on. As we drive by the parking pullouts, we recognize all the cars and know which routes our friends are on. Sometimes when I can't get to sleep, I think of handjams and granite domes and replay memory tapes of living in the most special place on earth. It never gets old.

Sally Moser fled the Midwest in the mid-1970s to seek her fortune in California. Fortuitously, she landed in Yosemite Valley and eventually began climbing. A move to Boulder, Colorado, allowed her to hone her communication and climbing skills. As managing editor of *Rock and Ice* in the late eighties and executive director of the Access Fund in the late nineties, she influenced and contributed to the climbing culture before the era of the internet. She also coauthored three guidebooks to the southern Sierra and worked as a climbing guide.

Continuing to ski and climb 5.Fun routes, Sally is a real estate professional in Boulder, Colorado. She still thinks there's nothing better than a good handjam.

MY FIRST TIME

Molly Bruce Higgins

This story first appeared in *Yosemite Climber*, edited by George Meyers and published in 1979 by Diadem Books.

It was the first warm morning after a week of rain, and I should have been racking my gear at the base of a climb. Instead, I chucked stones into a pothole in the parking lot and watched Jim load his gear into a pickup. Barb was still busy visiting her multitude of friends—first the Camp 4 ranger, now some new arrivals from Oregon. I wished one of them would finish so I could get on with my day. Finally Jim hauled his last trunk of gear onto the bed of the truck and approached me, obviously to say goodbye.

I looked up at him, loving him so much that my heart felt raw, yet still cursing him for leaving me.

He looked down at me with his warm brown eyes and said: "Do your best, Mol."

"If you would stay with me I'd do better," I replied bitterly.

His patient silence was enough of an answer. Furious, I turned and ran, grabbing Barb away from her friends and running off with her into the woods.

"He's such a creep," I said. "How could he leave me to go home? How could he sacrifice our ultimate climbing relationship?"

"I know you love him, Molly. It's certainly a shame, but he has his bad points too," Barb said.

He had the build of a gymnast and fists so huge he could jam a four-inch crack. His physique, combined with the fact that he was nice to me and had faith in my future as a climber, made it difficult for me to see his faults.

"Besides, now we'll have more time to climb with one another," Barb added after a pause. I agreed that it would be nice to spend more time together because routes were such an adventure with her. Since we had about the same ability, there was no one else to lean on except ourselves, and that made it a much more challenging endeavor. But I was worried about whether Barb would be as aggressive as me because I longed to climb as well as I possibly could, and some days she wasn't in the mood to push herself.

"What do you want to climb this afternoon?" Barb asked.

"Something hard," I answered.

That evening I slipped away from Camp 4 because I was in no mood to listen to the weekend crowd's sing-songs around the campfire. Barb was visiting a friend for dinner, and Jim was probably barhopping in San Francisco. My hands stung so badly that I could barely think. I felt like a lonely kid in the city of Camp 4, so I attempted to find some solace in the quiet woods of the valley floor.

I stopped at Eagle Creek to soak my hands; the skin on the back was scratched and raw in a few spots from being wedged so tightly in the crack. The climb had been desperate, so vertical and intimidating that I hadn't even glanced up at it once Barb and I arrived at the base. The crack had gone on forever (maybe 120 feet) and, at the end, when I was the most tired, it had widened by half an inch, just enough to make it bigger than the wide part of my fist. What a struggle! The last three feet of the crack took ten minutes. I tried to wedge my whole arm, a hand on one side of the crack, an elbow on the other, desperate for a place to rest. Finally I squirmed six inches higher and, reaching deep into the crack, I found an edge to lean against and was then able to pull up on to a small ledge. Jim's fist or any other man's fist would have wedged easily, but not mine. Barb had an equally bad time, and her hands looked worse! But maybe her friends had some hot water in which she could soak her hands.

It was a restless night and I awoke feeling uneasy and even more alone. I rolled onto my back and stared up at the stark trunk of a sugar-pine tree.

It was 200 feet tall and shot straight as a plumb line from the ground to the sky in one clean vertical line. "It's just like the rock walls here," I thought. It made me squeamish. Everything in Yosemite seemed bleakly vertical—the boulders, the walls, and even the tall barren pines! It was all so uncompromising, almost overbearing. Every climb that I examined had me craning my neck to see the top of a crack disappearing into a blank gray wall. In fact I seldom looked up from the bases of my climbs because it frightened me too much. I had a similar fear when I first began climbing, a desperate uneasiness that something might go wrong. But this late fear had surfaced when I began to dream about long and multiday routes, like Washington Column, *Steck-Salathé,* and ultimately the *Nose* of El Capitan. "By the time you do those routes you'll be competent," Jim had said. But I still imagined myself tiny and overtaxed on those huge walls, and I clutched to the thought of forgetting to tie into my jumars or rappelling off the end of the rope.

"THERE ARE SUPPOSED TO BE SOME DECENT LEDGES HERE WHERE WE can lie down," I said, leaning out on the rope and peering out from the depths of a chimney-sized crack.

"It's dark and I'm not moving," Barb stated. "Here, have some gorp."

I didn't really feel like moving either, for to move meant untying particular knots and unfastening certain carabiners, and I didn't want to undo the wrong ones. It was our first wall climb and our first time on a multiday route climbing a 1,000-foot face. We were well aware of the repercussions of a mistake, and with fatigue, an unusual routine, and now darkness, we had both got a little nervous and terribly conservative. We sat at the bottom of the V-shaped chimney and, leaning against each other, recounted the day's joys, horrors, and lessons.

"I don't swear anymore, it takes too much energy. I don't even sing. When I'm belaying I just sit with my head against the rock and doze."

"You nap when you're belaying me?"

After dinner I scooted 10 feet farther up the chimney and knotted my climbing rope to the eight anchors I'd put deep in the crack. Perhaps eight anchors were extravagant, but since I'd placed them in the dark, my vivid imagination required at least that many. Then I crawled out onto a ledge about the size of a toilet seat to spend the night.

It has always been one of my cardinal rules to avoid misery whenever possible, and this tiny ledge seemed like a ridiculous place to spend any time at all. It jutted out of a featureless vertical wall, and I could look straight down between my feet to Yosemite Village 700 feet below. I was prepared for the worst night of my life, but strangely I was more intrigued than disgruntled. "Jim has spent the night under more miserable circumstances," I thought. Besides, Barb and I were over halfway up Washington Column, and the fact that we'd get little sleep didn't seem to matter much.

We finished the climb the next day, delighted with ourselves for actually climbing a wall. With our ungainly packs we staggered happily down the trail to civilization, Kahlúa, and hot fudge sundaes. We spent two sleepy days identifying flowers along the Merced River before I again felt the rumbling need to do more difficult routes.

"El Cap next year!" I announced to Barb.

She hesitated, then said: "El Cap is three times bigger than the Column. We'd need seven days of water, and our sack would weigh eighty pounds. I think it would be too hard."

"We'll have to free climb the Stoveleg Cracks," I said. "That'll knock off two extra days."

Barb answered me softly and slowly: "Molly, you're climbing 5.9 and I'm climbing 5.8. The Stovelegs are 5.10, and with wall gear they'd feel even harder."

"Well, we'll just have to train! We'll do all the 5.9s at Arch Rock and the Cookie this spring, and then we'll be solid on the 5.10 by fall." I felt impatient; it seemed that Barb was stalling. We were both progressing so rapidly that it seemed ridiculous to waste time on less prestigious routes than The Captain itself. I loved to climb with her, but I loved the challenging routes more and knew that I could be leading 5.10 by the end of that spring.

Barb sensed my uneasiness and finally said, "You can do El Cap, Molly. I doubt that I ever will."

I felt wretched but I couldn't help answering, "Well, maybe we should free climb with other people for the rest of the month then."

"WOULD YOU PASS ME THE BAG, I THINK I'M GOING TO BE SICK," I SAID.

Barb reached across the ledge and retrieved some paper bags from the haul sack. "Are you going to be okay?" she asked.

"I'm so tired," I answered. "I've been living to climb El Cap for two years and I'm sure glad I didn't get here any sooner. I couldn't possibly have done this last year!"

Barb awoke early in the morning with the swallows, and as they darted and dived about us she passed out our allotment of granola bars, Tang, and one apple. She was in a typically cheerful mood. Barb was always like a little kid in the morning and especially optimistic on walls, as if that type of endurance and commitment most suited her strong body and will.

"Thanks to you, we made El Cap Tower in one day," I said. "You did a great leading in the dark."

"And we climbed the Stovelegs almost entirely free!" Barb exclaimed. Those beloved Stoveleg Cracks! For the last two years every crack I'd climbed had been a gesture of training for those cracks, and I was sad that they were over.

"Now all we have to do is climb the upper 2,000 feet of the route," I said. It seemed like a long way to go.

The first pitch that day was mine and it was nasty. A great vacuous chimney opened up like a yawning mouth for 40 feet and for the first time I was scared. There was no protection: if you fell at the top of the mouth you'd go slamming down onto the ledge. It was an awful image, and I whimpered and yelled down to Barb to come take the lead because she was better in chimneys. But no, that would take too much time. She sent up my better climbing shoes instead. Braver, I went up the chimney and finally hauled myself onto the top of the flake that formed its outside. This was the Texas Flake, but as I straddled its top I could have easily been a flea perched on a protruding mica chip on a huge boulder.

The whole day was tedious, for we often had to traverse sideways or pendulum into a different crack system. That night we were so exhausted that we slept like babes on a ledge so cramped that my rear end hung out over the valley below.

Jim once told me that if climbing were a religion, the great dihedrals on the upper 1,000 feet of El Cap would make a good cathedral. He was right. I felt fortunate, almost blessed to climb those great arching lines and roofs. Recessed in the back of each sweeping corner was an exquisite crack that one could write essays about. I envied the Stonemasters who had the time and talent to free climb those cracks, for they were all vertical or overhanging, and classically beautiful. I did my best, leaving behind my cursed stirrups, getting both hands and feet into the crack, and taking off for as long as I could free climb, resting on a nut, and then going again. I felt the way that I love to feel—elegant, strong, sure as a cat, and fast. I was so incredible that I kept reminding myself of how happy I was and, especially, how lucky.

And then there was the sack. A great red pig that had to be hauled up every pitch like a fat client who refused to jumar. The sack was so big and took so much energy to haul that it was as if our whole purpose on the climb was to haul the sack to the top; the climbing was for fun but the seventy-pound Grail was what really mattered.

By noon on the fourth and last day of our climb, I found myself reluctant to top out. I looked over at Barb, who had a yellow bandana holding back her long brown hair and accentuating her kind features. Her hands were well taped from her wrists to her cracked and bloody fingertips. She was my very best friend, and I wasn't sure how much I'd see her in the next two years because I'd enrolled in school, and my biannual trips to the Valley were about to cease. How could we relate if we couldn't climb together, or plan and train together? If our goals were not the same, could we remain such incredibly good pals? I had a feeling that the answer was yes, although it would never be quite the same again.

"Make sure you tie into your jumars," I needlessly advised. She gave me a sour look. I knew my comment sounded condescending, but I felt a surge of loneliness as I left her at the last belay and escaped to the summit. Everything had gone so well, but we both knew the story about the guy whose rope broke when he fell on the last pitch of El Cap.

But no, Barb and I were too thorough for such misfortune. We topped out safely and with enough food and water for our hungry friends who met us on the top. The friends emptied and carried the entire contents of the red pig, leaving us to descend the wooded paths together, down to my tent in Camp 4 where I found a note pinned to the door:

"Congratulations: first team of women up the *Nose*!"

Raised in a suburb of Philadelphia, Pennsylvania, Molly Bruce Higgins hitchhiked to Yosemite in 1974 with a friend with the goal of becoming a competent, independent climber. After a spring enjoying the Valley's granite walls, she traveled to the Pamir Mountains as part of the first American expedition allowed in the Soviet Union. Molly returned to Yosemite that fall, teaming up with Barb Eastman, with whom she would go on to share numerous important ascents in the following years, including the first all-female ascent of the *Nose* on El Capitan in 1977.

She works today as a microbiologist and lives with her husband in Whitefish, Montana, where they can ski, mountain bike, and climb to their hearts' content.

STEAK-SALAD: AN ASCENT OF THE SENTINEL

Carla Firey

We were dropped off at the pullout closest to the base of Sentinel. Julie judged that we had a late start because the sky had been light for fifteen to twenty minutes.

The approach zigzagged up ledges to a stretch of dirt hummocks stuck to steep slabs above a long drop. After mantling up the hummocks, Julie hesitated near the top of an open slab. I suspect I asked if we might ought to belay, but she said no, it was fine, and I would have no problem. The lack of any positive holds made it feel intensely like a problem. As I have never been a morning person, this was a rough wake-up. It also cemented my sense that I did not want to retreat off this climb and down climb those airy spots. I was completely onboard to do this climb. But it was Julie's idea that we could climb *Steck-Salathé* (known as Steak-Salad among many climbers) as a team of two women. We did not know of any other women climbing the route previously.

Julie and I had met in a rock climbing class at the University of Washington when she was a math undergrad and I was a senior in high school. We had also met the Seattle climbers who were pushing the limits of climbing in the Northwest. Junker cars and VW bugs were vehicles of choice for this demographic and were ideal, as long as they didn't break down or run out of gas. An old Volvo or VW van was a luxury ride. We didn't see less valuable cars at climbing areas until the bargain V-8 "Euro-wagons" showed in Yosemite.

Two years after meeting each other, Julie and I decided to hitchhike to the Tetons in the summer of 1972. The longest ride we had was in a tractor-trailer from a cheerful and respectful driver who listened to country-western radio. He made a point of telling us that in hitchhiking, even together, we were showing bad judgment. In the Tetons, we spent almost a week climbing out of Garnet Canyon. The most beautiful climb we did was Petzoldt Ridge, swinging leads on the white pegmatite with mica ribs and knobs, with a third climber we met at the climbers' ranch, Brian Cox from California. In subsequent seasons, Brian met us in Yosemite and, in this season of Steak-Salad, helped me train by joining me in climbing the *Northeast Buttress* of Higher Cathedral Rock.

The spring we embarked on *Steck-Salathé*, Julie and I were living in Camp 4 among the Seattle and Washington climbers, two of only a very few women there. One day as I was walking through the campground, one of the men in this group stopped me to ask a question: "You do realize, Carla, that this is a serious climb?" I can't remember my reply. This particular character, Don Harder, was one of the two Washington climbers who had originated the Steak-Salad name. The other would be Pat Timson, part of the yearly northern invasion of the inner sanctum of California climbing. Both were among the very top rock climbers in the West; both were no-nonsense and slightly intimidating. They would simul-climb *Steck-Salathé* in a few hours and wrap up the day by doing some additional climbs just for a workout.

The approach warmed us up, but we got cold on the first pitch. We had on long-sleeved shirts for the chimneys. Julie tied a windshirt around her waist; I had a thin wool button-down shirt for extra warmth. My pants were something like high-water khakis from either the surplus store or a second-hand store, held up with a piece of one-inch tubular webbing. We probably both wore Robbins boots for this climb, even though EB climbing shoes were the standard then. We had kneepads around our ankles ready to pull over our knees for chimneying.

Our harnesses were two-inch tubular webbing wrapped twice and knotted with a water knot. Mine was red. I had leg loops tied from one-inch tubular webbing. Our rack consisted of stoppers and hexes only, the largest being a #10 hex. We may have brought doubles of one or two of the larger hex sizes. Plus we would have had a few runners. Neither of us had climbed the route before; however, Julie had good information about the route and protection needed.

We had one quart of water between us, in the old flexible-type poly bottle that imparted an "eau de lab" vinyl flavor as the day wore on. It was tied by the neck to a short runner so the second could dangle the bottle below her hips to avoid interference with chimneying.

In my pocket I had a piece of jack cheese and some raisins in a knotted plastic bag, plus a book of matches. Julie had a candy bar and a space blanket. The matches and space blanket were because neither of us had a reputation for speed.

Not long before the day of our climb, a climber had gotten his foot stuck in a crack on one of the pitches. Unable to free his foot, he had fallen backward, hit his head on the ledge below, and died. This was not one of the crux pitches, but since it could be jinxed, it was determined to be one of my leads, and this set how we would swing leads from the bottom. This was not my idea, but it was clear I was expected to go along with it. At the same time, I remember feeling pretty sanguine about it; perhaps I was still young enough to feel immune to fate.

Julie led the Wilson Overhang pitch. We had been climbing routes like *Meatgrinder* and *Lunatic Fringe,* among other classic 5.10 crack climbs. I followed her earlier in the season and then led both later. This pitch was awkward and strenuous but otherwise not a problem. And since we had managed the crux without falling or hanging or leaving any uncleaned pro, surely all would be well for the rest of the climb(!).

There was plenty of dirt on lower-angle spots. Fortunately, more difficult sections were clean enough. I wore a large bandana that covered my head down to my eyebrows to keep dirt and sun out of my eyes and prevent "part sunburn" on the top of my head (as I'm a redhead, this was a real issue).

On May 13, 1976, Julie was our "topo manager." I'm pretty sure she reminded me, just before the rappel from the top of the Flying Buttress required to reach the ledge where the route continued, that once we rapped, we could not retreat. She did not realize that I had passed *my* point of no return after the exposed approach. After the rappel, we had a couple of pitches before the crux chimneys. I recollect feeling gripped faced with horizontal protection (a.k.a. a potential pendulum on slab) for "5.7" friction with Robbins boots. Ah well, I should have felt perfectly comfortable since my boots were well worn and I was probably second.

The first chimney pitch leading to the Narrows was mine to lead. In spite of being warned, I stemmed too far back in the chimney and then had to struggle sideways back to near the lip. There was no protection for a long distance, and I came close to panic when I got tired. I had to keep repositioning to effectively rest my wasted muscles between moves. And this was just the easy part of the chimney! At least I was able to place protection when it got slightly bomb bay—a term climbers use to describe a chimney that widens, threatening to drop you at any moment. At this juncture, I think I may have confided in my belayer that I could fall. True to form, Julie informed me I was not on anything that difficult, and therefore I would not fall.

I stopped to belay on the chockstone because I was uncertain the rope would reach an anchor above. Our rope was 165 feet long. Apparently I was expected to lead through the Narrows, and I received some admonishment about this omission. Still, this was probably for the best because I found it super awkward to clean and follow Julie's lead of the Narrows as it was. At this time, Julie was one of the best offwidth climbers in Yosemite (and probably in the United States), bar none. She had led *Twilight Zone* (an offwidth testpiece at that time) in a previous season without falling or hanging and probably did it onsight. And offwidths were not a strong part of my skill set. The anchor bolts at the chockstone were old and looked sketchy. I remember placing a #7 stopper along the chockstone for a backup. This belay was really cold, and I had to keep moving to avoid shivering.

I recollect hitting the proverbial wall on the last pitch. It was my lead. I told Julie I would lead it but I would probably have to hang to get up it. As a consequence, she took the lead, so we completed the route clean. It was late in the day and still hot in the last bit of light on top. I wanted to lie down and rest somewhere in the sand and granite blocks and manzanitas, but some taskmaster said we must move on.

We had enough light for the beginning of the descent, but then it became dark while we were hanging onto and battling downsloping branches of slide alder, using dirt-covered footholds over a short cliff—in the kind of pitch black where it's hard to see even a foot or two ahead. We could hear the creek to our right, so we knew we were more or less in the right spot.

After we had crept down by feel very slowly for a very long while, the May full moon came over the edge and we could see pretty well. Once down the gully, we crossed the meadow and walked back to Camp 4.

MY FIRST MEMORIES WHEN I SET OUT TO WRITE THIS REFLECTION, FORTY-four years after the deed, are images such as Julie's water bottle, the dirt hummocks, the pitch black of our descent, the moonrise. And the sensations of exposure, fatigue, cold, claustrophobia. I went looking through piles of old cardboard boxes for something I was sure I had thrown out. Miraculously, I found a box of old calendars with terse notes about climbs done, weather, people, and such. My present self is struck by the quantity of climbing my twenty-three-year-old self managed to do. I spent many other seasons in Yosemite before and after this one but never matched the amount of climbing I did in 1976.

My future husband would usually spend some or all of my Yosemite season with me, but this spring I was on my own for thirty-seven days, trying to settle some obsession with granite mastery or to test myself: Could I climb on my own? Still, many climbers around me did a lot more than me. At the time, it seemed to me I had a good season, but it felt unremarkable. Looking back, I see it was nevertheless an excellent season. My calendar notes for May 13 state: "was *hot* in the Valley—was cool on climb—we were in the shade—cold air came out of the cracks—did Steak-Salad *and* got down." I was reminded that the renowned Yosemite climber Werner Braun called this cold air "devil air" because it came from the "depths of utter darkness."

Yet I was still stuck on some questions and images. Was our rope 150 feet long? Or 165 feet? Did we do this route in the Robbins boots we both had used for years? Or EBs? I have discovered I have distinct visual memories of climbs and people in the past, yet the visual vignettes do not fall into a timeline; they form a wide-awake dream.

I had to get more facts. I cold-called Don Harder after my husband recalled he had a great memory. I knew he had been continuously climbing in Yosemite. Don shared his memories of doing the route three to four times. He also knew what gear was used and confirmed my recollection of our rack. I viewed online videos of the climb that Don forwarded.

Then I realized I needed a topo to locate the pitches in my mind. When my topo order arrived, I finally realized on which pitches I had been afraid of a lead fall, where I had struggled placing or cleaning pro, and at which belay I had been freezing cold.

Among the Washingtonians in Camp 4, we were often visited by California climbing friends on weekends and met new friends from around the country. There was nearly always someone to climb with among this talented and good-humored bunch, a bunch that had high expectations of themselves and others. A bunch you could count on to be conscientious about placements and anchors. Julie Brugger was a central personality in this group, and I was fortunate to be her climbing partner for many excellent climbs and adventures.

I am fairly certain we were the first women to climb *Steck-Salathé* as a team. I don't remember discussing this with Julie, but I have to think that climbing it onsight and in good form was a point of pride for both of us. I do recall that our lack of speed (descending after dark) was a mark against our performance in the minds of some. I think the climbers around us expected we would either succeed or fail. No one described it as an easy climb, but it was described as within our free-climbing ability.

Steak-Salad, for me, was one part all-day total body workout and one part high-level commitment characteristic of alpine climbs where you are on your own and responsible for your own fate. It echoed and prefigured the mostly alpine climbs I have also had the privilege to enjoy.

Carla Firey is the eldest daughter of Joan and Joe Firey, prolific Pacific Northwest alpinists, so it's no wonder she came to excel in the sport herself. Carla, too, identifies strongly as a Cascades climber, but her time in Yosemite helped shape the alpinist she would become. During the 1970s, Carla spent many seasons in Yosemite Valley, ticking off classic climbs with her female comrades from Washington. She became well known for her strength on the rock.

The allure of the alpine never waned; after leaving Yosemite, she traveled to various mountain ranges around North America, pursuing first ascents and big adventures. She lives in Seattle with her husband.

GROWING UP IN YOSEMITE VALLEY

Julie Brugger

The first time I went to Yosemite Valley, I hitchhiked there with my sister. She came to visit me in Seattle in the fall of 1969 before the start of our junior years in college. She was going to Ohio University and I to the University of Washington. That summer I had taken a beginning mountaineering course at the UW, and in thrall to my newfound passion for climbing, I thought she might enjoy climbing a small peak in the Cascades. She did not. After Seattle she was headed to Santa Barbara to visit a high school friend going to college there, and I was headed to the world's rock climbing mecca, Yosemite Valley. So we hitched to Berkeley together before parting ways. She bought me my first Yosemite guidebook there—the red one by Steve Roper—and inscribed the flyleaf with the date and the word *Insanity*.

That was the first of many stays in the Valley throughout the 1970s and '80s. My memory of when and which climbs I did is pretty poor: what I remember best is the feeling of being in the place and the people I climbed with. Most I have lost track of, although if they are still climbing and we happen to cross paths somewhere, we greet each other as old friends. Some were killed in the mountains. A few remain close friends.

Fall 1969, inspired by my first trip to the Valley, I took a rock climbing course from the UW. Several of Washington's best young climbers had volunteered to help the instructor teach the course. In the evenings, when we gathered around the campfire, they regaled us with tales of their nearly year-round exploits in the mountains and Yosemite Valley, and they introduced me to the possibility of being a "climbing bum." I had grown up envisioning only one trajectory for my future—the societally accepted one, college and full-time work—and they opened my eyes to other possibilities. One of them, Mark, became my boyfriend, and from 1970 to 1972 we lived the climbing life: traveling in his beat-up red Volkswagen to climb in the Cascades, the Bugaboos, the Tetons, the Wind River Range, Yosemite, and the Southwest deserts.

Many folks of the climbing bum persuasion had not acquired skills that enabled them to get well-paying jobs, but I was fortunate because I had a degree in math, knew how to program computers, and lived in the soon-to-be software capital of the world. For me, well-paying jobs were easy to find. That's how I came to be in the Valley in the fall of 1972 when I received word that Mark, who had stayed in Washington to make money harvesting fruit, had been killed alpine climbing in the Cascades. I went back to Washington for the funeral, but the next spring I was back in the Valley with his old Volkswagen, which his parents had given to me. After that, I was there for a month or two nearly every spring and fall for many years.

There was always a contingent of Washington climbers in the Valley. In the spring, we often went to Joshua Tree while waiting for the weather to warm up in the Valley. The dry desert air and sun on my skin after long, wet, dark Seattle winters felt like awakening from hibernation. Our crew shared the same campsite and bear locker in Camp 4 and often climbed with each other. Like-minded climbers from other states also joined us, like Neil from Oregon and Reed from New Mexico, who would roll into camp on his BMW motorcycle. We thought that in general climbers from California were too groovy and climbers from Colorado were too snobby, although I did meet great partners from both states.

On a typical day in the Valley, we dispersed with our various partners to our objectives for the day and showed up back in camp around dinnertime. I like to cook and would cook yummy dinners on my two-burner Coleman stove, often sharing them with whomever I had climbed with that day. I even rigged up a Dutch oven with different-sized pots and baked cakes for people's birthdays. Nevertheless, my food was sometimes pilfered from the bear locker, which really pissed me off, and I let it be known. Shortly after that our locker acquired an inscription inside the lid: *Munchkins are screwed.*

This was before climbing gyms, so even though I did weight training in the winters, we always arrived in the Valley in the spring out of shape. We had to do routes we had done before to get back in the groove, and they always seemed harder. My next boyfriend, Pat, was a workout fanatic and always brought a pull-up bar, which he put up between two trees in the rescue site. After a day of climbing we'd do pull-ups. After a while, other resident climbers added their training equipment: Bachar's ladder and Werner's slackline. Unlike the sport climbers of today, we climbed every day, maybe taking a day off a week, and then we felt like wimps. So we still did pull-ups. We thought you needed to climb every day to get better. On days off we might go swimming in the Merced, have Volkswagen races around the loop, or leave the Valley to go shopping in the city. There was also the magnificent Ahwahnee brunch on Easter and Mother's Day. But what to do after that? Rest days were boring.

In the spring when the weather was bad, and in the fall when it got dark early, we would hang out at the Yosemite Lodge lounge. The place was packed with climbers: I don't think I ever saw a tourist in there. I imagine we scared them away. Every once in a while, the Lodge management would kick us out of the lounge and we Washington climbers and our buddies would hang out in the hall between the lounge and the gift shop, sitting against the walls. Les from California, a Chinese guy with a long black braid, would play Neil Young songs on his guitar. To us he sounded just like Neil Young. To this day I think of him whenever I hear those songs and wonder what he's doing.

There are several smells that I always associate with the Valley. Bay leaves, from the trees at the base of many routes. Formic acid, from the ants that had nests in the trees and would swarm all over you if you disturbed them. Tincture of benzoin, which we used to apply to the skin of our fingers to make them tough and keep chalk on. We didn't use tape (it was definitely not cool), so my hands were usually covered in scabs from crack climbing. And the smell of the exhaust of the propane-powered shuttle buses, an innovation in the 1970s.

One spring, a friend named Bruce tried to talk me into doing the *Salathé Wall* with him the entire drive down from Seattle. I liked free climbing and was not interested in doing walls. I said no thanks, but he kept pestering me.

Finally, I agreed to go with him to fix the first few pitches and then we would decide from there. I was so painfully slow that he decided to solo the route, so I got what I wanted in the end.

One fall I met Larry from Colorado. We were climbing at about the same level and proceeded to do all the 5.9s in the guidebook, including very obscure ones that had long approaches with a lot of bushwhacking and that no longer appear in any guidebook. We were desperate because we were running out of 5.9s and we thought there was no way we could do 5.10. But we had finally climbed them all, so Larry asked his friend Steve, a top climber from the East Coast who was living in Colorado, to suggest a really easy 5.10 that maybe we could get up. (There were no 5.10 a's, b's, c's, and d's then, just 5.10. And no 5.11 either, just "hard 5.10.") Steve suggested *Sacherer Cracker*. It has a little offwidth on it and Larry hated offwidths, so it was my lead. We did it! And that was our first 5.10. Steve gave us more suggestions and we kept going.

This was during the transition from pitons to clean climbing. I was an instant proponent of climbing without pins, because they were heavy! Larry and I did all our routes clean and did a hammerless ascent of the *Steck-Salathé*. When I later did *Direct North Buttress* on Middle Cathedral with Will, he agreed to do it clean but then brought along a hammer. He said he was going to use it to test the fixed pins but instead used it to remove pins, which he placed again later. I was pissed.

One spring, chess was all the rage among Valley climbers. I hated chess and was terrible at it, but in order to find partners, I would take my chess set to the lounge, position it visibly next to me, and hope that some climber would come by and ask me to play. Then I could ask him or her to go climbing. One evening, who should show up but Steve. Uh-oh, I knew he was a killer chess player, that he would be bored to death with my level of play, and that no way would he be interested in climbing with me. On the third count I was wrong. After a very brief game, he proposed: "I know a new route Bridwell just put up. Want to go do it? I'll bring the rack and the rope."

We met the next morning, Steve carried all the gear (I wasn't used to my partner offering to do that!), and we hiked up to an obscure route whose name I can't remember, but I think it had *Eagle* in it. We got ready to climb. I was presuming I would belay, but Steve handed me the rack and said, "Your lead."

What? I thought. *I don't even know how hard this is.*

I expressed my uncertainty, and he said, "You can do it."

So I gave it a go, and I did it!

His next suggestion was *Meatgrinder*. I knew about that climb. Mark had done it and told me it was a burly layback, so I had no intention of ever trying it.

Steve again said, "I'll bring the rack," and I assumed I would be leading the short first pitch. But at the base of the route, he started gearing up for that pitch. We didn't do beta back then, but when he saw the look on my face, he assured me he knew a way to do the pitch that avoided the burliness. So when I got to the wide part, where I was supposed to "swing into a power layback," he told me to look for holds on the main wall and just face climb up inside it, occasionally chimneying against the flake behind me.

When I got to the top, I could see a bunch of people watching from the road below. I was later informed that one of the people watching from below was Bridwell. The words quoted above were purportedly his, and he was amazed to see *Meatgrinder* done without the layback.

Next, we did another new multi-pitch route that Bridwell had just put up on Elephant Rock. We were doing it at the same time as Jim Donini and his partner. I knew nothing about this one either. Steve led the first pitch again. I watched the guys ahead of us wrestle with the second pitch, a long offwidth. I had done quite a few offwidths by then, so it didn't look too bad to me. I think Jim was surprised to see me starting out on the lead. I managed to do it also. Only later did I learn it was *Plumb Line*, 5.10d.

I never knew why Steve chose to mentor me. It was one of the most memorable and moving experiences in my climbing life: I felt seen as an equal, and it opened my eyes to my potential. Climbers didn't project routes then (although I can remember watching Steve and Henry Barber climbing up and down *Hardd* without weighting the rope when they were trying to free it), so you had to have the confidence to be bold to push your limits.

Some seasons I climbed a lot with Carla, whom I met in the rock climbing course I took in 1969. We worked our way through the 5.10 thin cracks at the short cliffs in the Valley: Arch Rock, the Cookie, Five and Dime. Among others, we did *Stone Groove, Gripper, Lunatic Fringe, Outer Limits, Five and Dime, English Breakfast Crack, New Dimensions, Anticipation,* and *Leanie Meanie*. We also did many multi-pitch routes.

Catherine was Washington's best woman climber. She and I climbed together in the Valley one season. Her goal was to get better at laybacks;

mine to get better at offwidths. Offwidths were the in thing then: the hardest climbs, the hard-man climbs. After falling into disfavor for many years, they seem to have regained their cachet in recent years. But back then we protected them with tube chocks: no camming devices that you can push up ahead of you. The crux was often climbing around the piece after you put it in. I found that being small, I was pretty good at offwidths. I could get more of my body into them than most people, and I had good turnout, as Catherine called it.

I had done quite a few offwidths already, but it was hard to find partners who enjoyed offwidth technique and wanted to do them. When I did *Secret Storm* with a French guy, he laybacked the whole thing when following; Ajax from the East Coast did the same thing following on *Chopper*. I had worked my way through the grades: *Moby Dick, Chingando, Crack of Despair, Secret Storm, Vendetta, Ahab, Edge of Night, Chopper*, and *Twilight Zone*, my favorite. With Catherine I did *Steppin' Out* and *Cream*, and she did *Catchy Corner* and the *Good Book*. I also found a partner from California, Mark, who liked wide cracks, and we did *1096, Lost Arrow Chimney*, and *Basket Case*.

My favorite type of climbing was the long free climbs: *Royal Arches* and North Dome, everything on Higher and Middle Cathedral, *East Buttress* and *West Face* on El Cap, Elephant Rock, the Rostrum. But eventually I tired of spending so much time climbing in the Valley. I wanted to explore new areas. I was an alpine climber at heart and wanted to do more climbing in the mountains. I only went back to the Valley twice more after that.

In 1987, I went with Chris, a Brit I met while climbing in Joshua Tree. It was his first trip to the United States, and of course he had to go to the Valley. He wanted to do the *Nose*, and I agreed because most of it goes free at a pretty moderate grade. I sure am glad he convinced me to do it. We started up the route right after a storm and had the whole wall to ourselves: it was a magical experience.

In 1992, I went back with an exceptionally talented climber from South Africa whom I had met in the Alps in 1987 and married. It was his first time in the United States also, and of course he wanted to go to the Valley. We did a bunch of hard routes, with him in the lead, and a couple more walls that went mostly free then (and go all free now). After all that time away and climbing in so many other areas, everything felt so hard: the rock was slippery, there were no footholds, and there were too many wide cracks. And I did not enjoy staying in Camp 4, crowded together with strangers.

EXUM
Mountain Guides

PREVIOUS PAGE Catherine Cullinane, Margo Erjavac, and Gwen Schneider playfully mock the famous photo of Billy Westbay, Jim Bridwell, and John Long after the first one-day ascent of the *Nose*. *(Photo by Charlie Fowler)* ABOVE Chelsea Griffie makes her way up *Separate Reality,* Yosemite's fiercest roof crack. *(Photo by Greg Epperson)* OPPOSITE Sibylle Hechtel jumars on the *Salathé Wall*. *(Photo courtesy of Sibylle Hechtel)*

OPPOSITE Nancy Bickford Miller rappels after climbing the Lower Brother in 1955. *(Photo by Bob and Ira Spring)* TOP Sue Giller tapes for battle in 1979 on the *East Face* of Washington Column, now known as *Astroman*. *(Photo by Molly Bruce Higgins)* BOTTOM Barb Eastman swings for glory to enter the Stovelegs on the first all-female ascent of the *Nose* on El Capitan in 1977. *(Photo by Molly Bruce Higgins)*

TOP Climbing at night allows Babsi Zangerl cooler temperatures on a free ascent of El Capitan's *Zodiac*. *(Photo by Francois Lebeau)* LEFT Barb Eastman lowers out under the Great Roof on the *Nose*. *(Photo by Molly Bruce Higgins)* OPPOSITE Jo Whitford is determined on *Black Angel*, a finger crack in Tuolumne Meadows. *(Photo by Greg Epperson)*

Bea Vogel forges pitons in the engineering lab at Stanford University in the 1950s. *(Photo courtesy of the Vogel family and Stanford Special Collections)* PREVIOUS PAGE Lola Delnevo takes in the view of the Valley on an adaptive ascent of *Zodiac* on El Capitan. *(Photo by Diego Pezzoli)*

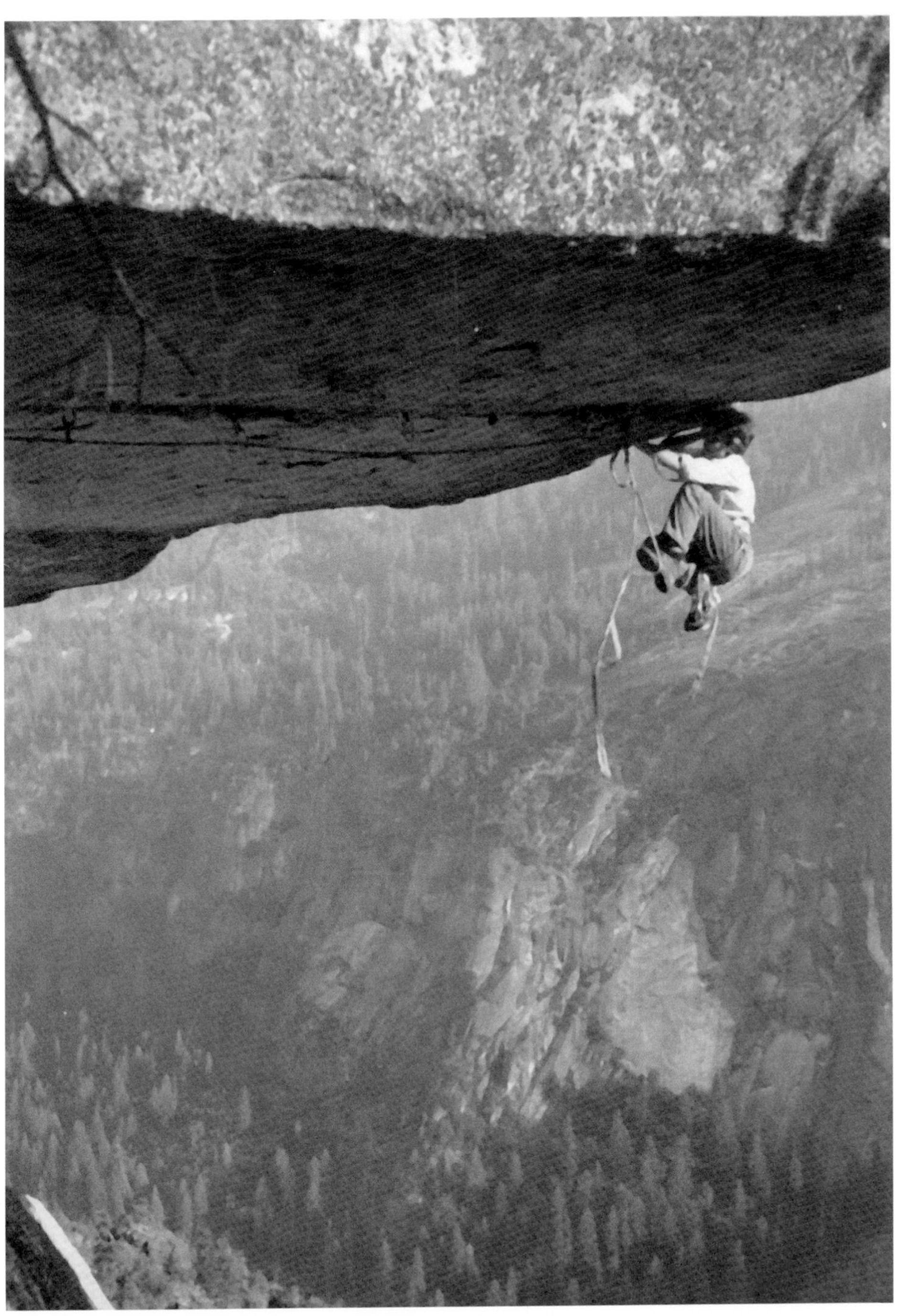

Meredith Little battles mind-boggling exposure on an early aid ascent of the *Owl Roof*. *(Photo courtesy of the Little family)*

TOP Shelley Presson Dunbar climbs *Crest Jewel* on North Dome with a fantastic perspective on Half Dome. *(Photo by Charlie Fowler)* BOTTOM Lisa Rands was the first woman to climb *Thriller*, a classic, very difficult boulder problem near Camp 4. *(Photo by Wills Young)*

CLOCKWISE FROM TOP LEFT Lydia Bradey takes a break on a portaledge. *(Photo by Duncan Critchley)* Beverly Johnson, known as "Big Wall Bev," sorts through gear after the first all-female ascent of El Cap, via the *Triple Direct* with Sibylle Hechtel, in 1973. *(Photo by Sibylle Hechtel)* Jane Jackson pulls the infamous last move of *Zodiac* during the first all-female one-day ascent of the route in 2018. *(Photo by Eric Bissell)*

OPPOSITE Nina Williams belays Katie Lambert on an ascent of Middle Cathedral Rock's *Father Time* *(Photo by Julie Ellison)* TOP Anne Carpenter on an early ascent of Higher Cathedral Spire *(Photo by Bob Kincheloe)* BOTTOM Josie McKee keeps her cool while demonstrating keen Yosemite finesse on *The Crucifix* on Higher Cathedral Rock *(Photo by Drew Smith)* FOLLOWING PAGE Hazel Findlay focuses on her next move on *Magic Line*. Findlay was the first woman and third person to climb the route. *(Photo by Eliza Earle)*

I haven't been back since then and have no desire to ever go back. From what I hear, it is much more crowded, there are lines to do the classic routes, fixed lines and camera crews all over El Cap. Nowadays it seems like Valley climbers keep track of what others have accomplished and strive to outdo them. We just did our own thing. The Valley was a place where I grew up as a climber: I learned a variety of crack-climbing techniques, got good at placing gear, and became efficient on multi-pitch routes. I also discovered what I really loved about climbing: being in wild places with no one else around except my partner and feeling and fitting in to the rhythm of the place in order to succeed in our objective. Yosemite helped me develop the solid climbing skills I needed to be able to do that in the mountains, and I am content to live with my memories of the Valley.

Julie Brugger first came to Yosemite in 1969 as a college student. Instantly hooked on the community, rock quality, and perfect weather that graces Yosemite in the spring and fall, Julie soon established herself as one of the best offwidth climbers—a strenuous type of climbing that many avoid—of a generation. Her early entrance into the emerging world of computer programming meant Julie could let her life revolve around climbing trips. Her love of the mountains soon took her to the great ranges of the world, snagging under-the-radar ascents of Cerro Torre in Patagonia, Cassin Ridge on Denali, and multiple prominent north faces of the Alps.

Later, seeking a change, Julie discovered a love of anthropology and pursued a doctoral degree. Her research interests center on natural resource management and climate change in the American West. She lives in Escalante, Utah.

A NATURAL PATH

Lucy Parker

Growing up in Yosemite, being born and raised in the tribe of the Yosemite Ahwahneechee Miwuk Paiute people, I lived in one of the last villages. It was located next to Camp 4—or Sunnyside, as we used to call it. As children we used to have to walk a couple miles to school (there were no school buses at that time), and we would walk right through Camp 4. I remember seeing a lot of guys there with rock climbing gear, and we'd just walk by without really knowing what was going on. My parents would tell us not to talk to anyone and to just walk through, but the climbers there were curious about who we were.

Later on, I started meeting people and understanding what they were doing with the ropes and how they were climbing up the rocks. Soon I started meeting all the guys, and they became my friends. At that time, the climbers didn't really climb like they were going to be world famous or get sponsored. It was nothing like that, it was just a sport they fell in love with. It never seemed competitive; everyone got along, and at the end of the day we'd all gather together.

Soon I could tag along with the climbers, and they said I could learn how to climb if I wanted to. I started hanging out at the base, and then I'd top-rope. We used to hike up and have a base party where we would haul up the haul bags and whatever we could carry and spend the night at the base to support our friends and send them off on their El Cap routes.

One time, Ron Kauk and I were out looking for climbs down by Cascade Falls. We were hiking through the boulders, and that's when he saw that roof up there, the climb that would become *Separate Reality*. But while we were scrambling up the boulders, I remember looking down into a cave and saying to Ron, "There's something down in this cave!" There was a small opening—not too deep—and I saw something in there, so we climbed in and found two baskets lying in there. We pulled them out of the earth. You could sit in this cave, which felt like it was for one person. All the rock was polished like someone had been going there, and these two baskets were preserved in this dark cave. They were both folded over and had been partly eaten by mice, but I recognized them as burden baskets, with their unique conical shape.

Climbing made me so much more aware of my surroundings. Growing up there, I heard the traditional stories in school about the rocks but never thought about climbing them. So when I realized what the climbers were doing, it really opened me up. The seventies were simply fun years. I never did any of the big walls, just a lot of short free climbing, but it felt like a natural path to climbing, and it was one of the best times of my life. Everyone loved Yosemite, and being from there, I was so happy to see that. Getting to climb what I did, learning the skills and to trust myself, was so valuable. It feels like it was only yesterday.

Lucy Parker is Ahwahneechee Yosemite Miwuk, Mono Lake Paiute, Coast Miwok, and Pomo and was born and raised in Yosemite Valley. She is the great-granddaughter of Lucy Tom Telles and the daughter of Dr. Julia Parker, both world-renowned basket weavers. Lucy grew up near Camp 4, where she eventually fell in with the campground's infamous resident climbers. Through their mentorship, Lucy learned to connect with her homeland in a different way.

Lucy travels the country sharing her family's craft with students of traditional art. She lives in June Lake, California, where she also works as a ski instructor. Lucy cares deeply about passing her family history on to her four children, including the traditional songs, cultural skills, and lineage that tie them to Yosemite.

LEADING BY EXAMPLE

Ellie Hawkins

When a friend told me there were rock climbers in El Rito, I bolted straight for New Mexico. It was August of 1969. When I arrived, all the climbers were out working on a fire crew except for the one who was seriously injured, Bruce Hawkins. We became inseparable.

Bruce had back surgery in the spring of 1971, and that September we arrived for the first time in Yosemite. In the camping site next to us was a group of foreign climbers with rich, colorful mountaineering histories: Tim Auger, a Canadian; Bugs McKeith, a Scotsman; plus Englishmen Rob Wood, George Homer, and Ray Gilles. That night they had a campfire, and I asked shyly, "Will you take me rock climbing?" I heard a deep voice in the dark say, "We do not like taking women because they are slow." I was young, naive, and impressionable, but they brought me climbing anyway, and the next day Bugs said he had never seen a beginner climb so well and so fast. I never whined or was hesitant because I knew that they would not have taken me climbing again. Because of Bruce's injury, if I wanted to climb every day, it meant being at the guys' campsite early each morning.

My third time climbing, Bruce and George had me lead a bolted 5.9 pitch. When Bugs and Rob found out that evening, they were furious. They had become protective and supportive, especially Bugs, when it came to safety, and they didn't think I was ready to be leading. At that time, we climbed in swami belts with slings in soft gray hiking boots called Kronhofers. Wide-eyed, I learned quickly to climb 5.9 to 5.10 offwidths and finger cracks. We had a lot of fun, and in late November I bought my first pair of EB rock shoes.

The following spring I met a variety of partners, and a group of us was able to acquire a site in Camp 4. The first thing I did that year was to swing leads on three Grade V routes with Bruce. I enjoyed the routes but was uncomfortable wearing a swami belt. Those slings were painful! However, the views, critters, and time in nature became intoxicating. Mike White introduced me to Beverly Johnson. Bev admitted she was extremely competitive, and I liked how straightforward she was. She knew where my camp was but never came by to partner up for climbing. One day, Bev was with Chuck Pratt at the Chapel Wall parking lot. Somehow she knew about my climbing. With dry humor she told me, "I have my spies out checking on your climbing progress." At first I was a bit embarrassed, but we both laughed. She had a reputation as a good climber, and I took what she said as a compliment. Years later after she met Mike Hoover, I got to know her better. I found Bev to be a compassionate, loving being who was exceptionally talented.

In the Valley later that fall, Keith Nannery asked Bruce and me to do El Capitan's *North America Wall* when we returned in the spring. This meant we had a lot to do in Seattle: lots of gathering of equipment, sewing, and organizing. A friend of Bruce's let us borrow his sail shop in the evenings. Using industrial sewing machines, I made slippery sailcloth haul bags. I used heavy-duty thread with a speedy stitcher to sew thick webbing straps on the bags. After collecting webbing and padded backpack straps from REI, I incorporated the materials into one of the first padded harnesses. Harnesses would become more common in the coming years, but until then it was just swami belts or improvisations.

The spring of 1973 arrived, and the guys we'd befriended in camp were excited for us as we prepared for the *North America Wall*. While I was organizing some equipment, a climber I didn't know came up to me to say that women were talented in cooking and sewing but didn't have the spatial intelligence for A4 big walls. He sincerely believed what he said. I smiled and walked away chuckling. When Bruce and Keith heard what this guy had said, they decided right then and there that I should lead both A4 pitches. Soon I was up there, staring up at Cyclops Eye, one of the most notorious pitches on the route. It was my lead. Standing on an RURP (an incredibly small piton not much bigger than a postage stamp), I felt it starting to shift. If it pulled, I knew that all the knifeblade pitons below would pop out and I would swing down and smash into a dihedral. Bruce said my eyes were as big as saucers, but I didn't fall. That was likely the fifth ascent of this route. The hauling did a number on me, prompting a visit to Portland to see both my family doctor and a cardiologist.

The doctor advised that I take some time to rest, so I headed back down to hang out in one of Yosemite's beautiful meadows, reading and stretching. The doctor cautioned me not to climb for nine months after straining myself so significantly, but after five months Bruce started bugging me about a new route. I finally gave in and belayed him on the first pitch. After cleaning the route, I was in no condition to lead the next pitch. He was not happy with me, and neither was my cardiologist. I made a rule that it was important for me to take the responsibility of swinging leads on every wall I climbed. Otherwise, I had no business being up there.

After I healed, I put all my concentration into building strength. Getting my body in better shape took time and patience. I was not as brave sometimes as I had been before, and I had less confidence in my body after being injured. When my body developed more strength and endurance again, I was willing to take more risks. Reinhold Messner's book *The Seventh Grade* was my bible. After a while, hauling was a bit less brutal because my legs were stronger. We climbed more big walls that year, including the *Salathé Wall* on El Cap.

It was an exciting time for all of us in North America. Barriers were being breached, many new routes were being developed, and a constant influx of new personalities from all over the world would arrive in Yosemite every year. After climbing big walls, we concentrated on lots of free climbing. We did many first ascents but rarely named or recorded the routes, including some on the Incredible Hulk in the Eastern Sierra. These have been climbed since, but at the time we were just focused on adventure.

Ever since the first time I saw El Cap, I knew I wanted to solo it. I started learning to solo by climbing two routes I'd done previously with Bruce on Washington Column, the *South Face* and the *Prow*. But in the next ten years, I spent a lot of time away from the Valley, climbing in Canada and across New Mexico and Nevada. It was October of 1982 when I returned and decided to start soloing Grade VI routes, the largest walls in the Valley. In the late 1970s I had bought some of the first Friends, a new camming device, from Ray Jardine. I wanted to solo *Tis-sa-ack* on Half Dome using these for protection on the route's notorious expanding flakes. It would have been perfect, but back then, Bruce and Jim Bridwell were convinced that the Friends would not work. Instead of me soloing *Tis-sa-ack*, they both suggested the *Direct Northwest Face* instead. I knew it would be one of the hardest routes for me to haul because of all the small roofs and lower-angle slabs, but to appease Bruce, I climbed *Direct* like he wanted. Just as I had imagined, the hauling on the *Direct* was incredibly hard. It took all my leg strength to get the two haul bags up. Years later, both Bridwell and Bruce forgot what they had said and contradicted themselves by claiming they couldn't understand why I hadn't soloed *Tis-sa-ack*.

In the late spring of 1985, I finally soloed El Cap via a route called *Never Never Land*. Bruce and our friend Mark Chapman had done the first ascent of this route in 1978. The hauling at first was slow, but after three or four pitches, it became steep. A peregrine falcon introduced himself on the first part of the route. At first, he would dive, trying to scare me because he thought I was a threat. But after a while we became friends, communicating with each other for hours on the climb. At the beginning of the twenty-first pitch, I ran into a problem. I reached a sloping ledge underneath a slightly overhanging wall featuring a long reach to the bolt stud with a nut on the end ready to pop off. Bruce was well over six feet tall and Mark around six feet, but since I only stood at five foot two, I couldn't reach it. Bruce and Mark had run out of hangers for the bolt, so there I was, teetering on that precarious sloping ledge with a huge, heavy rack trying to tighten that loose extended nut. It was impossible for me to reach. I stood up high and lost my balance, and the wire of the stopper I was using to reach as high as I could popped off. I fell 30 feet and injured my hand badly. But left with no choice, I got back up onto the route. Two pitches remained before the top. I don't know how I did it, but I finished the last A3 and A4 pitches, but not without taking a 100-foot fall.

These first solo adventures were to prepare me to make a first ascent in Ribbon Fall Amphitheater, a beautiful area with lots of wildlife. I called the route *Dyslexia*. It was interesting but loose and full of black silt from the nearby waterfall. Big balls of granite were stuck on the wall. As I put several cams under each ball of granite, the cams would expand, some completely opening and falling out. I was afraid that these hunks of granite, some weighing a couple of tons or more, would come off. Every evening while I was on the wall, a whirlwind would come screaming down the top of Ribbon Fall Amphitheater, making wild screeching noises and causing my sleeping cot to shake and twist all over. Then, about nine o'clock, it would come to a dead stop. I was on the route for eight days.

Today, at the age of seventy-one, I live in Joshua Tree. I wake up every morning feeling lucky to look out my window at this beautiful panoramic view. On crystal-clear summer nights, it's exciting to sit back and watch the incredible meteor showers. All I can say is that life has been amazing. I've met so many unusual people and have lived so many incredible adventures. Being alive has been a continual learning process. My life hasn't been without tragedy, but for me, it's a waste of time not to be happy.

Ellie Hawkins's childhood on the banks of the Columbia River in Oregon instilled a love for wilderness and adventure in her. On a trip to New Mexico, she met her future husband and discovered rock climbing. She quickly put her many years of dance lessons to use, perfecting the finesse required for scaling Yosemite granite. A background in clothing design helped her create much of the gear she needed for big-wall climbing.

By the mid-1980s, Ellie was among the leading figures in Yosemite Valley, with solo ascents of the *Direct Northwest Face* on Half Dome and *Never Never Land* on El Capitan. *Dyslexia*, named after the condition she had struggled with all her life but didn't have a name for until she was an adult, was the first big-wall route in Yosemite to be established solo by a woman. Today, Ellie continues to hike, climb, and enjoy the beauty and the critters around her in Joshua Tree, California.

SANDBAGGED BY THE STONEMASTERS

Maria Boone Cranor

This story originally appeared in a 2010 Patagonia catalog.

Swami belts? Check. EBs? Check. Stoppers? Hexes? Check. Nancy and I stuffed our packs into my tiny hatchback. We had pored over our yellow Meyers guides and pondered the Cookie, Arch Rock, Middle, the Apron. We'd picked out some routes we thought we could do, and we were primed for our first trip to the Valley—girls on the loose with rope, rack, and, we hoped, the chops to hold our own at the epicenter of the climbing universe.

In the days before the Park Service clamped down on the enjoyable, grubby anarchy of Camp 4, it was possible—and highly desirable—to live in the C4 parking lot, a fizzing social scene at all hours. Shortly after Nancy and I arrived there on this highly anticipated foray to Yosemite, we pulled out the stove and started organizing our dinner ingredients, which fatefully included the catnip of 1970s climbers: a gallon of Gallo Hearty Burgundy.

No sooner had the Gallo made its appearance than a couple of fit-looking locals drifted over, settling in to trade wine access for entertaining tales of derring-do on the crags. The evening wore on, the level of wine in the bottle sank lower and lower, and the stories got funnier and funnier. Eventually our guests retired, leaving behind an empty Gallo jug and a burning question: *Who were those guys?*

"Those guys" were Jim Bridwell and Dale Bard, a formidable welcoming committee. From that evening on, we were mentored (and tormented) by Jim, Dale, and friends from Southern California—the Stonemasters—who'd relocated to the Valley. The very next morning, and every morning thereafter, the lads wandered over with helpful—and, we would learn, profoundly unreliable—suggestions for routes we should do.

That first morning, we obediently headed off to the Apron to climb an obscure 10-pitch route recommended by Largo (John Long) and Gramicci (Mike Graham) in the strongest terms. Our first route in Yosemite! It was bound to be great.

The Apron was much bigger and more forbidding than our home crag, Suicide Rock; we knew its featureless expanse would test our minimal route-finding skills. "Where does this thing go? I can't even see the next bolt. Do you suppose that bush is the belay anchor? Nancy, watch me, I may have to downclimb back to the last piece of pro. Watch me, this looks like a hard move." And after what turned out to be a dirty, dubiously protected route that was about three times longer than anything we'd ever done before, we still had to get down via a series of long rappels that provided us a final jolt of anxiety.

That evening, the boys came by to find out what we'd climbed that day. "Well, of course we did that route you recommended, the *Punchbowl,*" we replied proudly.

"Ho, man," Largo boomed, amidst general laughter, "that must have been the second ascent!"

So began our sometimes terrifying, always entertaining, apprenticeship in Bridwell's Yosemite. "You guys told us that route wasn't run out!" I'd complain crabbily after yet another draining adventure, to which Gramicci, with his irrepressible grin, would innocently and inarguably reply, "But if we'd told you about that, you wouldn't have done it!"

Maria Boone Cranor is a sixth-generation Californian who spent two weeks of every summer making the pilgrimage from her childhood home in San Francisco to Yosemite National Park. Her introduction to climbing led swiftly to infatuation, and it allowed her the freedom to explore the walls of the park that had become her sanctuary. Maria's onsight, first female ascent of the 5.11 testpiece *Valhalla* at Southern California's Suicide Rock cemented her place in Stonemaster history and as a role model to a new generation of climbers.

Maria was one of the first employees of Chouinard Equipment; when the company dissolved, she and a few friends rallied to raise funds to start Black Diamond Equipment, a name of Maria's concoction. Today, Maria splits her time between the Bay Area in California and Salt Lake City, Utah.

THE SHIELD

Lynn Hill

This story is an edited excerpt from Hill's memoir, *Climbing Free: My Life in the Vertical World*.

The *Nose* introduced Mari and me to the cult of El Capitan. Back then, on the cusp of the seventies and eighties, climbers viewed the experience of living for days on end on a gigantic cliff as a mystical pilgrimage. These were heady times. We indulged in these "vertical retreats" as a means of reaffirming our belief in the virtue of abandoning material comforts in favor of the kind of character-building experiences that inevitably occur on these big-wall journeys. Through such intense experiences you get to know your partner's true nature without pretense. Mari and I were good friends and we worked well together.

The *Nose* had provided a good challenge for us and we wanted more, so we planned another El Cap route. This time we'd do one that was steeper, more difficult, and that would require us to learn more advanced aid climbing techniques. This time we'd spend more time living in the vertical world. If Yosemite Valley is to the world of rock climbing what the Himalayan Range is to mountaineering, then for us, doing El Capitan by a route like the *Shield* would be the equivalent of tackling Everest.

The *Shield* is a big-wall experience altogether different from the *Nose*. While the *Nose* is steep, especially in the upper third of the route in the huge corners, the *Shield* is so overhanging that a drop of water falling from the top of the route would land in the forest 200 feet out from the base. The last chunk of the climb—a thousand-foot feature known as the headwall—juts over the floor of the valley so dramatically that the first time I watched a party climbing up it, I was reminded of two flies crawling around the underside of a giant hot-air balloon. The only way to climb this overhanging wall is by slow and methodical aid climbing tactics. Up on the *Nose*, Mari and I had often been able to stuff our hands into cracks and quickly free climb long sections of the route. But the cracks of the *Shield* are not much wider than a piece of string.

Into these we'd have to hammer tiny pitons, one after another for hundreds of feet. Hanging from our pitons in ladderlike slings called aiders and inching our way upward, it could take hours to climb 100 feet. Though I was more enthusiastic about the natural movement of free climbing, the dramatic, wildly exposed position that we'd put ourselves into on the *Shield* made the labor of aid climbing—which I have no interest in if taken as a style on its own—seem worth the effort. Aid climbing would take us to a place on El Cap that no other method would allow us to reach.

The other aspect of climbing the *Shield* that would be a new experience for us was the way we would have to live on the wall. On the *Nose* we found spacious ledges to sleep on each night. The *Shield* offered no ledges until the top. Instead we'd have to take our own portable ledges for sleeping on, which we'd suspend from the belays on the overhanging wall. Sleeping, eating, climbing, even answering calls of nature, would all be done in an overhanging environment. We were entering the arena of hard-core big-wall climbing.

To say we were apprehensive about doing a climb as wild as the *Shield* was an understatement. But once the work began, there was no more time to be nervous. At that stage in our climbing every experience was new, so we were used to finding new ways to adapt to whatever situation we were in. We always seemed to find a way to make it work. On the *Shield,* we would just have to find a way. Once we climbed onto the headwall, we would have no choice about backing off; rappelling back down such an overhang becomes nearly impossible because the rope swings free from the rock. So once we passed this landmark we knew we were committed. More common to mountaineering, this aspect of the sport is all about the mental space you occupy when you know there's no turning back.

Prior to setting off we learned that two other teams wanted to jump on the route too—Randy Leavitt and Gary Zachar, both Californians, and another team from Arizona. Both teams had a wealth of big-wall experience under their belts. We agreed to let these all-male parties step in line ahead of us, and we stalled our departure for a couple of days. We figured that letting the faster, wall-hardened climbers go first was the "gentlemanly" thing to do. We were surprised to see, on our first day on the wall, both teams rappel past us on their way down. First Randy and Gary came down because Randy had gotten a splinter of metal in his eye, then the team from Arizona followed.

"What's wrong? Why are you retreating?" I shouted up to one of the Arizona climbers above me. I wondered if the storm of the century was bearing down on Yosemite. Yet the sky was blue.

"We heard someone take one hell of a fall early this morning. There was a terrible scream. He must be way fucked up, or dead. It kinda freaked us out, so we decided to bail," came the reply.

Mari and I eyed each other, then explained the story behind this bloodcurdling scream. Mari's boyfriend, Mike Lechlinski, and Yabo [John Yablonsky] had set off at midnight to climb the 3,000-foot-long *Triple Direct* on El Cap in a day. When Mari and I arrived at the parking area below El Cap early that morning and saw the two of them standing by their car, we knew something had gone wrong. Mike was arranging their gear while Yabo leaned against the fender, smoking a cigarette, staring into the forest.

"What happened?" Mari asked.

"Yabo took an eighty footer!" Mike shot back.

At this Yabo uttered one of the staccato sniggers he was known to emit whenever nervous or unsure of himself.

"Yabo, are you okay?" I asked, looking him up and down from head to toe, searching for blood or bruises. He appeared unscathed.

"Yeah, I'm fine. I was climbing in my tennis shoes since it was easy up there. I was climbing with a pack and a full rack of gear, but I didn't bother to put in any protection. It was four thirty in the morning, so it was a bit hard to see. I was cruising fast until I was nearly at the top of the pitch, and suddenly I realized that I messed up my hand sequence. Just then my foot popped off the face and I took a huge whipper," came his sheepish admission.

"He was a hundred feet up, on the tenth pitch!" exclaimed Mike. "When I saw him flying through the air, I reeled in slack through the belay device, but I could see he had no pro between me and him. I thought for sure, we're dead, he's gonna rip us off the wall. Strawberry jam, here we come. But then his rope hooked around a mysterious knob or feature just barely big enough to catch Yabo's fall. If he had fallen 10 feet farther, he would have come crashing down onto Mammoth Terraces. As soon as Yabo scrambled back down the last few feet onto the ledge, I flipped the rope and it came tumbling back down! I don't know how the rope snagged on that chunk of rock, but if it hadn't, Yabo would have gone another 80 feet! I knew Yabo was not badly hurt when he said, 'Let's go for it. We can do it.'"

The *Shield* was still there, though, awaiting Mari and me, so after hugging the boys and saying goodbye, we started jumaring up our ropes to Heart Ledge, where we had fixed them a few days earlier. Now that the last of the men had retreated due to the horror of Yabo's primal scream, we had the wall to ourselves. It amused us to know that despite the more impressive range of experience that these teams had over us, we remained the determined ones, going to the top.

"A wall without balls," I jokingly said to Mari, referring to the term Bev Johnson and Sibylle Hechtel had coined when they did the first all-female ascent of the *Triple Direct* on El Cap in 1973. The *Shield*, which loomed frighteningly steep over our heads, was now the sole domain of two women.

FOR THE FIRST TWO DAYS OF THE CLIMB WE INCHED UP EL CAP'S GLACIER-cut face, slowly gaining height by the unfamiliar mode of aid climbing, and even more slowly dragging up our haul bag. For good reason, climbers refer to the haul bag as the "pig." Haul bags are heavy, unruly, and obnoxious, and they do not obey. They often get stuck behind a flake or small roof and stubbornly refuse to budge. Whenever our haul bag got stuck, one of us would have to rappel down to the bag and maneuver it around the obstacle, then herd it upward. Ours was loaded with so much equipment, water, and food that it outweighed both of us combined. So on the first few hundred feet of the wall, Mari and I rigged a two-person hauling system. We each pulled out backward with all our might on the haul line, winching the bag's weight through a small pulley. Our pig crawled up the wall in small surges. Our skin was rubbed raw from pulling on the rope. Sweat poured out of us.

After two days on the wall, we became accustomed to living in a reality where survival required us to concentrate on each move and to evaluate the consequences of every action, whether it was hammering in a piton or clipping ourselves into our batlike hanging bivouacs. During those intense moments of total engagement, I would become acutely aware of that little voice of intuition that on the ground is so often obscured by the clutter and command of our day-to-day thinking. On the sixteenth pitch off the ground, while bashing a piton into an expanding crack (a crack that opens as the piton is driven deeper into it, making for a very unstable piton placement), the thought occurred to me that perhaps I should have hammered this piton a little harder. In the next instant, after I had clipped my little 4-foot-long ladder of nylon webbing onto the piton and stood up in it, the piton ripped out with a loud ping. I flew 30 feet backward before a well-placed piece of gear caught me on the rope. The fall was over in less than a breath but the memory of the need to listen to the quiet internal voice of warning was never forgotten.

Night was a precious time when we could relax, eat, drink, and gaze up at the stars—but only after we had fiddled for an hour rigging and suspending our sleeping bunks. Mari had it good—she owned one of the first portaledges ever made. This newfangled gadget was a six-pound collapsible cot consisting of an aluminum frame strung with a nylon sheet. It hung from six webbing straps all sewn together into a single loop, into which she clipped the anchor. It made a comfortable sailor-style bunk. My bed wasn't so deluxe. It was a banana-shaped hammock in which I slumped like a caterpillar in a cocoon. My first night in this was dire. In the corner of a dihedral, I hung in a bent position all night long, shifting from side to side in discomfort.

On the fourth day Mari led us up to the headwall. The pitch she followed to get us there was dubbed the Shield Roof, and it was indeed a giant of a roof. Hanging upside down under the roof to place each piece of gear, she dangled in her aid ladders, whacking in pitons and placing nuts whenever possible. Among the more dubious devices she hung her body from were "copperheads." These are blobs of copper clamped onto the end of a thin wire cable, and they are used whenever the crack is too shallow to accept the blade of a piton. The copper blob is pounded with the pick of the hammer until it softens and molds around the irregularities of the crack. It then has the adhesive quality of a piece of duct tape, and you can hang a while on it before it gives up its grip and pops out. If you find yourself placing a lot of copperheads in a row, you know you are headed into territory with high potential for a big fall.

Hours passed while Mari led to the end of the Shield Roof. Finally shouting down through the afternoon wind that blew our hanging rope in a swirling dance, she let me know that she was off belay. I jumared up while removing a few precarious-looking copperhead placements she had hammered in. When I pulled around from the underside of the ceiling and joined Mari at the lip of the roof and at the start of the headwall, I found that we were poised in an outrageous position. Under our feet, there was nothing but air. Above us rose 1,000 feet of smooth, overhanging orange granite. To either side of us the walls curved around out of sight. We seemed to be suspended on the edge of the world, and the two of us and our pig hung from three steel bolts the length, yet not quite the thickness, of a half-smoked cigarette. Feeling vulnerable, I instinctively checked the knot at my waist, the only thing securing me to the anchor. I could see now why this climb had been named the *Shield*: the feature we were on resembled the curving shield of a warrior.

We had reached the point of no return. It would be impossible to rappel down from here. It was now summit or bust. But we grew accustomed to the exposure of our perch, and once we set up our portaledge and hammock for another bivouac, the calm of twilight descended and Mari and I were finally able to rest. A distant strip of clouds in the west, over the plains of the San Joaquin Valley, glowed with brilliant colors. Hanging side by side in our bivouac cocoons, we munched bagels, tuna, and canned peaches to add hydration to our dry pemmican bars that were loaded with calories. We had no fear of the height, only an enhanced sense of intimacy between us. Up here in this giddy place I felt as if we were the last people left on earth and secrets were of no use.

Our progress slowed to a snail's pace as we coped with the difficulties of the headwall. Poking out of the crack ahead of me were occasional RURPs that had been hammered in so tightly by other ascents that they could not be removed. Old and tattered bits of skinny webbing tied to these "fixed" RURPs flapped in the breeze. These little slings creaked like ripping fabric when I hung from them. They felt ready to break, so I hurried on to the next placement. The only thing in my favor was that my weight—around a hundred pounds—exerted less force on the RURPs than other climbers. The more solidly built Charlie Porter, or any other guy who had climbed the route since him, likely weighed nearly twice as much as me.

On the fifth day we exited the headwall, hauling onto a large, sloping rock platform called Chickenhead Ledge, so named for the black knobs of intrusive diorite that poke through the bed of white granite. Sometimes these bumps resemble a head with a narrow neck, and some wit in the climbing world had likened the grabbing of them to strangling a chicken. With only one day left before we topped out, we slept well here, knowing we'd be on flat earth by the next afternoon. Some of our pitches had taken us five hours to lead. I wondered if I would bother doing another big "nailing," or piton-bashing route, ever again. It was so slow and tedious and I missed being able to walk around and sleep on a flat, horizontal surface! We'd later learn that in the time it took us to lead three pitches on the headwall, Mari's boyfriend, Mike Lechlinski, with John Bachar, had climbed all thirty-three pitches of the *Nose*!

We also learned that the guys in Camp 4 who knew us "girls" were up on the *Shield* and were occasionally checking our progress from the meadow below, had all made bets about when Mari and I would retreat from the wall, as the other two teams of men did. But Mari and I believed in ourselves and were willing to "put our backs into it," as Mari liked to say. We would do whatever was necessary to get the job done!

The next day—our sixth since leaving the valley floor—we pulled over the edge of El Cap. Twenty-nine pitches lay behind us. The relief of the climb being over and the elation of finally standing on top was enhanced by the presence of John Long, otherwise known as Largo, and Mike, who had hiked to meet us on top, just as Mari and I had done when our boyfriends had reached the top of the *Shield*. In fact, that was when Largo had suggested that Mari and I climb this route together. After hearing about what a sensational climb it was, Mari and I had looked at each other and said, "Yeah, why not? Let's go for it." Though it was a lot of work, living in such a spectacular vertical world had been well worth the effort. Weighed down by our haul bag and by coils of ropes and racks of pitons, we wobbled on our legs, but we were grateful to be able to walk again and return to the comforts of a hot shower and some fresh food.

Years later, after I had done the first free ascent of the *Nose*, and then again in one day, I had read with some chagrin in Galen Rowell's book *The Vertical World of Yosemite*, "Women are conspicuously absent from the climbs in this book. I have no apology to make here because it is not my place to change history. There simply were no major first ascents in Yosemite done by women during the formative years of the sport."

Our sport back then was directed by a fraternity of men, and there was little encouragement or, frankly, inclination for women to participate. Yet women climbers were out there. There were women such as Beverly Johnson before me, who had done the first ascent of a big-wall route on El Capitan with Charlie Porter, the same person who also did the first ascent of the *Shield*. The fact that this woman who had done the first ascent of a big-wall route in Yosemite back then was not given credit or even an acknowledgment during those times was disgraceful to me. It was very important for me and others to know that there were other women out there who shared a passion for climbing and adventure.

I had learned early on as a little girl that what I believed was appropriate or even possible was dependent on me: not on what others projected onto me because of my gender or appearances. In fact, these types of stereotypic experiences throughout my life have become a dominant theme of my career. The underlying motivation for my most noteworthy ascents was that I felt the need to demonstrate that women can do whatever we set our minds to. Believing in ourselves is the most important quality of all. It's amazing what we can do when we put our heart, mind, and soul into it to achieve something much greater than ourselves.

A natural athlete, Lynn Hill competed as a gymnast and runner and immediately excelled at rock climbing after roping up at the age of fourteen. By the late 1970s, she was climbing near the top standards of the day. After pushing the limits of sport climbing and succeeding on the world competition climbing stage, Lynn returned to Yosemite to complete the climbs she is undoubtedly most famous for: the first free ascent and the first free one-day ascent of the *Nose* on El Capitan, feats that changed the definition of what's possible in rock climbing.

Lynn's climbing spans all disciplines: she was the first woman to climb *Midnight Lightning*, a very difficult bouldering problem, as well as the first to succeed on difficult aid climbs on El Capitan. There are few Yosemite walls Lynn has not transformed. She lives in Boulder, Colorado, where she climbs, guides, coaches, skate skis, and is raising her son, Owen.

SUNKIST

Lydia Bradey

Back in the early eighties, I spent three seasons climbing big walls in Yosemite Valley. I got started because I found free climbing quite scary. I wasn't very sporty, kind of a roundish body with thin arms and legs, but I was an acolyte of those who told adventure stories, and would hang around the likes of Mugs Stump listening to tales of "being up *there* . . ." I *had* to get to see the scene.

Zodiac was my first Yosemite wall, climbed with none other than John Middendorf, whom I had met shortly after he'd taken a soloing fall and sported a crisscross of rope burns. I pestered him for three days to take me "up *there*." "I'll belay the whole way if you want!" I'm sure his friends were eye-rolling at this seemingly inexperienced Kiwi chick as a belay partner. I may have been relatively inexperienced as a big-wall climber, but I had suffered a lot of alpinism and knew the ropes. I led a third of the climb and concluded that big walls were boss! Eight walls and two seasons later, I eyeballed *Sunkist*.

I was super lucky to have two big-wall partners, a Brit named Duncan Critchley and a Californian named Chuck Wheeler. Duncan liked me to rack the gear in order of size as I cleaned a pitch, and with Duncan, we never ran out of food; he was organized, and of course it paid off! Duncan was very funny. Chuck was easygoing and quieter; we could clean a pitch and rack gear in whatever pattern we liked—we could forget the bagels and cream cheese and have to eat carrots for a whole day. Our debonair approach was fun but caught up with us at the top of *Sunkist*, 300 feet below the top of El Cap.

I had fallen in love with the art of copperheading and thin, fine piton placements. These were the days before beaks, and I was sniffing around for a "fine" climb to do. When I heard that *Sunkist* was all copperheads and RURPs, we went hunting for information. Rumor had it that the big-wall guru Dale Bard had come down from the first ascent of *Sunkist* saying, "Now I know what A6 is like!" We heard we needed about seventy 'heads and twenty-five RURPs, but there was no topo to be found in Camp 4. It was decided that our best potential source for a topo would be the famous Jim Bridwell.

It took me three days to psych up the courage to call Jim and ask him about *Sunkist*. Jim was reticent. He seemed dubious about a Kiwi girl wanting to climb the route and didn't give any advice, just a few grunts. Another three days of gathering courage were required to call an enthusiastic Greg Child, who was making aluma-heads to order. We bought about fifty, including circleheads, ten zeros, fifteen ones, a light rack to go with the twenty-five RURPs, and a fat bunch of hooks.

The aesthetics of *Sunkist* were what most held my attention: it was fine and it was beautiful. The most beautiful part of the climb was a golden overhanging wall. *Sunkist* wasn't a long climb, but with no route map and no fixed pieces, we found it challenging. The theme of the climb was that we were searching for the "A6 pitch," both wanting to lead it. We swung pitches from Heart Ledge, up part of *Jolly Roger*, branching onto *Sunkist* proper. As the climbing became incrementally harder, the leader would issue a nervous mutter, causing the belayer to look up and politely inquire if perhaps this was the A6 pitch? Once, we started up a smooth wall completely in the wrong direction, because it *looked* A6. Gradually we were drawn high up onto a proud piece of rock several pitches long: the Golden Wall.

The headwall of *Sunkist* is like the *Shield* but sunken, overhanging just slightly, the first pitch of it long, sustained, leading straight to a bivouac anchor of four bolts, where we felt we slept in the air. Plenty of time to think about tomorrow, my lead. The smooth golden granite was sliced by a single seam, a seam that was not a crack, and on the second ascent remained completely clean. *This* was what we'd come for, utter beauty matched by the physical challenge of staying attached and gaining ground.

Above the portaledge, I high-stepped on my sixteenth consecutive RURP. The seam was closing down and allowed one last RURP with only the bottom edge hammered in, a half-RURP placement in a slot too thin and the curve of the granite rolling away from the tiny semicrack too rounded and open for anything else. I leaned my head gently on the rock and prayed. I was so scared. I didn't think this was A6, but it felt A5 and I was just a twenty-year-old clumpy Kiwi girl who wasn't any good at sports. Pull this, zipper the pitch. Time ticked, Chuck at the anchor below, fully focused on me, nothing moving, everything on edge. How did I top step without moving? What did I place next? I think I welded in a fat aluma-head, clipping it with joy as it was so solid compared to a half-RURP. More 'heads, then rivets and hooks, and I was away to the anchor. Yes!

Chuck used almost all our #0 and #1 heads in the vertical and curving obtuse corner; this was the crux of *Sunkist*. He was all scrunched up on the etriers directly above me. He placed the second zero and shifted his weight, and it pulled, stripping the pitch, landing on me, and breaking a bolt on the belay. We were down to two good (5/8ths) bolts for the anchor, we didn't have a bolt kit, and we had only one more #0 head left. The wire had pulled out, leaving the aluminum swage stuck in the corner, so Chuck needed to aid up again and pry the metal away from the granite before making the remaining #0 stick. He had to succeed. We figured the same had happened to the first ascensionists, as there was one rivet before the circle-head traverse, but Chuck didn't see that until it was too late and climbed on through. Once again, we were quiet and focused; once again we were two climbing as one.

We slept under the exit for *Sunkist*, the final five pitches of *Son of Heart*. These are steeply overhanging, alternating corners that required a full rack of long Lost Arrow pitons. We'd left *all* of ours at camp. One hundred meters away, across the upper shield of El Capitan, we spied some fluffy sun-bleached ropes, fixed and seemingly forgotten. We aid climbed two pitches horizontally to the bottom of the ropes. This was no route. We did rock-paper-scissors to see who would jug the ropes, and Chuck lost.

We hauled up, exiting that golden mecca, the wall to which we had both whispered, back to the grits of Camp 4, leaving the gold but feeling we'd won the treasure. Chuck Wheeler and I had climbed the most beautiful and delicate big wall we'd ever been on. We'd lain awake hanging in the bivouac at nowhere. We'd kissed the rock pleading safety, and I'm not certain we ever took all of ourselves away.

Lydia Bradey started mountaineering in the Southern Alps of New Zealand as a teenager. Within a decade she had climbed in eleven countries, participated in and co-run seven Himalayan expeditions, and become the first woman to climb Everest without oxygen. Always afraid of free climbing, Lydia embraced aid climbing on Yosemite big walls as a means to immerse herself in the vertical environment, wanting the experience of "being up there." In three seasons she climbed ten big walls, making seven first female ascents.

Certified as an IFMGA mountain and ski guide, Lydia has guided Mount Everest five times and has been on more than thirty-five expeditions higher than 6,000 meters.

DANCING IN THE SKY

1990–2010

If the Golden Age was the era of big walls, and the Stonemasters began the era of free climbing, the climbers of the 1990s and early 2000s took it one step further. Free climbing Yosemite's biggest walls and climbing them as quickly as possible was the name of the game, and women were right there, holding their own.

The so-called Stone Monkeys ushered in a lifestyle-driven approach to climbing that sought to carry the torch of the Stonemasters. The Monkeys may very well have been some of the world's best athletes, but their disregard for rules and tendency to eschew law enforcement is what they're often remembered for. Free climbing walls once deemed impossible pushed the athletic potential of this era's climbers. In 1993, Lynn Hill free climbed the *Nose*, returning the following year to free climb it in a single day. By the early 2000s, other women were following in her gigantic footsteps, Beth Rodden and Steph Davis some of the most famous among them.

On the other end of the big-wall spectrum, climbers were using new tactics to climb Yosemite's largest faces faster than ever before. The women's speed record on the *Nose* started to take hold of the Valley's best climbers. Nancy Feagin upped the ante by climbing El Cap and Half Dome in a single day, though it would be a few more years before a team of women would complete that together.

The Stone Monkeys epitomized pushing the limits, combining strong athleticism with the obsession required to spend enormous chunks of time on Yosemite's big walls. Women's full participation there mirrored mainstream American society, where women occupying places of power was becoming a normal part of life, not the taboo phenomenon it had once been.

THE MANY GIFTS OF CLIMBING IN YOSEMITE

Abby Watkins

I'm like a spider made of climbing gear and body parts dangling below the roof of the final pitch of the *Nose*. Below me stretches 3,000 feet of mind-boggling exposure, only I can't see any of it in the dark. My whole world is the small sphere of light emitted by my headlamp. I check my backup knot, shift my weight onto one ascender, and confidently remove the other from the rope. I replace the ascender uphill of the piece, adeptly remove the piece, and continue ascending. As I turn the final lip of the roof, the day's adventure flashes before me. At five this morning, trotting up to the base and stepping off the ground and straight into a well-practiced rhythm, our teamwork so seamless we barely had to speak. All day, inching up the soaring cracks in the shining granite, peregrine falcons dive-bombing the swirling swifts. And now, just after dark, following Vera's final lead up and over the roof to the summit.

We planned this moment to include a full moon to light our way over the lip. We did not plan for the moon to be entirely obscured by the shadow of the earth. A total eclipse! I pause and look in awe. It's magnificent, although impractical at this moment. This temporary shadow, however, matters as much to us today as the #4 Camalot I accidentally left on Sickle

Ledge at the beginning of our ascent. Vera found and removed someone else's stuck #4 from the Stovelegs almost immediately. Now I belly flop onto the slab and drag myself and the ropes up to Vera. We high-five, hug, check the time, drink a little, have a snack, and head for the descent in the now-unobstructed bright moonlight. We've done it.

It was 1996 when Vera Wong and I climbed the *Nose*-in-a-day. Back then, we were only the second all-woman team to have done so (Sue McDevitt and Nancy Feagin had done it a few years before). I knew it was a significant achievement at the time. I did not realize, though, the lasting impact the experience of the *Nose*-in-a-day would have on me. The experience included not only that one impactful day but also the years, months, and days of becoming a skilled enough climber to complete the *Nose*-in-a-day. As I reflect on it twenty-five years later, I realize it was a rite of passage that bestowed on me important gifts that have helped shape my life and who I am.

YOSEMITE DRAWS ME IN FROM THE FIRST MOMENT. NATURE'S POWER IS tangible in the Valley. The soaring walls pulse with Earth's energy. The story of a vast geological and glacial history is laid bare, reminding me that I am part of this, the culmination of deep time. Every time I approach the Valley from Berkeley, where I live for the decade I climb regularly in Yosemite, I feel the pull of it. As the car strains up the foothills, my heart quickens with the anticipation of my first glimpse of El Cap. Then, there it is, the familiar outline standing silently, proudly, whether in the perfect sun of another California day or ghostly and massive in the moonlight. Over the years, once I have climbed El Capitan by the different routes weathered into its gigantic face, that familiar outline becomes like the face of a close friend.

When I first see El Capitan, I am not yet a climber. My awe is massive but not yet intimate. I don't know anything about rock climbing, outside of the rock scrambling I did naturally as a kid. Standing there in El Cap Meadow, I can see tiny people up there. Soon after, a friend brings me along on a weekly Friday evening buildering session on the Berkeley campus. We traverse rock retaining walls, offwidth up hanging balcony features on the library, chimney up features on the engineering building, and climb trees. This all comes naturally to me, as I have been recruited to the university on a gymnastics scholarship from my native land of Australia. This kind of Friday evening is far more interesting to me than the usual activities of a university student my age: drinking, partying, and hooking up. I simply don't fit into that scene. From these humble beginnings climbing around on buildings, it's inevitable that I will find my way to Yosemite. Once there I know I have found my place. I have found a magical world and subculture to nourish me for the foreseeable future.

What a revelation, this discovery that not only can I drink in the power of these vast walls, but I also can develop a relationship with the rock! Rock climbing invites me to get to know this vast amphitheater in a personal way. I learn to fit all or part of my body into the cracks. I learn exactly how much pressure to apply to hands, elbows, shoulders, back, knees, thighs—whatever helps me wriggle and push my way up. Granite climbing is not about pulling, and once I master the subtle skill of the precise distribution of weight between body contact points and the rock to make upward progress, it is sublimely satisfying. I come to understand how I can find my way from the valley floor to the rim up the well-known and classic Yosemite cracks.

But it doesn't always come easily.

I SPEND MUCH OF THAT FIRST CLIMBING SUMMER OF 1989 IN YOSEMITE. My good friend Deb Wolfe and I become regulars in Camp 4, where we meet a group of British climbers. We tag along with them on most days, following a lot of pitches, learning how to remove and place gear and how to crack climb. I'm adamant that I don't want to lead yet. I want to know what I'm doing before I take on that kind of risk. Toward the end of the summer, however, one of the British climbers, John Elwell, and I decide to climb the *East Buttress* on El Cap. John is confident he can lead all twelve pitches with me as a beginner following him up. I don't have the experience to have a say in that, but I'm game.

What he doesn't plan for is the rope cluster mess that occurs at each belay. We're climbing on two ropes (very British) and because he is leading every pitch, he is leading out from the bottom of the rope stacks each time. At the top of the second pitch, I find myself sitting in an ant nest with ants running all over me and the ropes while I simultaneously try to feed both ropes out smoothly as John leads. The sticky, dead-ant-smelling ropes are hopelessly tangled, and John constantly has to stop as I work to untangle them. Neither of us has enough experience in our respective roles to solve the rope mess.

But we keep going up. The pitches are physical and relentless in the middle section of the route, but we're dogged. With three more pitches to go, we are really committed and have completely underestimated the climb. The sun is sinking toward the horizon, and we don't have a headlamp between us.

"You're going to have to lead," says John.

"Oh . . . ," I answer doubtfully. I think about it for a minute. We really are in a bit of trouble. The mess and cluster of the ropes have been exhausting for me and frustrating for him each time he leads. A retreat from here is more dangerous and committing than heading up and over the top now, especially since we don't have headlamps.

"Okay," I say. I see relief wash over John's face.

I take the rack (we carried them on gear slings in those days) and get myself organized to lead. I step up and out onto the airy 5.7 arête. The exposure is dizzying. The Valley feels distorted, like a fishbowl. The ground, so far below, looks like an Impressionist painting. The breeze lifts my hair and brings me back. I look at the climbing right in front of me. The rock is polished, and I could slip off if I make the wrong move. A flash of doubt hits the pit of my stomach. *How did I get here?* It doesn't matter now. I have to find a way. I wiggle a nut in between features; I think it's good, but I don't want to find out.

No falling, I say to myself as I place a foot up onto a higher hold.

I shift my weight. It feels okay. I'm still hanging on and starting to feel a bit more balanced. I settle into it quickly because I have to. It's kind of like the balance beam, but I don't have to do any flips and I have handholds. I can do this. The leading comes naturally to me, but it has taken the whole summer and getting backed into a corner to find out.

We top out late in the evening and head for the East Ledges descent. The lack of headlamps means we must get down through the rappels before dark, or we'll be sleeping on top with no food or water. The descent goes smoothly, luckily, and just as we touch down on the last rappel, it's completely pitch black. We spend the next hour or two crawling over, under, and around boulders down the gully to the road in the dark, having lost the trail immediately. Back at camp, I am more exhausted than I have ever been, but I'm elated, strangely. What an amazing experience. I could never have imagined I could have such adventures. I'm hooked.

I CLIMB COUNTLESS FEET OF YOSEMITE GRANITE IN THE NEXT SEVEN years leading up to the *Nose*-in-a-day ascent with Vera Wong. My skills and confidence grow with each new climb. I have found my true love, and it is climbing. Every weekend, on all breaks from school and work, I spend climbing. There is so much to nourish me: the unmatched and very real adventures, the satisfaction of getting better and better as a climber, living in wild nature, sleeping under the stars most nights, the ancient trees and silent forests, the rushing snowmelt waterfalls, the icy rivers, bear encounters. Meeting climbers from all over the world who have the same sense of adventure, who are part of the tribe. I settle into the simple pleasures of climbing road trips. What an amazing thing I have discovered: I can travel the world and find rocks to climb almost anywhere. But I always come back to Yosemite. Everywhere else, the approaches seem too long and the climbs too short. Yosemite is paradise.

I meet Vera at a climbing festival in the Blue Mountains of Australia in 1995. I am taken by her quiet strength and deep confidence. I am impressed by this, and also her experience in the big mountains: she's climbed in New Zealand and the Himalayas. We immediately recognize in each other a similar drive and a complementary skill set that can be honed into an amazing climbing partnership. Vera suggests we climb the *Nose*-in-a-day soon after our first meeting. I have never considered it, even though I now have the perfect résumé. My climbing friends in California do the *Nose*-in-a-day as a matter of course. I haven't put myself in the league of climbers who can achieve that rite of passage.

Vera arrives in the United States from Australia at the beginning of the summer of 1996, and we go on a mission to train for a *Nose*-in-a-day ascent. By pure chance we meet two other Australian women who are also on climbing trips in the US that summer: Nik Woolford and Kate Dooley. Nik and Kate join us on the quest. The four of us pair off in all versions of teams of two or three and climb many amazing routes in Yosemite and Tuolumne. As the temperatures climb in California, we drive north, climbing everything made of granite that we can find. Index in the Cascades, a brief stop in Squamish before being rained out, a memorable trip to the Bugaboos in British Columbia. When Vera and I complete the *Beckey-Chouinard* on South Howser Tower in ten or eleven hours from Applebee camp to Applebee camp, we know we are ready for the *Nose*-in-a-day.

By then, I am down to my last twenty dollars. I get into my Honda Accord hatchback and drive toward Portland, Oregon, where my dad lives. I watch the gas gauge descend toward the red, then use those twenty dollars to fill up somewhere in the middle of nowhere in Washington State. I stay a night in Portland, borrow twenty dollars off Dad, and drive the rest of the way back to Berkeley, where I have a couple of weeks of work shifts lined up at the climbing gym to keep me in food and fuel.

Vera, Nik, and Kate take their time coming back to California, climbing all the way. I want to keep my training going, so I hatch a plan to climb six routes in a day on Fairview Dome in Tuolumne with my friend Hans Florine. In our planning, we can come up with only five routes we consider safe. The sixth route, *Hemispheres,* is rarely climbed and is run-out in the way that only Tuolumne slab routes can be. We climb four routes up and over the dome, then start on the scary one. The crux is mine to lead. By now I am feeling good about my climbing. I have covered acres of granite in the previous few months and can't imagine making a mistake. Hans and I have a discussion at the belay.

"The bolts are pretty far apart . . . ," I say, balling up my courage, squinting up the shining, golden slab in the High Sierra summer sunshine. A line of three very sparsely spaced bolts is the only indication there is a route up the smooth rock.

"At least there are three of them in 150 feet," says Hans, in his characteristic wry and ever-positive way.

"If I fall, I'll turn around and run," I say hopefully, having never (perhaps thankfully) practiced this technique of avoiding flipping up on a slab fall.

"Sounds good!" says Hans.

I have always valued Hans's generosity. He is genuinely thrilled when people do well at things, and I feel that Hans thinks I can do anything and am an equal partner when climbing with him.

Confidently, I step out onto the slab, ready to head into some really scary, insecure climbing. I have to be confident to even think about doing such a ludicrous thing. All the skills I've learned so far are embedded in every move I make. I feel poised, balanced, focused, and determined as I shift my weight between slightly rougher bits of stone and tiny sharp edges. Occasionally there is a bigger crystal to stand on, but these are less trustworthy. I clip a bolt and commit again into the hands of friction. A second bolt, then the third. I squint hopefully up at a vague dish ahead and a rounded flake. Will I be able to place a camming device behind that flake? I hope so. This route is supposed to be 5.10c, but in all reality it is probably 5.11, considering when it was first climbed and the age of the rusty bolts.

Taking a deep breath, I look down at my shoe rubber and marvel that it is somehow sticking to the shiny rock. I look back up. The rock is steeper, and the holds, already tiny and sparse, are thinning out even more. I have to put my hands and feet in a vertical line and then lean across and step to the right. As I do, I know it is an irreversible move, but now I have done it. I look down at the rope trailing away below me. I'm getting very high above the third bolt. I somehow muster more terrifyingly insecure moves and am now at the flake. Of course, the TCU bounces out of the flare, and my heart sinks. I wiggle it in, and it hangs by a corner. I know it won't hold a fall. I clip it anyway.

I am so far above the bolts now that it doesn't matter if I go farther. I won't hit the ground if I fall (we are three or four pitches up), but it will be massive. I have little choice. I should be scared, but it wouldn't help me, so I just focus on keeping my balance. Carefully and slowly, I shift my weight to the next foothold, take a breath, paste my foot, and shift again. There is nothing to hold onto, and just friction is keeping me here; any false move and I will fall. I'm now stemmed across a shallow dish, and I'm looking at a giant crystal. Once I have both my hands on it, I will be able to pull up and get to easier ground. I will get to a crack to build an anchor.

Then, *crack!* The crystal under my right foot explodes and I am airborne. I turn around to run, but the slab is so steep that I touch nothing. I plummet, facing the upcoming trees as they rush toward me. The fall seems to go on and on, and I can vaguely hear Hans whooping in surprise or awe at the size of the fall. Then the bottom of the fall violently twists me back upright, the rack peppering me as it's wrenched by my abrupt change of course. My face smashes into one of the three bolts, breaking my front teeth.

"Are you okay?" Hans yells. When I nod, he shouts, "Wooooo-hooooo! That was amazing!" I had fallen about 40 feet.

We have only one rope with us and therefore cannot descend from here. I come back to the belay for a breather. After a discussion, Hans takes over the lead and ends up making a pendulum into an adjacent climb. We manage to get ourselves up to the top of the dome safely.

"How about another climb?" says Hans when we reach the summit.

"How about a dentist?" I say.

"I don't know that route," says Hans, trying to get a smile out of me. I give him a closed-mouth smile, my tongue feeling the jagged edges of my broken teeth.

This lesson comes at the exact right time for me. I'm heading into some of the biggest climbs of my life—Half Dome in a day, followed by the *Nose*-in-a-day. I was so confident I had begun to cut a few corners in terms of safety. This impromptu training day turns out to be an important lesson in humility. Yes, I want to complete the *Nose*-in-a-day, but I do not want to die or get injured doing it. Although I cannot control that completely, I can make my decisions differently and widen my margins of safety.

A COUPLE OF WEEKS AFTER MY BIG FALL ON FAIRVIEW DOME, VERA AND I round out our summer of training by completing the *Regular Northwest Face* on Half Dome in a day, a fabulous day. Finally, we are ready for the *Nose*. The ascent goes smoothly; we are well trained and ready. Our successful one-day ascents are the women's speed records on both Half Dome and the *Nose*. These records stand for the next seven years. But we are not aiming for a record. What we want is the mastery required for such an ascent. And what we get as a bonus are gifts that last a lifetime.

Knowing I can complete the *Nose*-in-a-day means I am confident to take on other big climbs. It opens up a whole world for me that I hadn't imagined was mine. Vera, Nik, and I go on to complete the first ascent of a 1,000-meter granite tower in Pakistan on an expedition two years later. Shortly after that I move to Canada, where I truly become an alpine climber and mountaineer. I master waterfall ice climbing and backcountry skiing. Sponsors take notice of the *Nose*-in-a-day ascent, which leads to a decade or so as a sponsored athlete. I climb in the Himalayas. I become a certified guide, a profession that lasts eighteen years in the mountains of Canada and New Zealand.

Now, looking back, what I really gained from climbing in Yosemite resides in my heart and my being. The courage to take on big things even if I'm not sure I can do it, and the deep confidence of knowing I can back myself to get through real difficulties. The perseverance to do the hard work that leads to mastery and success. Deep friendships based on the sharing of difficult tasks. Seeing my climbing partners meet their edge and their demons and watching them shine. Knowing they have my back if I need them to, and that I have theirs. And through all of this, a deep and abiding love of the natural places we are privileged to spend time in, getting to know the Captain like an old friend. Living right amongst the wildlife, furred and feathered. Sleeping in the forest under the vastness of the Milky Way.

I have rich memories of lying in El Cap Meadow and running my eyes up the lines I have climbed. These lines contain my stories. And the scores of crack lines weathered into El Cap's face contain countless personal stories of other people. Like tiny drops, these stories make an ocean filled with triumph, defeat, discomfort, fear, mirth, wonder, pain, friendship, and awe—and sometimes grief and loss. Those of us who have been lucky enough to climb in Yosemite have been touched deeply and carry the gifts of our experiences with us into the world.

Raised on the beaches of Australia, Abby Watkins moved to the US to attend the University of California at Berkeley in 1988. Naturally, she found her way to nearby Yosemite, where her skills as a gymnast were quickly put to use. Less than a decade later, Abby had climbed the *Nose* in one day with Vera Wong, setting the women's speed record at the time. Her success as a rock climber led her to alpine and waterfall ice climbing. Abby worked as a mountain guide in Canada and New Zealand for nearly two decades in addition to climbing and establishing alpine routes in Pakistan and the Himalayas.

For the past few decades, Abby has also performed for vertical dance companies on cliffs, buildings, and other aerial spaces. She works as an environmental biologist and resides near one of her other favorite places to climb, Mount Arapiles in Australia.

FULL CIRCLE ON ASTROMAN

Nancy Feagin

In the summer of my junior year of high school in Jackson Hole, I worked in the office for Exum Mountain Guides. One of my favorite guides was Chuck Pratt. Chuck was a pioneer of Yosemite climbing, and in 1959, he had done the first ascent of the *East Face* on Washington Column (renamed *Astroman* when it was free climbed). Chuck told me stories of the perfect granite and the variety of climbing skills needed to climb the twelve-pitch route.

On one of my first trips to the Valley with my mother and Chuck back in the late eighties, we climbed a classic route named *Royal Arches*. On the hike down, we had a great view of *Astroman*, and it looked both incredible and intimidating. From then on, it was a dream of mine, although I had a long way to go to have the skills and fitness to be able to climb it.

My climbing progressed and the years passed. In 1994, I met Sue McDevitt. She was a climbing guide and accomplished big-wall climber. On our first outing together, Sue and I teamed up to climb the *Nose* of El Capitan in a day. I had done the *Nose*-in-a-day with my boyfriend, Hans Florine. He was a great, supportive partner, but he was faster and stronger than me. Sue and I would be more equal partners. On our *Nose* climb, we were focused on climbing fast and not on free climbing. We would pull on gear or clip straight into a piece when the climbing got hard. We had a great time together. We laughed a lot and supported each other when we got scared and tired. We managed to do the *Nose* in twenty hours, the first time it had been done by a women's team in under twenty-four.

A year later, I was back in the Valley. At this point in my life, I was working as a climbing guide in the summers for Exum Mountain Guides, and I would try to go to Yosemite in the spring or fall. Sue had some time available, so we started talking about what route(s) we wanted to do. *Astroman* was at the top of our list. Our friend and climbing hero Peter Croft had done the first solo of *Astroman* a few years earlier. We were totally in awe of his solo, and it made the climb legendary in our minds. I'm sure women had climbed the route, but neither Sue nor I knew who they were, and it didn't really matter to us. It was a mythical climb to us, and we wanted to do it!

It would be a big challenge for us, testing all our abilities. The route has twelve pitches—five rated 5.11—and we wanted to do every pitch free. It's a Valley testpiece and has it all: an 11c boulder problem, an 11c endurance crack, a technical 11b, a crazy bomb bay chimney that led to a squeeze called the Harding Slot, and to top it out, literally, a grainy, run-out, insecure 10d. Sue had climbed and projected a few 5.12 cracks, but I had never free climbed any cracks harder than 5.11c. After a few warm-up climbs, we felt ready.

We swung leads, and I was doing the even pitches. It was hard going, but we made our way up. It was hotter than expected, and we didn't bring enough water. I was super dehydrated by the time we got to the last pitch, which is notorious for being run-out and insecure. When I was in the middle of the crux section, I got a bicep cramp. It was bad! I wish I could say that I dealt with it well, but I freaked out. I got really scared because the fall would have been ugly. The protection wasn't very good, and if I blew it, I could easily pull the gear and hit a spike down at the base of the hard climbing. Thankfully, Sue talked me through it, and I sent the pitch. We were thrilled to make it to the top!

What an amazing day we had. *Astroman* had lived up to its incredible reputation. The pitches were stellar. The next day we went swimming in the Merced, and we started talking. What would it be like to lead the other pitches? How would I do leading the Boulder Problem, the Harding Slot, or the Changing Corners pitch? Sue wondered about the even pitches. We decided we had to go back up and find out. After a few days of rest, we went at it again, each leading the pitches we hadn't led the first time. It was a relatively uneventful outing, and we both successfully led our pitches. But it was still at the upper end of our abilities, and we were stoked!

Then I had a little nagging thought. *Could I lead every pitch? Was I strong enough? Did I have both the physical strength and mental stamina?* I wasn't sure . . . and in my mind, if I had any doubt, that would mean I would have to give it a try so I would know unequivocally.

We decided we would round up a couple of guys to belay us. It was fun trying to figure out who to ask. Sue had a friend, Josh, in Camp 4 who she asked. I chose Mark Chapman. Chapman had done a significant amount of Valley climbing in the seventies and eighties, and he lived across the street from Sue in Yosemite West. In recent years, though, he had been working in movies as a stunt rigger. Even though he wasn't in climbing shape, he was game to be my belayer.

OFF WE WENT A COUPLE OF DAYS LATER. MARK AND I CLIMBED ON A ROPE ahead of Sue and Josh. Since I was the leader, I barely had a chance to see Sue during the climb, and I never got to see Josh. He was at the bottom of Sue's rope belaying her.

Things were going pretty well until we got to the Harding Slot. It's a formidable overhanging squeeze chimney. It starts out with a few thin, overhanging handjams. Then you reach the bomb bay section. You can barely get one hand in a poor jam, and the rock is slick and smooth for the feet. At one point the feet cut loose and dangle wildly into space. For Sue and me, who are five foot one and five foot two, after the initial few hard moves, we could get into the slot and do traditional chimney techniques for the next 30 feet to the belay. But Mark was a big guy with a broad chest. When he got through the initial moves, he was panting loudly. From where I was belaying, I could look down the slot and see his head and shoulders. After some minutes, his breathing was more panicked, and he was yelling that he had gotten his chest stuck in the slot. He was wedged. He couldn't go up or down, and he sounded really desperate.

There was nothing I could do. After a few more tense minutes and lots of cussing, Mark somehow managed to eject himself out of the slot, turning upside down, and he ended up swinging around in space. In his process of turning upside down, one of my small cams necessary for protection up on the top pitch came off the sling around his shoulder, and down it went 500 feet or so to the ground. He was exhausted but utterly relieved to be out of the slot. He swung back onto the rock, laybacked the outside edge of the slot, and climbed it relatively easily up to me. Mark and I regrouped on the ledge and continued up the climb. While the rest of the climb was tiring, my fitness had greatly improved from the past weeks of climbing.

But my key cam was now gone. Looking up at the last pitch, I was apprehensive and worn out, but I kept up my positive self-talk. We took a short break and enjoyed the view across the canyon to Half Dome. How fitting for this goal to have the top be the final challenge. After the break, I stepped up off the belay ledge fully committed. I knew I couldn't hesitate. Move by move over the ball-bearing-gritty granite, I patiently made my way to the top, where I gave my standard, "Woo-hoo! I'm off belay, Mark!" In a short time, Sue and her partner were with us at the summit. What an incredible day and culmination of Valley climbing challenges.

I remember the beautiful walk down and the immense satisfaction of the success of leading every pitch and proving to myself that I could do it. I thought about Chuck Pratt and tried to imagine what it would have been like to do the first ascent. It would be great fun to see him back in Jackson and share stories about the climb with him. I could already visualize his smile and the twinkle in his eyes.

Nancy Feagin hails from the mountains of Wyoming, where she started climbing as a teenager. As a playful young gymnast, she immediately took to the movement and within a few years was mastering the techniques of big walls and big adventures. Her years of climbing in Yosemite solidified her role as one of the best; her long résumé includes the first female one-day linkup of Half Dome and El Capitan, the first all-female one-day ascent of the *Nose* on El Capitan, and an all-female thirty-hour ascent of *Salathé Wall* on El Capitan.

Nancy pursued a long career in mountain guiding before becoming an accountant. She lives with her husband and son in Salt Lake City.

MEMORIES

Sílvia Vidal

This story was originally written in Spanish and translated by Cris Valerio, in collaboration with the author.

To write about Yosemite means to rummage through a trunk of memories, to scratch away so as to reveal the light of distant and remote memories. It's a place that—alongside Montserrat in Catalonia—marks the start of my big-wall climbing.

The last time I was in Yosemite was in 2000. The first time, in 1995. Since then, my relationship with big walling has changed, both in manner and location, and yet it has kept its essence. I climb to experience new sensations, because every new lived experience marks a before and an after, and the more intense those encounters are, the more indelible a footprint they leave behind. Emotions that started in those two places, Montserrat and Yosemite, soon became necessary to find elsewhere, precisely so as to experience as much variety as possible.

Changing places is a way to up the ante. Altering your commitment to a project, or the manner in which you approach a wall, is another. To be able to add new ingredients to the soup, that's what makes it all so interesting. To leave in search of remote and wild places with higher levels of commitment and in pursuit of solitude is part of a deep-seated need for variety. Still, Yosemite is one of those places I assume I'll return to one day. I imagine that since my last time there, many things in the Valley have changed, but others stay the same.

My memories are primarily of that big wall, El Capitan, because I probably spent more days hanging from that wall than below in the valley. My memories are also full of the individuals whose paths I crossed and whom I met on those trips, for although I spent much time climbing alone, there was always a cadre of watchful, encouraging people below ensuring it went well.

Of all the routes I climbed on that amazing wall—in 1995, *Mescalito* with Juani Espuny, *Zodiac* solo, and *Zenyatta Mondatta* with Pep Masip; in 1996, *Sea of Dreams* and the *Shield* with Pep; in 1997, *Reticent Wall* with Pep; and in 2000, *Wyoming Sheep Ranch* solo—the route that first comes to mind is my solo of *Zodiac*. It's not that it's the most beautiful route, nor the longest, nor the most difficult. It's also not the one that required the greatest effort, nor is it the first route I did on the wall. But it was the first route I rope soloed on El Cap and my first bivy on a big wall alone. Because of that, there was a before and an after.

I hold a special memory of that ascent, for it has the stamp of a first and because memories from solo climbs are conjured differently, because they are lived distinctly.

IT WAS 1995 AND THE FIRST TIME I WAS IN YOSEMITE. IT HAD BEEN ONLY A little more than a year since I started climbing. I had gone from barely knowing what a carabiner was to climbing A5 routes in Montserrat: *El Mirall Impenetrable* (A5) Montserrat with Pep Masip and *Vudú* (A4) Montserrat with Pep and Pere Vilarasau. In that brief period of time, I had climbed only one route solo, an aid climb: *Roca Regina* (*La Festa del Paca*, A3). After these short but intense experiences, I left for Yosemite, hopeful to discover this place that the whole world spoke of.

As I was looking for information from those trips to write this story, I found an incomplete diary entry that I wrote about climbing *Zodiac*. I have no memory of writing it; it came out of a box, long forgotten. Here's what I wrote at Camp 4 that summer of 1995 before and after my solo ascent of *Zodiac*:

> *It's hard to explain the series of sensations and experiences that I've felt, equally new and intense. Everything has been very quick*

and sometimes it takes time before we can assimilate and share these experiences. I spent the night thinking and ruminating on a new idea: I'd like to do a rope solo on El Capitan, but I feel a deep respect for the idea. When I say I have a deep respect, what I'm trying to say is that I am scared.

There are many things to keep in mind: the type of aid (so very different from the conglomerate rock that I am used to), the numerous big-wall techniques (which I have to do all by myself, and the haul bag certainly weighs a lot). The nights on the wall will be long. Many hours to turn things over in my head. These are all factors to keep in mind.

My experience with rope soloing is minimal, only on a handful of routes (with no haul bag nor bivy) and only one of those involved aid climbing. And yet, despite it all, there is something drawing me toward trying it: PSYCH.

I am highly motivated, and I think that is more than enough of a reason to try it. I know enough big-wall techniques; the only question is, Can I actually do it? If I don't try, I'll never know, and I don't want to have that kind of doubt. Were it not for that sense of restlessness, I suppose I wouldn't be as interested in this objective.

When you face a challenge, there's a series of thoughts and emotions that make you feel as if you are not in control of the situation. You get the distinct feeling that it might be just out of reach. That feeds a sense of anxiety, to know whether or not you are truly capable of doing it, and finally that's what pushes you to try it.

Noon. Preparations and water (18 liters), food and supplies (climbing, clothes, sleeping bag, portaledge)...

Evening. I porter to the base of the wall (some friends help me). Goodbye and... The night starts horribly. My nerves and fear of all the animals that are running around, real or imagined, and, well, I didn't sleep at all. If the first rivet had been slightly lower, I would have hung my portaledge on the wall to feel safer. I'd prefer to be hanging in the vertical.

The following morning. I leave my sleeping bag and the first thing I do is lay out all my gear on the ground and pick what I will use for the first pitch. I start the pitch, placing RPs and nuts, and at one point, while rummaging through my gear sling looking for a cam, my last piece comes out and I tumble. Well, I can attest to the fact that my "solo" system works and it stopped the fall! This fact alone brightens my morning.

Hauling was hard. The bag weighed so much and I so little. I finally managed to get it off the ground and onto the next anchor. I was on my way!

My first bivy was at the third anchor (with a portaledge), the second at the top of the seventh pitch (on a small ledge) where I spent a horrible night thanks to a cut on my finger. I spent my third night at the tenth anchor (with a portaledge) and the fourth and last night at the thirteenth pitch, on a good ledge that I shared with a mouse who also wanted to join me for dinner.

THAT'S HOW MY ENTRY ENDS. THERE'S NOTHING MORE. READING IT NOW makes me smile because I keep talking with the animals, as they appear in every single one of my expeditions. Much like the way I live these adventures. That doesn't change. What does change, however, is the challenge.

During my past expeditions, many things have changed: the scene, the manner in which we climb, the commitment. But the essence has not: the restlessness to keep experimenting and pushing limits. When you try to push your limits, you are facing situations that you consider, well, limiting—barriers that we all have because one day we chose to believe in those constraints. To explore those barriers allows us to learn that they are not, in fact, so limiting and allows us to find new ones. Because there is no end.

People sometimes reproach me for not carrying a phone or radio, going completely isolated and alone for months in remote and wild places. It is not thoughtlessness but the knowledge that we cannot control everything, no matter how much we believe that technology keeps us protected. For me, being protected is being consistent with what I am and what I feel I want to do, and doing it. The rest is not in my hands.

I just returned a few weeks ago from Chilean Patagonia. I came back in the middle of the pandemic. I had spent two months isolated, alone, without any means of communication, with total autonomy and above all with joy to be able to overcome both the good and the difficult moments—bad weather, cold, uncertainties, fears.

Those fears that always come with me, that creep into the haul bag, sometimes they don't want to come out. They hold on with all their might and no matter how much I want to rip them out of there, there is no way. But when I get them to stick their heads out of the opening of the haul bag, the wind appears and takes them away. Far. Sometimes they come back, and I don't know how they managed to sneak inside again, but eventually they end up jumping into the void or catching on to another gust of wind and disappearing again. And one day, they don't come back anymore.

This last adventure is far from the first adventures on El Capitan. Each climb takes you to the next one. What is possible now depends on what went before. Every time I go on a new expedition, doubts, hopes, uncertainties, illusions are activated. This does not change. Nor does the magic of each new adventure. I named the last route I opened in Chile *Sincronia Màgica* (*Magic Synchrony*) because there were many situations and moments of blockage when it seemed as if the expedition would end abruptly, as if it would not be possible to continue, and suddenly something happened that unblocked the situation as if by magic and allowed me to move on. Things flowed, with effort (because the two are not incompatible), day by day, on the fly. I was able to climb that virgin wall of 1,200 meters, spending thirty-three days hanging on the wall and living a new experience, which, like all intense experiences, marks a before and an after.

These days I am writing about this latest adventure. But unlike the writing I found from *Zodiac*, now I do it with a computer. Where are the pen and paper? Some things really have changed, but only in form, not in essence.

Zodiac, Sincronia Màgica—the memories of both ascents make me smile.

Sílvia Vidal is a world-renowned climber from Catalonia, where she learned to climb as a university student. She quickly fell in love with the challenge and adventure of big-wall climbing in remote places, and her desire for solitary travel flourished. She has pioneered numerous first ascents in a pure solo style, carrying no communication devices nor GPS trackers.

Sílvia's accomplishments in Yosemite prepared her for massive expeditions to places like Pakistan, India, and Chile. Although Sílvia has been climbing since 1994, she has never lost her desire to test her limits and see what is possible.

HUMBLED BY YOSEMITE

Sarah Watson

This story was transcribed from "Sarah Watson: Humbled by Yosemite," a video produced by James Q Martin and released by prAna.

Stepping into Yosemite Valley for the first time, I knew my life would never be the same. The granite walls towering over me were like nothing I had ever seen before. What a change from endless miles of cornfields and hay bales. I hitched a ride to this place having started rock climbing a short time before. I had no idea how consumed my life would become with the sport. Before I left the Midwest, a friend asked, quite concerned, "Are you sure you're ready for the Valley?" I replied, "Of course not. But here's my chance to go learn!" And I learned. In the summer of 2007, I quit my summer job last minute to deal with a "personal emergency." I didn't reveal that the pressing matter was my need to stay in the Valley and climb El Cap for the first time. It had been my dream since the day I started climbing.

My first big-wall experience was epic, to say the least. A gnarly accident left a German guy in the party ahead of us bleeding out on a ledge after taking a 150-foot fall. A helicopter rescue directly overhead and the sheer amount of blood present had scared my partner to the point of retreat. After a few traversing rappels, he almost killed me when he somehow let our haul bag loose while I was on rappel below him. I thought, *This is the end,* as it whooshed past my head a foot and a half behind me. I didn't ever want to be scared like that again. I was ready to walk away from climbing and never look back.

That morning in the meadow, I met Sean Jones. He convinced me to check out a new route he was working on on the south face of Half Dome, and I once again leapt into something way over my head. Two and a half months after meeting, we finished a new twenty-one-pitch 5.13a/A0 route up the center of Half Dome. We named the route *Growing Up,* fitting in so many ways.

The next three years would prove trying for me. I got really sick for a while and ended up in the hospital a few times. Months floated away in the fog of painkillers, surgery, and IV antibiotics. When finally back to my old self, I endured a gnarly knee injury, one that doctors said I would never recover from; they said I would most likely never walk again without pain. I didn't believe them. I couldn't. I had to try to get back simply for my own sanity. I had to be patient. I had to learn how to be still and accept that my life might never be the same. In reality, it never would be the same because I would never be the same.

Eventually, I started to climb again in the gym with one leg. Then I started to go on easy hikes. Then I could carry a light pack, and now a full one. This spring was the first time I had a chance to return to Yosemite in years. The knee that doctors had dismissed works just fine. Every day I wake up with so much appreciation in my heart. I feel so blessed to feel strong and healthy, to be able to climb on these granite walls once again, to stare up and dream of future adventures, and to be free once again to run around in this magical place.

Despite her Midwestern roots, it wasn't long before Sarah Watson discovered the wide adventure of the West and never looked back. After graduating from the University of Wisconsin–Eau Claire, where she was first introduced to climbing, she settled into the community of Yosemite, eventually becoming the first woman to establish a new route on Half Dome. Sarah quickly excelled at crack climbing, repeating some of the Valley's hardest routes.

Since then, Sarah has carried on traveling the West and has learned to skydive and BASE jump. These days, she makes art and explores the desert that has become her home.

I REMEMBER

Chelsea Griffie

For a number of years, I lived in El Portal, the tiny hamlet just west of Yosemite, the nearest town to the Valley. I wasn't thinking of big walls at first. I just wanted to climb harder. Climbing is something that made sense to me once I tried it, since I studied gymnastics as a kid and then modern dance in college. So I always knew where I was and where my center of gravity was. Of course, there are climbing routes to follow, but a lot is still up to you. And whatever I was climbing, I thought I should try climbs that were rated just a little harder. Once I lived in El Portal, I started to think about El Cap. If you're a climber and you live so close, it's practically required.

I remember climbing a bunch at Cookie Cliff and Pat and Jack Pinnacle because they weren't too far from El Portal. I also bouldered a lot in the Valley and in Tuolumne Meadows. If you didn't have a partner, the boulders were always available, and if you bouldered in Tuolumne, you could go eat at the Mobil gas station in Lee Vining, where the food was awesome and there was often a band playing.

At five foot two, I always preferred crack climbing. Sometimes with sport climbing, the bolts are placed way high, and I would have to climb the crux before clipping a bolt. With crack climbing, I got to put the protection wherever I wanted it. I liked the *Rostrum*, except for one pitch that's often described as a fist crack. My fist is too small, and I have to do arm bars, which takes way more energy. Some folks say size doesn't matter, but it truly does in that case.

At some point, I started to aid climb routes that I had successfully free climbed. I just tried to keep up with the people around me who were climbers. They all pushed me. Most of those people were white dudes, since white dudes were the majority of climbers at that time. They probably still are. I did climb with women, and in fact, most of my big-wall partners were women. I didn't compare myself to other climbers—I just tried to do as well as them.

Lurking Fear was my partners' idea. It was my first time up El Cap, and I was the free climber. My partners were definitely more experienced with aid climbing. I hadn't aid climbed much at all, and my partners were bummed out with me in some respects, as they thought I was slow. I pushed myself to climb as fast as I could. I had trained that way, and when I was leading, I made the times I wasn't climbing as short as possible. It was a long day, twenty-six hours and change, since we didn't sleep on the route. When we came down, I just remember being pretty tired and having slightly sore legs. I could move them, but I definitely noticed they weren't as fresh as I was used to!

Over time I became better at being in charge. On a wall climb, all of your decisions become very important—your success is a direct result of the decisions you make during your preparation. I didn't fully realize it then, but I grew in many ways simply because I was surrounded by top-notch climbers. They impelled me to become better because I had to try my best to keep up with them.

Yosemite made me think anything was possible.

Chelsea Griffie grew up in the suburbs of Chicago and started climbing unexpectedly on a trip to Brazil, but it didn't take long for her to be hooked. By 2001, she had moved to the Yosemite gateway community of El Portal to be closer to the rock, enabling her to make her first bid at El Capitan. After twenty-six hours of nonstop climbing, she and her partners topped out on *Lurking Fear*, making her likely the first Black woman to climb El Cap. She climbed El Cap three times after that and has climbed in Greece, Spain, and Thailand.

Her passion for sharing the outdoors with others grew, and she led the first women-of-color backpacking trips in the country every year from 2004 through 2017 for the Yosemite-based Balanced Rock Foundation. Her work with Balanced Rock as well as the National Outdoor Leadership School, Outward Bound, and Bay Area Wilderness Training led her to found Los Angeles Wilderness Training in 2011. She lives in the Bay Area.

ILLOGICAL PROGRESSION

Heidi Wirtz

Every spring, it was time for the pilgrimage. From wherever we happened to be, the sweeping granite walls, raging waterfalls, swaying giant pines, lush meadows, soaring ravens, and tan-skinned friends began to call us. Packing my little '82 Toyota pickup as snow turned to mud after yet another season of powder hunting and refilling my bank account in Crested Butte, I soon was making my way on the road toward the Valley.

A stop in Indian Creek, where my friends would also appear, was the norm. Without a phone call or a hint of a plan, we found ourselves cramming body parts into splitter cracks, turning our bodies and clothes a grungy red hue. Once we had achieved the optimal shade of desert red and our bodies were sufficiently tired and trained in all things crack, we would once again hit the lonely road to the final destination.

Rolling through barren desert and past snowcapped mountains, I would listen to cassette tapes and daydream about my days soon to come. Typically in spring the pass would be closed, so I would take the high route, visiting my buddies at Lover's Leap along the way.

The first rock formations coming into view sent a thrill through my veins as I rounded the final bend into the Valley. Cruising onto the loop road, I was anxious to get to the meadow to see who was already there. I always made one last stop at Fern Spring to refill my water bottles. This is still a ritual of mine, as l love the pure, clean water gushing from its clear, cold pool.

Flowers popping on the dogwoods; the smell of pines, firs, and granite... yes! Granite everywhere. Then the thundering roar of Bridalveil Fall to my right. And then the Captain, soaring like the grand master of it all, high above the meadow. A peaceful and awe-inspiring formation. The reason Yosemite is what it is, one of the greatest places on earth and a place that still to this day feels like my home.

It's not the people or the rest of the Valley that makes me feel this way as completely as just being in the meadow, under the giant oak tree gazing up at this beautiful piece of granite heaven. The center of the universe!

THIS PARTICULAR TRIP WAS A SPECIAL ONE, DEDICATED TO A DREAM OF mine. I wanted to link up El Cap and Half Dome. I had friends who had done it, and I wanted this accomplishment under my belt as well. I also wanted to do it with a woman. My chosen partner was Vera Schulte-Pelkum. She wouldn't be arriving for another few weeks, so my mission was to get as fit as possible so that I was ready.

I walked the worn path to my favorite tree in the Valley and plunked down next to smiling and welcoming faces as if we had been here all along. We chatted of climbs done and climbs to come. Some of my friends had been here already for a while and some had just arrived as I had, ready to immerse ourselves into life in the Valley. This life was a balance, as is all of life. Our balance went something like this: number one was climbing, number two was friends, number three was finding a place to bivy and (just as important) staying away from what we called "the tool" (a.k.a. law enforcement), number four was food, and number five was rest days.

Number one, the climbing: pretty self-explanatory. We climbed every day that our bodies would allow. Our training center was the very walls that surrounded us. Our training was romping up the classic and sometimes obscure lines that filled the small 7.5-mile-by-1-mile valley. Some people had missions, and some were here just to climb anything and everything they could. I was typically in the second category and wanted to climb as much as possible without coming to total failure. I did want to climb harder, for certain, but typically I was quite content climbing 5.11 all day, every day, as long as I didn't fall off. I was from the old-school philosophy that the leader never falls.

My plan was a bit different this trip as I had a mission: to climb as much granite as possible in a day. And this mission would require me to be in perhaps the best shape I had ever been in. So I set to it, climbing every day that I could, on climbs that pushed me to try as hard as I could and push my body to its limit. My favorite thing to do!

By the time Vera showed up, I felt ready. I had climbed so much granite over the past month that I felt prepared to do the linkup the day she arrived. Unfortunately, she was not as ready and hadn't actually climbed for four months. Not a worry, I thought. We can get fit in a week! So poor Vera started my impossibly unrealistic training program. We would start out by climbing *Astroman,* a 1,000-foot 5.11 mega-classic Yosemite hardwoman climb. Of course, Vera walked it off the couch because she is a phenomenal climber. She actually made the notorious Harding Slot look like 5.9 instead of 5.11. I thought to myself as I watched her performance, *We're going to crush the linkup!*

Our next objective was the *West Face* on Leaning Tower in a day. Eleven pitches, 1,000 feet, with a bit of an involved approach and descent. This one went down fairly quickly, and we were back in Camp 4 after only half a day's romping. We were on a roll!

My logical progression meant we would tackle the *Regular Northwest Face* of Half Dome: 5.9 C1, 2,200 feet, with a 2,500-foot approach. This climb is twenty-two pitches of awesomeness. Before the chimney pitches fell off, this was one of my favorite climbs in the Valley to do in a day. We managed to get up this one in not my fastest time, but still a respectable five hours.

By this climb, Vera was beginning to show signs of fatigue. I led all the pitches while Vera jugged with her best gusto, leaving me waiting, rope stretched tight to its end, frothing to go higher faster. In hindsight, I should have eased off a bit and perhaps allowed some rest days. But being a driven—perhaps slightly psychotic—climbing-hungry youth, I pressed on, thinking Vera needed some tough love to get fit enough for the linkup. She was, after all, an amazing climber and could definitely do this if I could only get her fit enough. So . . .

Next up on our training circuit, we strolled up to El Capitan in the wee hours of the morning. Headlamps shining brightly, sweatbands donned, we began our ascent of the *Nose*: 5.11 A1, 3,000 feet, thirty-one pitches. This would be our final training day, I thought, as we would then be ready to send the linkup. *Weehooo!*

I began my run up the wall, pulling on gear, freeing when possible, and moving with rhythm and precision up the rock. I was in the flow and soon found myself through the Stovelegs and scampering across the Lynn Hill Traverse. I opted for this variation as I thought it would be quicker with harder free climbing but avoiding the sometimes-complicated King Swing. With sweat dripping into my eyes despite my amazing sweatband, I reached for a hold, grabbed, and felt my fingers slip. I found myself cascading down the wall, only to be caught some 30 feet below. *What the?* I thought to myself. I regained my composure quickly and pulled back up to my high point to commence my jog for the base of the Great Roof, a classic pitch on the route.

Now, to be fair, at this point Vera was likely quite worn out from my idiotic decision to do so many big routes in a week to train up. Most climbers would have been stoked to do just a couple of these routes in a week, much less all of them. Vera, however, has the ability to never complain and to always (or almost always) have the stoke needed to get up nearly anything.

Anyway, I quested on to where Vera was to take over. Three hours had passed, and we were twenty-two pitches up the wall. Not bad for a couple of girls. Vera, who is a far better aid climber than me, took over to conquer the Great Roof. However, I think at this point she hit a wall. Hours went by before she finally pulled to the anchor. I came across to where she was, a slight panic starting to rise within me. She took off on the next pitch, and it was the same slow going. Now I was panicked. We were losing too much speed. I needed to take over.

She led one more pitch, and then I took over. I managed to pull out some energy to take it to the top as Vera jugged behind, likely happy to have given up the lead. We scrambled to the top and slapped the ceremonial tree that all speed climbers tag at the top of this famous wall. We still had managed to do the wall in just over twelve hours. Not a bad time; however, not fast enough in my mind to do the linkup. We wandered down the slabs to the valley floor, my mind spinning on how I would get us fit enough for the linkup. Vera wandered behind, likely thinking about something completely different.

To my dismay, that evening as we shoveled food into our depleted bodies, Vera announced that she was going to leave the Valley. "What?" was all I could say. She said she just wasn't up for it. I could not fathom her giving up. It made no sense to me at the time. We had a commitment. We had a goal. My heart sank and my dream vanished under a dark cloud that immediately rose above my head.

WHEN I LOOK BACK ON THIS TRIP, THIS LITTLE BLIP OF TIME, I HAVE TO think, *What would have happened if I had actually been a good partner?* I was so focused on the goal that I was willing to push my best friend and partner into a state of defeat instead of triumph. She definitely had it in her to accomplish this goal. She was for sure a better climber than I ever was, and if we had gotten fit together instead of me pushing her to catch up, we could have done it, I'm sure. Unfortunately, I was too young and inexperienced to know how to get us to the finish line. I pushed too hard.

After Vera left, I was bitter and sad and dejected. I looked to no avail for partners to finish what was now just *my* goal. I couldn't find someone fit enough or psyched enough to do it with me that season. It wasn't meant to be. Thus, I missed out on using my hard-earned fitness to achieve my dream climb. I left in a state I deemed to be empty-handed.

It was an incredible week of climbing. My thoughts now are that if I hadn't been so goal-oriented and had just been into the moment and having more fun with an amazing partner, we may have succeeded. This I will never know, and it's a slight regret. But what I do know, now that I can reflect back with perhaps more wisdom, is that partners are more important than goals. If you have a good one, hang on to her, don't piss her off if you can avoid it, and work together to reach your potential.

Heidi Wirtz grew up in the suburbs of Sacramento, California, but it wasn't until a trip to Crested Butte, Colorado, that she started to discover a passion for the mountains. Frozen waterfalls first pulled Heidi into the climbing world, but within a few years she started leaning toward rock. She learned the ways of the hard-core trad climbers around her, honing her skills in the Black Canyon and Indian Creek. A 1994 trip to Yosemite saw her first El Capitan climb, and within a few years she was setting speed records on the Valley's biggest walls.

Since then, Heidi has climbed all around the world, exploring big new routes on remote mountains. Her travels inspired her to cofound Girls Education International, an organization that seeks to bring educational opportunities to women and girls in underserved areas. She is also the founder of Earth Play Retreats, an adventure yoga retreat company. Today, she enjoys life on the road, bouncing between Colorado, Utah, Wyoming, and Nevada.

ALL THE WAY: SALATHÉ FREE

Steph Davis

This story first appeared in Davis's collection of essays, *High Infatuation: A Climber's Guide to Love and Gravity.*

I had planned five days on the wall: three climbing days with two rest days in between. The first day would be hard since we had a lot of vertical gain. It would also be Cybele [Blood]'s and my first climbing day together. I was nervous about the second day, having to climb the Huber pitch, the dihedrals, and the Salathé Roof. Though I had stuck the Huber pitch on my one-day climb of *Freerider*, after twenty-two pitches of climbing I still dreaded it on this ascent. The sideways jump I have to catch to reach the final handhold is "low percentage," and increased traffic on *Freerider* had recently caused one of the setup crimpers to crumble and become less positive. I didn't feel sure I would fire it. I also worried about sending the Salathé Roof after climbing several crux pitches that day. I haven't figured out why it's rated 12a in guidebooks, because it seems so difficult. Like the headwall pitches, the hardest moves come at the very end, and I worried about the strenuous, insecure moves over the lip. Cybele would also have to do hauls with our sleeping bags and clothes, which could slow us down. The third climbing day, our fifth day up there, would be the two headwall pitches and the final pitches to the top.

Cybele and I blasted off in the dark, and I started the chimney above Hollow Flake just before dawn. Despite unseasonably hot temperatures that day, the climbing went well, and we spent the next day resting at the Alcove. Cybele turned out to be one of the most interesting people I've ever met, with endless stories and unique world perspectives. Unfortunately, the day was not completely relaxing. We heard news of an impending storm. Since the date was exactly one year after the freak October storm that had killed climbers on El Cap, all the weather forecasters were erring on the side of caution, afraid to take a firm position about the storm. We spent the day calling friends on our cell phones, trying to find some consistency in the predictions. I hated to think of going down already, after all of this preparation. We decided to keep going.

We woke in the dark the next day, to start the Huber pitch in morning shade since it had been so hot the day before. This day dawned stormy and cold instead. I stood at the belay, shivering, and an aid party approached. Rather than waiting at the Sloping Ledge belay below us and giving me a chance to climb this crux, the leader aided right up under me and hung on a piton, waiting. I tried to ignore it and went for the pitch. Nervous and cold, I whipped off the jump move. I lowered back to Cybele, deeply upset. I felt too pressured to rest, so I tried again immediately. This time I got my hand on the big hold but not deep enough to stay on, and I whipped off again. After my third rapid-fire try, nearly in tears and feeling my crimp strength fading on the opening moves, I told the aid climber to just go through. He slowly went up. Instead of backcleaning to leave it clear for me, he left his rope clipped all along the final crack that I would have to reach for after the crux. I waited in disbelief, shaking with cold. Thoughts of rapping filled my mind. Suddenly it started sleeting. I looked at Cybele and started laughing. This scenario seemed like a joke. It could hardly be any more epic. I started up, brushing sleet from the bigger footholds. I stuck the jump, pulled their rope out of my way as I laybacked up the crack, and sped past the other climbers.

I had wasted way too much time and energy on the Huber pitch. As we reached the Block, it started to rain. We opened the haul bag and crouched inside our bivy sacks, wondering what to do. The rain stopped, winds kicked up, and the rock dried, so I kept climbing up to the strenuous dihedral below the Salathé Roof. Freezing wind blew straight up the giant corner.

Miserable and wretched in tight rock shoes and thin clothing, I reached the belay below the roof. Worn out from the cold, I looked up at the daunting roof. I had to climb it now to stay on track for a shot at the headwall. I fought through the Rifle-esque overhangs, trying unsuccessfully to shake the pump out of my rock-hard forearms. Too tired to recover, I rushed into the final crux. My mind blanked. I screwed up my double-knee-scum sequence and gracelessly pawed at the sloping holds over the lip in a last-ditch attempt to hit the final flared handjam. I whipped off, flying into space below the Salathé Roof, thousands of feet off the deck with nothing below me. Believe me when I say that is *really* scary.

I was too cold and exhausted to try again, but blowing this pitch today threw off my plan for the headwall pitches. The day had gone so badly that I knew I should just call this attempt and leave. I felt like I had flailed all day—and I hadn't even reached the headwall yet. But if I bailed now at pitch twenty-eight, there was a chance I wouldn't be able to organize again for another attempt this season. I would have to replace all the water and food we had used at the Alcove, find another partner, and start all over. It would be more effort to do all that than to keep going, despite how bad things were looking. In terms of effort and supplies, I was fully committed to this seemingly doomed attempt. On the bright side, after this day of repeated falling, I fully trusted Cybele's belay! We got on the fixed lines and went up to Long Ledge to sleep on it.

Fortunately, the storm passed, and we roasted all day in the sun on Long Ledge. El Cap—always too hot or too cold. The next morning, we woke up in the dark and rapped back to the roof. With no warm-up, I got instantly flash pumped. My forearms were as hard as rocks, and there was no way to pull the last moves. I lowered down to Cybele, trying not to feel demoralized. The Salathé was turning out to be a battle, even more than I had imagined. On the second try, I finally felt good. I pulled the last moves, this time in control and climbing right, and I heard my husband, Dean, make his characteristic raven call, clear as a bell from El Cap Meadow. I knew that he and Fletcher, my dog, were down there in the grassy meadow, watching me climb. I wondered when I would see them. I was only 3,000 feet away from my little family, but in a whole different world.

It took some time for Cybele to jug and for me to organize the rack for the endurance headwall pitch. As I left the belay, the sun hit the wall, making it hard to see small footholds. I climbed through the lower cruxes and through the increasingly strenuous crack, feeling weak. In the dreaded overhanging flared splitter crack, I climbed until my body couldn't go on, feeling the greasy, sunny rock slime out under my opening hands. It was over.

I didn't know what to do. Things had been going so wrong ever since the Huber pitch. I felt like I had struggled all the way up this route, and that maybe I was forcing this attempt when it wasn't meant to be. My last free climb on El Cap had been so magical—not easy, but flowing—and I had wanted to feel like that on the *Salathé* too, not like I was fighting to the death. But I felt like I hadn't had a real shot at the headwall, which was really the driving force behind climbing all the way up here on all the same pitches as *Freerider*. My original plan was irredeemably shattered. We only had food and water on Long Ledge for two or three days, and we had already spent a rest day on the ledge and this climbing day. I wasn't physically recovered from the trying storm day, despite the rest, and was now even more worked. Realistically, I didn't think I could do the headwall tomorrow. I just wanted one good chance. "So we take another rest day, and you try again," Cybele said reasonably. "We have some food."

We spent another day on Long Ledge, watching the birds and listening to music. The next morning, at first light, we returned to the base of the headwall. I was freezing cold, and my feet were completely numb as I climbed through the lower crux. I kept thinking they would come to life as I warmed up, but even after I fought through the flared splitter, I couldn't feel my toes at all. Giving it everything I had, I tried to place my feet by sight instead of feel on the tiny footholds through the final crux. My right foot popped off as I hit the second-to-last handhold, 150 feet up, and I whipped below the anchor, which I had already clipped. I was two moves away from the hands-off stance above that final anchor. Totally spent, I hung on the rope and felt my feet come back to life. Great.

Back at Long Ledge, I looked at Cybele shamefacedly. "Cybele, we've been up here seven days. I can't ask you to stay up here any longer. Plus we're almost out of food."

"Hey, at this point, what's another day?" Cybele said. "You fell off the last move. Obviously you can do it. We have a little food. Try again tomorrow."

The next morning, deeply tired, I fell from the flared splitter and finished the pitch with one fall. I had completely underestimated the added difficulty of leading this endurance pitch, having worked it from above, freeing it every time on my top-rope system. When I climbed above the pieces at the end of this ultralong pitch, I could feel the weight of the rope pulling me down throughout the most strenuous crux sections. I was leading on the thinnest possible rope, an 8.9 millimeter, but on the last clips of the pitch, the cord was so heavy that my thumb couldn't push it into the carabiner gate. I had to get to a stance, pull up a loop of rope, clench it in my teeth, and push the loose section into the carabiner at waist level. I was so close. But we had been up here for eight days. My muscles weren't recovering. It was starting to look hopeless. Still, the thought of just giving up and forfeiting all the effort didn't feel right.

Demoralized and sad, I told Cybele that I thought we should go down. She'd already been up here longer than I had asked her to be. Plus, she had put her elderly little dog in a kennel in LA to be here and had rented a car to drive out to the Valley. Both were racking up bigger bills by the day. I was torn with guilt, knowing that the geriatric dachshund was all alone in a strange place without her human, all because I selfishly wanted to free the *Salathé*. But despite a few comments about feeling like she was on Gilligan's Island, Cybele wasn't having any of it.

"Look," she said, "I'm going to jug those fixed lines to the top and go down to the valley for food. I'll spend the night there and come back the next morning. Then you'll get a rest day and you'll be able to eat tons of food. Your body is getting too weak up here. You hardly eat anything. It seems like you're about to do it. I don't think you should give up just because things haven't been perfect." I was truly awed at Cybele's generosity, and I couldn't believe what she was doing for me. Later she would insist over and over that it was really no big deal. But not many people would be hanging in there with me like this, and I knew my instinct about Cybele had been right on.

I decided that since I had a four-gallon water stash hidden just at the summit, which Cybele would never be able to find, that she shouldn't carry an additional thirty-six pounds of water weight in her pack. I also would certainly never impose on Ivo or Dean or the Valley crew by calling them on my cell phone and ordering them to hike up, get my stash, and rap it in to me as I waited diva-like on Long Ledge. Grabbing the water stash would be a ten-minute chore of jugging and rappelling. If that simple task left me too tired to lead the enduro pitch, then it was time to go down anyway!

When Cybele left, I sat alone on the ledge, missing her. Hours later, I saw my truck pull away from El Cap Meadow and watched her drive off in the direction of Yosemite Village.

At this point, it seemed equally likely that I would do this route or that I would fail. I had lost sense of time, but I also felt like I had been on the *Salathé* forever. As long as it didn't storm and we had food, I actually liked being up here on El Cap. I've spent weeks in a snow cave, and this was pretty luxurious by comparison. What wasn't comfortable was the stress I felt at having put so much into this climb knowing I probably wouldn't complete it. I also felt sad that things had gone so wrong when I had tried to plan everything perfectly for one good attempt at the *Salathé*. Partially, my careful plan had slipped out of my control with the other climbers and the storm. But I knew I should have anticipated how much harder the lead would be on the enduro pitch, and maybe I should have tried to lead it a few times last month by rapping in from above. That was my own oversight and harder to accept. My solo system of working the route had been definitely far less efficient than working it with a partner. I had loved my summer days alone on El Cap, but now I was feeling like I wasn't as ready as I could be to complete this project.

THE NEXT MORNING, CYBELE RETURNED TRIUMPHANTLY, BEARING SPINach, tofu, alfalfa sprouts, salad dressing, nutritional yeast, juice, forks, a full bottle of red wine ("for consolation or victory"), a "You go, girl!" card with a vial of lavender scent labeled "Pussy Power Potion" from my friend Adonia, an astonishing supply of other carefully planned and packed treats, and best of all, a travel Scrabble game. With excitement like this, I could stay up here another week! I felt fortified and ready, but an aid party of four arrived at the headwall. I had learned from the Huber pitch debacle that when aid climbers approached cruxes of the free route, I was better off just waiting until they climbed through. "What's another day?" had become my new mantra. We played a thrilling game of Scrabble and ate. My harness was starting to feel too big, the leg loops hanging loose. You get what you need, I think, and I figured losing a few pounds could help if I ever got to the Boulder Problem pitch.

That night I lay in my sleeping bag looking at the stars. Despite the festivity of new food, psychologically this climb was getting hard. Two extra days in a row on this narrow ledge was a little much. Cybele was a hero, but I couldn't ask her to stay much longer. I couldn't stand the guilt of her elderly dog languishing in the kennel, made worse by the fact that Fletch was comfortably at home with Dean, all because of my climbing project. If I couldn't send the enduro pitch the next day, I was going to call it. At least I would feel like I'd had a real try. At this point, that was all I wanted.

We had a radio that Ivo had given me to take on the wall. The task of perking up my battered spirits was too big for Cybele alone at this point. Our cell phone batteries were on their last legs—from the early days when we were anxiously checking weather reports—and now I lived for the few minutes a day when Ivo's encouraging voice would come onto the radio with his distinctive Bulgarian accent. "Steph. You can do it!! Thomas says you can absolutely send the enduro pitch next try—he fell off the flared part too, and he knows you will get it next time. You are doing super good! We're super impressed that you are not coming down! All the monkeys are rooting for you down here!" He would pass the radio around to a circle of friends in El Cap Meadow, each giving me words of friendship and support. I was in a raw, stripped state, and hearing their voices over the walkie-talkie touched me to tears. It meant so much coming from this tight crew of true, hard-core El Cap climbers, who understood completely why I was still up here.

The next morning, I started up the headwall feeling great, my rack perfect, my feet finally not numb. I got unbelievably pumped through the flared splitter. I fought through the bulging wall to a strenuous stance, so pumped that I couldn't even pull the trigger to place the next cam into the crack, nearly dropping it as I klutzily shoved it against the rock. Finally I got it in and, after another fight, got it clipped. A few more moves, and I was hanging straight-armed off a handjam, trying to recover, staring at the final crux section.

In early September, I had rapped in to work this section and met a climber who had used my rope to play on the headwall. Climbing up that day, I'd realized with horror that my most important foothold in the final crux section had been broken. A crumbly micro-edge, an inch lower than the original smooth, nickel-sized edge, was all that remained. Now, instead of climbing hard moves to a useable stance before the last desperate crux, I would have to climb hard moves to no stance into the desperate crux. I immediately went into denial when I realized the foothold was gone. At the time, I determined to think positive, take it in stride, and tell myself it didn't really matter since I could still get through the moves. But the truth was that the final crux had become significantly harder without that decent foothold, which was not what I really needed after 140 feet of hard climbing.

"Get mad!" Cybele shouted up, as I stood at the final "rest" stance, shaking out the pump in my arms. The days and the failures up here had taken their toll, and at this point I felt more like a hostage than a warrior. Finally, I embraced the fury that I had been suppressing since the day I discovered that crux foothold was gone. Yes, in fact, I was super pissed that someone had broken it off just before I was ready to send the *Salathé*! Exhausted but full of rage, I climbed ferociously until I was on the last handhold, and I grabbed the flat hand slot like it meant my life this time. I threw my leg up into the hole, with the anchor below my waist, and—hands-free—clipped the rope into it. I started screaming with astonishment. The sun had arrived. As Cybele cleaned gear from the pitch, I decided to leave the Boulder Problem pitch for tomorrow. At this point, another day didn't matter. Trying the hardest crux pitch in the sun would be silly, and now I really didn't want to blow it.

The next morning I woke feeling like hell, physically and mentally. I was thrilled to have sent the enduro pitch, but the pressure was now huge. After such a long, drawn-out ordeal, it would be heartbreaking not to finish, just 50 feet away from freeing this route.

"I feel great," I told Cybele, unconvincingly. I felt horrendous. Sore, worn out, and kind of sick to my stomach. I swallowed three aspirins and squeezed my shoes on. The crux pitch of the *Salathé* is not the best warm-up at six in the morning. Unbelievably nervous and tense, I fell again and again on the bouldery, powerful moves of the second headwall pitch, one move higher each time. Cybele tried to calm me, but mentally I was a wreck. I wondered how many times I could stick the first deadpoint moves before my fingers gave out. The sun moved onto the headwall. I tried desperately to empty my mind, but my thoughts spun with how much I had gone through to get here, how much I wanted to go to Patagonia this winter and not be in the grip of a *Salathé* obsession, how tired and sore my fingers felt. I had focused so hard on the first headwall pitch and now my mind was fried. A little part of me wished I were freeing this route team-style and could have a stress-free top-rope up this last crux and just be done. Not very zen. I was too broken down to even be dismayed at my lack of spirituality.

I started up again, knowing I would try until my fingers gave out. I barely stuck the first deadpoints, my mind full of failure. Just then, a loud whoosh sounded, like a BASE jumper. Almost in slow motion, in the middle of crux moves, I turned my head. A dark cluster of birds rushed past, the wind from their wings washing over me. Joy rose through my body. The word *magic* flooded my mind, driving everything else out. Immediately, I broke free.

I cranked through the steep finger crack and, with a shout, jumped to the flared handjam at the base of the tiny cave in the middle of the pitch. I crawled in and waited till my breathing slowed. The close air in the little crevice filled with the scent of lavender and sweat, and I waited longer, knowing this was the final test—it was literally now or never. I didn't have it in me to lower all the way back to the anchor again and climb the first part of the pitch if I blew it now. And this last, hardest crux was the one section of the *Salathé* that I had never consistently been able to climb when I was training.

Emerging from the cave, I stood up aggressively on the tiny footholds and gripped the flat arête above, rocking my body around into the changing corner. I stood up, strenuously balancing into the tight, flaring seam above, and stopped in the precarious position, gathering my force. With detachment, I noticed that I felt nothing. There was nothing to feel. I breathed deeply, brought my feet up to waist level as I clamped onto the slick, rounded layback edges, and floated way out onto the face to catch the final granite knob. I was light as a dandelion seed, completely in control, perfect at last. For a few precious seconds, I reached the inexorable flow I had been craving on the entire route. I was finally free.

FOR WEEKS I WAS IN ECSTASY. I HAD GIVEN MORE THAN I HAD TO THE *Salathé*. I had used every scrap of reserve I possessed and had to fight harder than I ever thought possible to climb it. That, even more than having freed the route, gave me an enormous feeling of confidence, and I was high from elation. For the first time in my life, I truly believed that I could do anything I put my mind to, and it was an amazing feeling.

But after the flush of success faded, I began to feel drained. I have always experienced a matching low after a big climbing high, and this time was no exception. The low was every bit as intense as the high, to a degree I had never experienced before. I was flattened. And for the first time since I'd started climbing, I felt crushed by doubt. On the *Salathé*, more than any other climb I'd done, I'd succeeded ultimately through sheer refusal to give up. I felt intensely proud of the effort I gave. But from nowhere, I suddenly saw that effort as diametrically opposed to the spiritual philosophies I have been trying so hard to grasp.

I have always revered climbing as a path to knowledge, a way to learn lessons that are lacking in my materialistic, competitive culture. Every Eastern religion I have studied tells the aspirant to surrender to the flow, to never force outcomes. For the first time, I recognized the conflict between my spiritual philosophies and my personal ethic of hard work and determination, and I was filled with confusion. Didn't working on something I couldn't do qualify as "forcing an outcome"? And if I truly practiced the philosophies I aspired to, shouldn't I have given up on the *Salathé* the first time I ever tried the headwall and found it too hard to do immediately? Every time something went wrong on my free attempt, should I have "surrendered to the flow" and started rappelling instead of refusing to be defeated and persevering with everything I had? And if my goal in life is to become a better person, shouldn't I be teaching myself not to force the outcome? Or would that just be forcing a different outcome? These questions rained down on me, filling me with confusion and angst. I didn't know what to believe anymore.

When you spend a lot of time inside your head, things have to be right in there or nothing else works. For months I struggled through a kind of crisis of faith. Later, in Rifle, a friend would say sensibly, "Obviously you were exhausted after *Freerider* and Patagonia and the *Salathé*. That's what happens—your adrenal system was shot." Whatever the cause, hollowness consumed me, physically and spiritually. For the first time since I'd started climbing, I questioned my motivation. I felt fragile and helpless in the face of my emotions, and I insulated myself from people even more than usual. I didn't have the strength to stay centered in my own mind, and I had become too sensitive to handle the force of outside energy.

I have to admit, when I first started climbing I assumed I was on a path and that eventually I would get "there." I loved that feeling. Now I am starting to discover that there is no "there," and there may not even be a path most of the time. I hear a lot of voices and a lot of ideas swirling around. It can be hard to figure out what I really think about anything. In some ways it seems like the answer is buried inside the question, and maybe I'll never be able to pull them apart. Maybe I shouldn't even try. In a way, I wish for the clarity I once believed in, though perhaps it was naive. I think some things, the good things, really are that simple . . . Fletch, touching rock, living naturally, breathing, moving, laughing.

In the last few months, surrounding myself with true friends and their positive energy, I am unfolding, emerging renewed. Climbing, I touch rock and feel the rush of infatuation. In a way, it feels like being reborn. I will always push hard. At times, I will be caught by inspiration, and when that happens I will never give up. That's who I am. But what I know now is that climbing is more than that. I'm more than that. So much has happened, but in some ways nothing has changed. Climbing, simply and joyfully, is the way I love the world.

After a suburban East Coast upbringing, Steph Davis was introduced to rock climbing while in college and not long after followed her newfound joy west. Her climbing career is as long as it is varied, from free solo ascents of some of North America's most prominent walls to difficult alpine ascents in Patagonia, Pakistan, Kyrgyzstan, and Canada's Baffin Island. Her Yosemite career often revolved around free climbing El Capitan, becoming the first woman to free climb *Freerider* (the second female free ascent of El Cap) and *Salathé Wall*.

Soon, Steph gravitated toward skydiving and, eventually, BASE jumping. She lives in Moab, Utah, with her husband, dog, and two cats.

A GOOD DAY

Katie Brown

Darkness has long since fallen as we drive through the Valley in my friend's large white van. "Stealth bivying," as climbers refer to it, doesn't allow for a casual early night in. Even when you're planning to start before dawn the following morning, you must wait until at least nine or ten at night to drive through the campgrounds in the Valley looking for a vacant site. The prevailing theory is that the later you pull into an unoccupied spot, the less likely you are to be awoken by an RVer wishing to claim their campsite. You see, sometimes people book campsites but don't arrive the day their reservation starts, resulting in an empty site for a night that we can effectively steal. It's a gamble, but it *usually* works.

Once we've found an open site, my companion and I begin racking up for the following day. He's climbed the *Regular Northwest Face* of Half Dome innumerable times, but I'll be attempting to onsight it. Twenty-three pitches and 5.12—not that difficult a grade, but the longest onsight I've ever attempted. A full day of climbing without any mistakes or slips.

"It's a good thing we never really dated," my companion says casually while we sort gear. This particular climbing partner says what he's thinking, no matter what. It's refreshing because I never have to wonder what's *really* going on in his head.

I laugh a little. "Yeah? Why's that?"

"Because you probably would have driven me crazy in the long run. You're like the least motivated, most talented climbing partner ever."

I can't help but laugh again. It's kind of a compliment, and kind of an insult, but also strangely true. My tortured relationship with this sport has defined my life. I have so many aspirations, but the voice in my head berates me relentlessly, and I start each day exhausted before I've even climbed anything. I never train, and truth be told, I don't know how. I rely on this climbing partner to motivate us both, which must be annoying for him. But when we're on the rock, I can carry my own weight. It's all the stuff leading up to it that I'm strangely apathetic about.

"Yeah, I know," I sigh with a bit of sadness, but also with a half grin playing on my face, picturing what he says. "It would have been a shit show. But seriously, thank you for helping me do this." Without a partner like him, I wouldn't have the strength or bravery to attempt this route onsight. His experience and belief in me make me feel like I can do it.

The next morning, we don't have to worry about getting out before the camp host arrives to check campsites. We're climbing Half Dome in a day, so we start hiking long before sunrise. Our photographer friend is hiking around back to rappel down and take photos, which only adds to my nerves. All my other hard onsights have been basically whims, when there is no pressure, no expectations.

We scramble up the slabs below Half Dome, eventually reaching the base of the route. My climbing partner will carry our water and food for the day so that I don't have to worry about anything but climbing. I'm touched. I've never been supported in this way before, at least not in a way that makes me feel like I don't owe my partner anything in return. I honestly feel that he is offering this to me, well, just because. No strings attached.

We start out simul-climbing through the easy parts low on the route. There are some wide chimney sections where I feel tucked in and secure, safe from the inevitable exposure of the hard pitches above, and we move quickly through this area.

The first truly hard bit of climbing comes after Big Sandy Ledge. It's called the Zig Zags, and the climbing suits the name. Up and sideways, up and sideways, the route progresses. On the third and hardest zigzag, the route cuts to the side, and I find myself underclinging a thin crack with my feet pasted on the rock below me. I look at a piece of gear below and to the left of me. I've progressed well past it, so I fumble to place a small cam underneath, gauging the size by feel alone. I can't see it go in, so I try to lean down to see the placement, but it feels precarious, pushing me off-balance and out from the rock. Given that my arms are in a permanent bicep curl position, with just my first digit fitting into the thin undercling, and my legs are under a lot of pressure to maintain friction on the rock, I know I will pump out if I fiddle with the gear too long. I look to the right, where I can see the anchor. I know I can make these moves without falling, but I don't know if I can do it if I expend all my energy trying to put in gear. In the briefest of moments, I decide to just "punch it" to the anchor.

Weird, I think to myself as I move toward the anchor, trying not to think about the fatigue in my biceps, breathing heavily, scowling in concentration. *I should be scared right now, but . . . I'm not*. It's a strange thought to have at that moment.

"Well, I'm super impressed," my belayer says as I finish the route and glance back at him, a look of glee and triumph on my face. I've been told before that I'm strung too tight, but in this case it pays off. He looks at me with a goofy grin on his face.

After the Zig Zags comes Thank God Ledge. It's just wide enough but also not quite wide enough, so there are two ways to move across it: crawl, or face your back to the wall, your front to the open expanse of air, and scoot sideways. I honestly don't remember which way we traversed this piece of rock—I probably crawled.

We sit on the wide ledge, feet dangling into the abyss of air and sky, and eat our snack. There's basically one more hard pitch above us, but it's a slab. I'm terrible at slab climbing; it scares me, and I'm not confident. I try not to think about the fact that the hardest pitch (for me) is at the very end of the day, when my skin is thin and my mental endurance is lagging. If I think about it too hard, I'll talk myself out of it.

So instead, we sit and eat, and my climbing partner tells me about his own experience on the pitch, when he allowed one finger to hover over a fixed piece during the hardest section. The idea that he could possibly catch himself with that one finger should his foot pop gave him the confidence to keep going. I think about it as I chew, wondering what it must have felt like for him in that moment.

Finally though, it's time to start climbing again, and if I wait any longer, I'll overthink it. Movement, action before thought, is what I need now. This habit of mine sometimes gets me into trouble—the whole "leap before you look" adage—but sometimes it works in my favor. I consciously click off the part of my mind that tells me I can't do it or that I will give up or get too scared. I rack up—with only a handful of quickdraws, slings, and protection needed between here and the summit—and put on my shoes, then get into position swiftly, before I can have another intrusive thought.

The day has been long, but it could not have been more perfect. Warm, probably a bit too warm for some but just right for me, with a breeze but not so much so that it feels unnerving this high up. I'm unencumbered by the extra layers needed for ideal conditions, or "sending temps," and I feel light and airy as the sun begins to slant in the afternoon sky. Our photographer friend pops his head over the summit and offers calls of encouragement. I hear his camera: click, click, click. It feels comforting somehow. I'm not alone up here.

I arrive at the crux of the slab pitch and clip the fixed piece that my friend's finger once hovered over, not touching, just offering a whisper of invisible support, and I begin to move past it. It feels like I'm holding nothing, stepping on nothing, just smeared on this blank piece of granite, splayed out like a lizard with nothing but air below me. I prefer steep rock, something to grab, even if it's tiny, so that I can get my foot up high and pull my body in tight to the rock, safe and compact. I have to remind myself that on slab I'm better off having space between my body and the rock, when all my instincts are screaming at me to lie down flat and hold on for dear life. I can see the hold above me that I need to get to. It's a jug, and if I can get there, then I've done it.

But what if I can't? my mind begins to whisper at me. I hear the encouragement from below and above me as I stand, frozen, on a smear of a foot, afraid to commit to the move I can see that I need to do. *What if these two people have put an entire day into supporting me, and I fall right now? I'll have failed them.* My mind is tired. The mental tenacity of onsighting for twenty-two pitches has left me feeling drained.

But then I hear my belayer below me, an indistinguishable garble of gentle encouragement, and I snap out of it. *No,* I think, *I* want *this*. I'm terrified, but I feel as though I have to do this. I let out a loud, guttural yell as I pull through the couple of delicate moves. It's a not-so-delicate response to this style of climbing.

"Aaaaauuuuugh!!!"

Everything I've held in all day comes out, and I latch onto the final jug. I feel a little embarrassed by my outburst. Above me there's a hoot, below me there's a hoot, and I feel so thankful for these friends.

I've done it. In all honesty, the grade doesn't even matter. What matters more is that I've conquered my mind. That is a huge hurdle for me, and it makes this—hands down—the most special day of my life.

I top out to the smattering of tourists who have hiked the nine miles up the backside of Half Dome. I sit in the late afternoon sunlight, feeling complete and whole, as my partner comes up behind me. It's been a good day.

Katie Brown's rise to climbing fame came swiftly and at an astonishingly young age. She was introduced to the sport as climbing competitions were growing in popularity, and before she turned twenty she had won the X Games, Rock Master, and the World Cup. Outside of the gym, she racked up an equally impressive résumé, including the free onsight one-day ascent of the *Regular Northwest Face* of Half Dome in October 2008 described in this story. Though often called one of the best female rock climbers of all time, Katie had complicated emotions about climbing and soon left the sport.

Katie lives in Boulder, Colorado, where she's reintroducing herself to the movement that she fell in love with as a teenager and writing a memoir about her life in the spotlight of the climbing world.

MELTDOWN

Beth Rodden

It's always weird starting a new project, especially one that has never been done before, especially one left unfinished by one of my climbing heroes. So many questions run through my mind: *Is it possible? Is it good? Is it worthy?*

In September 2007, I started working on a thin, discontinuous crack through a dark black wall next to Upper Cascade Falls in Yosemite. Ron Kauk had worked on it but had abandoned it many years earlier. The week before, I had surprised myself by completing a route of his, *Peace*, up in Tuolumne. Embarking on another one of his routes (this time unfinished) felt ominous but made me appreciate his eye for beauty and location in a climb.

I had spent the spring and fall of the previous eight years in Yosemite, slowly working my way up from *After Six* to El Cap, learning to trust the polished granite and convince myself that my swollen knuckles and bruised ego were all part of becoming a better Valley climber. At some point during that period, I realized I only had eyes for El Cap. I obsessed over free climbing in the vast amount of granite and endless possibilities. But after a handful of years up there and three free ascents, my body and mind were exhausted. I was tired of vertical manual labor. I wanted fresh food, a toilet that flushed, a refrigerator, and a fluffy pillow.

I had become that person who was a topic of shit talk around the cafeteria tables, but I didn't care. I had paid my dues and experienced the fulfillment of free climbing the *Nose* and other routes. But more important, I knew what parts of me remained unfulfilled. At the time, I thought I just wanted a break. I convinced myself that shorter routes, ones I could walk to, ones where I could stand on the ground in between attempts, would be a worthy temporary substitute.

The route, which I would later name *Meltdown*, is striking. It's directly to the right of Upper Cascade Falls. All of the rock within 20 feet of the ground is polished and pitch black, in stark contrast to the famous, sought-after white and light gray granite of El Cap.

Some people can dive in and start putting together the pieces of a hard project right away, but I spend the first days and weeks just identifying the pieces, as if it were a giant jigsaw puzzle. Then, over the next months, I see if and how they come together. For *Meltdown*, this process took me six months.

Tommy Caldwell (my then husband) and I had just finished building our house in Yosemite a year earlier. Growing up in Davis, I had long had a love for the Sierra; our voracious love of climbing and obsession with Yosemite funneled us into wanting to make a home there. We had a rhythm of either trying a project together or alternating supporting each other on individual ones. Tommy had completed the first free ascent, and then the first in-one-day ascent, of *Magic Mushroom* on El Cap the previous spring, so this fall was mine.

I liked the somewhat civilized nature of this project. We had spent the previous decade sleeping in our cars and vans, running from the rangers, poaching campsites—the typical rites of passage for anyone wanting to be called a Valley local in the early 2000s. But now I was settling into waking up in a warm bed, warming up on my home climbing wall in the garage, and driving to the project. It felt soft, but I secretly loved it.

By January 2008, I had found all the pieces and was stringing them together. I was making links from the bottom of the climb to the crux, and then from the crux to just before the anchor, and then to the anchor. My progression was steady, which gave me faith that I would be able to do it. The skin on the sides of my knuckles was raw from the sharp and precarious finger locks, and I wore through shoes every other week from standing on incredibly precise footholds. But for the most part, it was a progression that kept me coming back, that fed my desire to set loftier and loftier goals. I pushed my body to exhaustion each day on the route and then returned home and trained for another three hours. I thought that by pushing my limits I could extend the sport of climbing into uncharted territory. It felt oddly virtuous at the time, even though when I think about it now, it seems so inconsequential to climb a 70-foot piece of rock for the first time.

This was our first full winter in Yosemite (except for the one when we built our house, when we didn't climb at all), and at that time the Sierra got consistent, massive snowstorms. It snowed a typical 4 feet in this storm, and two days later we were hiking up to see how many more days I needed to let pass before I could try the route again. As we walked up the river wash, carefully balancing on one slick boulder after another, my face became wet with spray about 50 feet earlier than any other day we had hiked up there. As we continued up, my face got wetter and wetter and my spirits lower and lower. When it warmed up after each snowstorm, the waterfall grew and grew, making the climb wetter and wetter.

For someone who hung most of her identity and self-worth on making each climbing objective harder, the thought of nature putting a stop to all my hard work of the past five months felt unjust. I felt tears welling in my eyes; my face became hot and my hands started sweating. I looked up at the climb, and the entire bottom half was glistening. Spray was engulfing at least 20 feet of the thin crack all the way to the crux. My heart sank. Was this the end? Did I have to pack up and wait until next October? Would I forget everything? Could I ever get back to where I was? I knew the route like the back of my hand. I could practically mime the sequence in my sleep. I loved how fit I had become. I loved the precision of my hands going into the crack, knowing how hard to flex and turn; I loved how decisive my feet had become in each placement, sticking to improbable minuscule polished bumps. The thought of leaving all that alone for the next nine months felt devastating.

I looked at Tommy. "How many days? Can we put up a tarp? Should we let our cars idle for the next week to promote climate change so it will never snow again?" My brain just dumped all my fears and irrational thoughts out of my mouth.

Forever the optimist, Tommy said, "Let's come back in a few days. You are so close, you can do this." We turned around and walked back to our truck, where we could continue listening to *Harry Potter* on tape, my one escape from obsessing over this climb.

FOR THE NEXT MONTH I MADE SLOW PROGRESS, AT FIRST HANGING THREE times on the route, then twice, and then just once. Each time gave me a little more hope. After my work on the route each day, I would train until I couldn't lift my arms above my head. But each big snowstorm brought a meltdown of fear that I wouldn't be able to do the route before spring came.

On Valentine's Day 2008, I was getting to the point where I was over it. That may sound funny, since my obsession was with a random 70-foot crack on an arbitrary wall in Yosemite. When you really think about it, climbing is altogether pointless, but when you're so deep into it, when it's your professional life and your personal life and your identity, it seems crucially important. I was getting tired. I was burned out and wanted to take a break. I wanted not to have to worry about what I ate each day, the size of my waist, if my skin was good, if my shoes were perfectly broken in but not worn out. I knew I could do the route. I was strong enough, I was fitter than I'd ever been, and it was the hardest thing I had ever tried.

On that day, I got to the base and felt a light spray on my face. The waterfall was slightly bigger than the week before. It was slightly warmer, which meant a little more snow from the high country was melting and draining out through Upper Cascade Falls. Each warmer day, the waterfall would get bigger and bigger. I felt a sense of urgency, but somewhere inside I squashed it with a rare feeling of confidence. I put on my shoes, pulling them tight and placing the velcro perfectly. I cinched my harness and clipped on my gear in precise order. I put my hands in my chalk bag and looked up at the route. I knew it. I knew what to do. I knew how hard to try. The waterfall was loud, but I could hear my thoughts. *Just fucking get this done,* I said to myself. I put my hands in the crack and started up.

Climbing my hardest for me is a balance between listening to the thoughts in my head that I need to and filtering out the ones I don't. When I listen to the chatter, the worry, the doubt, the questioning, that's when I get distracted. But filtering these out is not some zen moment where I don't hear anything. I talk to myself the whole time, my mind racing through the information I've learned over the past six months, all of the smallest details: how hard to clench my abs, how much to turn my finger, when to breathe, where to put my gear in, how to check it, how many times to shake out. It's a constant track in my head, sometimes on loop like breathing and relaxing, sometimes specific like *tighten your abs, twist here, crimp but not too hard there*.

Getting through the crux surprised me, but I didn't let that emotion distract me. I knew there were still hard parts, that I was tired, that I still needed to keep my attention on the climb, not what I had just accomplished. I could hear Tommy below, but I didn't let my attention go enough to hear what he was saying. Another 30 feet of climbing and I clipped the anchors. I slunk onto the rope and immediately felt relief. I felt lighter, I felt proud, I felt lost and found all at the same time. It was a huge endorphin rush.

We celebrated the only way we knew how, at the hot food bar of Whole Foods in Fresno after a two-hour training session in the garage.

It's been more than a decade since I completed *Meltdown*—a route that was not repeated by anyone until November 2018—and since I last climbed El Cap. Tommy and I divorced; I fell in love and remarried and started a family with the birth of our son. *Meltdown* was the pinnacle of my accomplishments in climbing. It was the culmination of fifteen years of wanting to push myself and the sport of climbing forward. But on the other side of *Meltdown*, I realized, slowly, that pushing climbing forward couldn't fill all the gaps and holes in my life, that accomplishment and achievement were not the only ways to happiness. I had achieved more than I could dream of, but there was still something missing and an underlying unhappiness that I couldn't get rid of. I started to notice that with each climb I did, with each cover I was on, with each video I was in, I only felt pressure to do more and bigger and better. It was time to stop.

I still live in Yosemite, but my life here looks quite different from before. Our son goes to school in the Valley, and his friends are the kids of rangers, the same group of people I used to hide and run from when I was in my twenties. I now spend most of my climbing days on the boulders below the cliffs I used to climb. Occasionally we'll venture up on a route where I remember the unique feeling of the wind and sun and birds on the wall. Sometimes I miss the simplicity of sleeping and camping in a van. But we've been able to turn this magical valley into our home, into a way of life for our little family. I love going on hikes and climbs with my husband and son that I would have scoffed at in my younger days. *After Six*, a five-pitch 5.7, is now my favorite climb on earth. If I could do only one climb for the rest of my life, it would be that.

Beth Rodden started climbing in a gym in Davis, California, at the age of fourteen, and by the time she graduated from high school, she was traveling the world for climbing competitions. She left college after just one semester to follow her passion for the mountains. In the following years, Beth would make three free ascents of El Capitan, including the first free ascent of *Lurking Fear*; be held hostage for six days by militants on a big-wall climbing trip to Kyrgyzstan; and establish what was Yosemite's hardest single-pitch climb (5.14c) at the time, *Meltdown*. She then stepped away from the climbing spotlight to focus on balance, healing, and family.

She lives with her husband and son in Yosemite, where they can climb, play, and bask in the beauty of the natural world.

THIRTY BRUISES

Kate Rutherford

I have approximately thirty bruises—give or take a few (some blend together)—and five scabs: one on my left ankle, one on each shoulder, a small one on my hand, and a tiny one on my wrist. Despite all my injuries, I feel like I fared pretty well on that huge physical endeavor we call freeing *Freerider*.

Sixteen years ago, I thought freeing El Cap was an impossible goal. The huge scale of Yosemite Valley, with granite towering above on all sides, always made me feel like a baby chipmunk looking up at a redwood grove. The pot of golden calories is at the top of a massive tree on the end of the most delicate branches. The logistics, plus the physicality, of freeing a big wall seemed beyond me until I started asking for help and learning the ropes.

Over the years, climbing started feeling easier. I spent more time on big routes with great mentors and started to really fall into a rhythm with my favorite partner, Madaleine Sorkin. We started to build up our endurance together. As a team we laughed and cried our way up the first all-female free ascents of Zion's *Moonlight Buttress* and the *Regular Northwest Face* of Half Dome. We learned tricks to hauling a bag, what snacks to bring, and how to be patient and wait for shade, or sometimes how to wait for the sun to warm our stiff bodies. We learned from the mountains and each other to break down intimidation by focusing on one pitch at a time. Concentrate calmly on the task at hand and then move on to the next one. Most important, we learned how to have fun together, to take the lead when the other was tired, to coax talent from tears, and to sing songs with each minor success.

WE STARTED UP THE INITIAL PITCHES OF *SALATHÉ WALL*, CALLED *FREEBLAST*, early on a Monday morning, planning to spend the five-day workweek on El Capitan. A long time, yes, but even after doing our homework by rappelling in from the top to figure out the harder pitches, we knew we would need time to rest our bodies and use the shady parts of the day. The first day went pretty smoothly, the slabs a bit slow, but soon we were climbing down, over, and up the Hollow Flake, an intimidating maw of a crack that has broken many a bone and punctured the lung of many a talented climber. That first night we slept on Hollow Flake Ledge, where our friends Hayden, Ben, and Katie had left a bag of food on a rainy retreat, a gift for us. We were feeling set up for success.

Waking up on day two, we were stiff already. We ate avocado, apple, and cheese wrapped in tortillas for breakfast. We climbed a few mellow pitches and then tiptoed into the Monster. The 200-foot offwidth is just big enough for one of my butt cheeks and is an intimidating rite of passage, both literally and figuratively. I had chosen to take two #6 Camalots for mental fortitude and was so glad I did. After slowly wiggling my body up the seven-inch fissure, we met photographer Mikey Schaefer at the Alcove and hauled our bags to El Cap Spire, a contender for the world's most beautiful place to sleep.

Day three was exciting. We both fell off the infamous Boulder Problem a few times before I changed my sequence at the last minute, allowing me to send it on my third try in the hot sun. Madaleine followed, and then I struggled my way up the muddy jungle of the Sewer. As the sun sank, I shivered in my muddy, wet clothes and smiled to myself as I watched a granite-colored frog ascend the crack above me while I belayed Mad up the sloppy chimney.

We set up camp there on the Block and planned to stay two nights. This awkward sloping bivy for two people had a cache of friends' gear, including a double portaledge, which we set up for a very comfy sleeping arrangement. It seemed like we were getting the princess treatment. Mikey broke out a flask of whiskey, and a few sips put us straight to sleep.

Morning came with high clouds, and the day was perfectly cool for the three 5.12 pitches on the agenda. I had a minor meltdown when I thought my forearms were going to explode on the first corner. I fell off. I was furious. My arms hurt so badly, and it was only day three. Mad gave me a ginger chew and a pep talk. I pulled the rope and was fine on the next go—turns out it helps to warm up a bit.

Pitch twenty-eight was wet. It's a distinct crux on the route, the last pitch under the roof of the Salathé Headwall. I mumbled encouragement and gave Madaleine the actual shirt off my back. She tagged it up and shoved it into the key finger locks to soak up the water. Now that the holds were dry, she calmly cruised up the kneebarring, laybacking Enduro Corner. Thrilled by our progress, I followed.

Freerider then traverses left on wild pitches. Pitch twenty-nine is one of the most exposed and beautiful. It has no footholds but huge handholds. Unfortunately, Madaleine broke a crimp all the way at the end, fell, and had to aid all the way back to the anchor. I was freezing (thanks to that wet cotton shirt), but it was my turn, and I quickly warmed back up by traversing out left and ultimately freeing my nemesis pitch. I sat in the glowing evening sun in a place named Knights of the Round Table, and it dawned on me we were sending!

Our strategy, passed down from our Camp 4 teachers, prioritized hauling less by spending two nights on the Block. Thus, we fixed our ropes and sailed down to our deluxe bivy, celebrated with a touch more whiskey, smiled a lot, watched the clouds light up pink, and drifted off to sleep. We awoke to a fine drizzle in the dark. I tensed with the fear of wet granite destroying our summit dreams and nulling the years of learning and love donated by our friends. We had only a few hundred feet to go to reach the summit. I nudged Madaleine with my elbow. Together we grimaced and then pulled our sleeping pads over us to act as a rainfly.

The rain was brief, and the morning lit the mist rising off the river. Images floated like notes in a summer solstice melody: green valley, birds chirping, clean granite rising above. But on that final morning, the Scotty Burke Offwidth gave me most of my bruises. The thirty-first pitch (of thirty-five) is rated 10d, but it's wide and *steep*. I think I tried harder on that pitch than any other. I walked my #6 for half an hour, pressing my tired body against the rock for friction and inching up with my tender toes. When I finally got to a handjam, superpowers rushed into my arms, and while scampering to the belay, I let out a little wolf pup howl of joy, thankful for the relatively simple final few pitches above.

Atop the smooth, flat summit, I counted my bruises and belayed in a daze. I realized how much we had asked of ourselves, our bodies, our friendship, and our community. The Valley had prepared us for this: the granite mentors, the detailed maps, the specific instructions gifted by friends, equipment shared, jokes told, frogs viewed, and dinner parties given to nourish body and soul.

My last thoughts as Madaleine crested the rim were, *How can we ever reciprocate this gift? Can we draw a map of inspiration for others?* I hope this story is a start.

Adventure might truly be in Kate Rutherford's blood. Her first home was a family-built cabin in rural Alaska, where she learned to experience the mountains through the seasons, and she spent most of her childhood on Vashon Island in Washington. Kate has followed her innate sense of exploration to every corner of the globe. She has spent the last twenty years seeking adventure on some of the biggest walls around, from Yosemite to Zion, Greenland to Venezuela. Kate has climbed all seven of the skyline peaks of the Patagonian Fitz Roy Massif, upon which she established numerous first ascents.

She lives with her husband in Bishop, California, where she enjoys a range of climbing experiences and makes jewelry inspired by her travels and love for the natural world.

ON THE SHOULDERS OF GIANTS

2011–PRESENT

It becomes easier to draw out the themes and lessons of an era when the passage of time allows us to look back and reflect. So how do we summarize a time period that is ongoing? Yosemite climbers are more diverse than ever before, pushing the limits of every discipline of climbing to heights that not long ago were unfathomable. While developing the first few eras required concentrated research to identify female climbers, selecting the women who would represent this era was far more challenging, as there were so many to choose from. Rock climbing is less countercultural now than at any other point in the sport's history, and with the proliferation of climbing gyms and climbers in the media, more women are involved in the sport than ever before. Today's climbers cannot deny the strength and courage of the women around them.

Yosemite climbing still demands the most of climbers, requiring a wide array of skills and talents. The women's *Nose* speed record became a coveted trophy in the first part of this era, falling from a record time of 10 hours and 40 minutes in 2011, to 7 hours and 26 minutes in 2012 as part of the first all-female El Cap–Half Dome linkup, to a mere 4 hours and 43 minutes in 2015. And while the *Nose* is perhaps the route most often climbed in a single day, other El Cap routes have been subject to speed ascents as well. The *Salathé*, *Zodiac*, *Triple Direct*, and *Lurking Fear* have all seen all-female one-day pushes, and certainly more are to come. Another milestone fell in 2016 with the first solo female one-day climb of the *Nose*. And while a small group of women are pushing the absolute limits on El Cap's hardest free routes, more than a handful have found success on routes like *Freerider*.

We can't be sure when the tide will turn, signifying a new era, or what it will look like when it arrives. What we do know is that women are involved in every facet of climbing in Yosemite. They're climbing bigger, faster, and harder than many people imagined was possible; they're establishing new routes and repeating many of the park's proudest lines. They have fulfilling careers, as park rangers and rescuers, mountain guides, doctors, biologists, engineers, and professional climbers. They support their families and communities, as mothers and caregivers, as leaders, allies, and advocates. They fight for equality on and off the walls so that climbing will be more diverse, inclusive, and welcoming. They are strong and humble, brave and proud. Through their actions and stories, they carry on the legacy of our foremothers, of the generations of women who came before them.

VALLEY OF GIANTS

Libby Sauter

When I showed up in Yosemite Valley in 2009 for my first season on Yosemite Search and Rescue (YOSAR), I was so intimidated I couldn't get out of my car. Sitting in my almost-new yellow Volkswagen Beetle in the Camp 4 parking lot, I was surrounded by the beat-up dirtbag-mobiles of true Valley hardmen and women. I had never even attempted to climb El Cap or Half Dome, and the only big-wall routes I had tried had resulted in failure. My application to YOSAR had been padded with 5.12 crack routes at Indian Creek, slackline rigging knowledge, and international nursing experience—little that prepared me for being on one of the world's most elite high-angle rescue teams.

After several long minutes of staring at the Reserved Parking—Search and Rescue sign, I got up the nerve to walk to the famous SAR compound at the back of Camp 4. I was relieved to be greeted warmly by the eclectic group of climber dirtbags, the "monkeys," that composed the team. "We're gonna go solo *After Six*! Wanna come?" one monkey asked as he mounted a haphazardly spray-painted yellow cruiser bike with black electrical tape encircling the frame to make it look like a bee. Terrified at the thought of onsight free soloing the six-pitch 5.7, I declined, saying that I had a lot of unpacking to do. As everyone biked away, I stood there alone, feeling as though the walls around me were growing even taller.

My self-doubt was only exacerbated a few nights later when a former YOSAR team member known as Mega G Force stopped by camp for dinner.

"Back in my time here, you couldn't be on the team unless you'd climbed El Cap ten times, and the *Rostrum* was a warm-up," he said, unaware of my inexperience. I couldn't even fathom climbing the *Rostrum*, an eight-pitch classic 5.11c route, let alone thinking it was a warm-up. My feelings of being out of place, of insecurity among the giants of the park, burned in my gut as I took another swig of the climbers' malt liquor, King Cobra.

A culture of competition and bravado has always pervaded the Valley climbing scene. In the 1950s, climbers Warren Harding, a wine-drinking, philandering renegade, and Royal Robbins, nicknamed the Valley Christian by Harding for his pioneering advocacy of pitonless clean climbing, fought to one-up each other and established contradictory ethical styles. It was in this environment that I found great motivation that first season.

Knowing that it's impossible to feign excellence in Yosemite, my first few months on YOSAR were spent inching through the classics, mostly under 5.9. Groveling my way through the sandbagged moderates, I began to realize that in Yosemite you don't actually have to be a very talented climber to succeed; you just have to be willing to work hard—and suffer. The history of Yosemite climbing is one of submission more than of harmony; Warren Harding's famous first ascent of El Cap took forty-five days spread out over eighteen months, and Tommy Caldwell's *Dawn Wall* took seven years. So while I couldn't exactly dance my way up the rock, I did have the determination to fight my way up.

A few months into that first season, I had ticked off a lot of the sub-5.9 classics, and I had also begun to get used to the feeling of being surrounded by the climbers who seemed to casually set and break records in the Valley. Alex Honnold came and went. Beth Rodden did a photo shoot in the YOSAR site. My teammates on YOSAR left camp early and came back from big missions full of energy and in time for dinner. My perception of the possible, of normal, began to shift, and I began to seriously contemplate larger objectives that only months before would have seemed outlandish.

"You know, the women's speed record on the *Nose* is over twelve hours," said Papa D, an ex-parajumper medic for the Air Force and one of my YOSAR teammates that first season. That was all I needed to hear. This was the lofty goal that would enable me to feel worthy of the prestige that being on YOSAR confers. I was so stoked about the idea that I lined up a partner and a training plan to break the women's speed record on the *Nose* before having ever attempted El Cap in the more traditional, multi-day style.

Consistent with its capricious origin, my journey to setting the *Nose* record was not graceful. The first time I climbed El Capitan with my friend Chantel Astorga, I cried at every anchor, frustrated by my inability to construct clean, efficient anchors. When Althea Rogers and I climbed *Lurking Fear* on El Capitan in a very average twenty-one hours, we topped out in the dark. Nervous about the descent off El Cap from the far west side, we curled up on our coiled ropes and spooned and shivered until the sun rose. When I finally attempted the *Nose* for the first time, I wanted to lead every pitch with my then-boyfriend Jake Whittaker jumaring behind me. I was so nervous that I vomited the entire contents of my stomach before we even roped up, thus beginning one of my most grueling days of climbing ever with no fresh calories to draw on. I topped out the *Nose* later that day feeling exhausted and sick, yet more exhilarated than I had ever been before.

Through these trials and tribulations, two things became clear to me: that I could push myself further than I had ever imagined, and that these pursuits were fueled by the greater community of climbers that settle in the Valley. The band of misfits, the monkeys, that inhabit the tents and illegal boulder caves set a high bar of excellence. Knowing that your best friends have the ability to run up the walls and that they will risk their lives to save yours is essential in the process. My first ascent of El Cap with Chantel would not have been possible without her ability to calmly help me uncluster the ropes. Climbing El Cap in a day that first time would not have been possible without Althea, whose big-wall rhymes and indefatigable attitude kept the mood light when the sun set and stress levels rose. Leading every pitch on the *Nose*-in-a-day would not have been possible without Jake, who could have gotten us off the mountain with ease if my will or my muscles had faltered. Mega G's history lessons kept me humble, while Papa D helped me dream bigger. And the ever-present knowledge that YOSAR was there, often cheering from the meadow, gave an undercurrent of confidence through it all.

After four years of working on the *Nose* with various lady friends, I eventually teamed up with the German-Kiwi climber Mayan Smith-Gobat. Her determination and drive were second only to her biceps. Over two seasons and at least six ascents of the *Nose* together, we broke the record three times, finally settling at 4 hours and 43 minutes. The combination of our boldness and Mayan's free-climbing ability created a successful team.

Years after we set the *Nose* speed record, the cascade of inevitable tragedies that plague climbers led me to realize that as much as the walls of Yosemite had taught me lessons, so too had the giant personalities. As much as climbing is an individual pursuit, it is ultimately a team activity. My success in Yosemite was born of inner grit and a desire to fit in, but in the end it was made possible by strong partners and good friends. The subtle competitiveness and high expectations set by the local climbers coax you to dream bigger. While the climbers, like the Valley walls, are massive and foreboding, they are, unlike the walls, ephemeral. The people come and go. Some drift with the seasons, and others leave this world forever, too often falling from those same cliffs that brought us all together. But their lessons remain. To be a successful climber in Yosemite, you must be driven to master the technical skills that allow passage up the towering walls. But to truly reach your potential, you must dig into the community. Because the true route to Valley success is through the monkeys.

Libby Sauter grew up in Las Vegas, Nevada, where she was introduced to rock climbing at a youth camp. Her passion for the sport blossomed in college and drew her to Yosemite, where she landed a coveted spot on Yosemite Search and Rescue. She honed her skills on the Valley's walls, making use of her ability to keep calm and collected under pressure. During her tenure in Yosemite, Libby was part of the first all-female team to complete two routes on El Capitan in a single day, and with Mayan Smith-Gobat, she set the female speed record on the *Nose*, a record that has stood since 2014. She has since become the youngest person ever to be inducted into the American Alpine Club's Mountaineering Hall of Fame.

It is this same ability to perform well under pressure that has led to impressive success in her career as a pediatric cardiac nurse, for which she's traveled all over the world. Though she has backed away from the high-risk game of big-wall speed climbing, Libby still enjoys a good granite romp with friends.

SEVEN WALLS IN SEVEN DAYS

Quinn Brett

I'm not sure where I got the idea for seven walls in seven days. I wanted to run around, I wanted to do something different from male climbers—to climb as part of a female team on a new adventure. First, I mapped out the walls, the gear, who would lead which pitches. The fact that Lost Arrow Spire, one of the formations I wanted to climb, has seasonal peregrine falcon closures in the spring left us with seven big walls: El Capitan, Half Dome, Liberty Cap, Leaning Tower, Washington Column, Mount Watkins, and the Gold Wall, according to the book *Yosemite Big Walls* by Chris McNamara and Chris Van Leuven.

I asked a few gal pals of notable ability if they were interested in giving it a rip. One was definitely not, in a kind, "that's too much for me" way. One was interested but not as experienced. I was so stoked that someone was interested that I did my best to assure her that her skills and her ability to move were more important than the enormity of the walls themselves. I flew to Yosemite to do a practice round with her and welcome her to the big walls. She was coming off an injury, psych was low, and I think the overwhelming nature of the Captain looming above did not help my cause. Darn.

That winter, I was on my habitual rotation of climbing in southern Patagonia. Josie McKee and I were acquaintances with mutual friends all over the climbing world and similar ambition. We attempted a climb in the

Fitz Roy range without success, but it ignited a friendship and the stoke to share a rope and try harder goals. I mentioned my far-fetched climbing goals: the Triple Crown in Yosemite (climbing El Capitan, Half Dome, and Mount Watkins in a day... or, I was hoping, in a push), a weeklong linkup of three classic ridges across the American West (like *Evolution Traverse* in the Sierra, part of the Picket Range in the North Cascades, and the *Grand Traverse* in the Tetons), and climbing seven big walls in Yosemite in one week. She might have looked at me with the usual "Josie eye," a mix of skepticism and excitement, but she agreed to work our way up to it. Looking back, I realize I put a lot of confidence in my partners. Libby, Josie, Jes, to name a few, were strong and capable. Sometimes I forget that we all, myself included, have insecurities and often don't think as highly of our own abilities as others do.

My seasonal work as a climbing ranger in Rocky Mountain National Park ended in late September 2016. I packed my car and drove west, intending to stay in Yosemite for the entire month of October. I had changed the detailed notes I had taken in 2015 just slightly. Because it was fall, we could now climb Lost Arrow Spire, which we swapped out for Gold Wall. I had never climbed it, so the desire was high. Josie and I still hadn't roped up together for anything more than a few pitches of sport climbing or bailing in Patagonia. We decided to spend a day climbing on *Royal Arches*. While we didn't rope up, it was nice to move across terrain we both were familiar and comfortable with. We chatted about weather and wondered if we were in the right mental space to put in a really big effort. I was fit from playing at high elevation most of the summer, and the weather looked like solid California sun for a week at least. We had better go!

OF THE SEVEN WALLS, EL CAPITAN HAS BY FAR THE MOST VERTICAL CLIMBing. It is also a wall that we were both very familiar with, so we took advantage of our combined experience and fresh minds and bodies. Our plan was to climb the *Nose* in two blocks, me leading from the start to the top of the Boot Flake, with Josie doing the King Swing and climbing through to the top. This day we chose to do a variation to the left of the first pitch as there was another *Nose*-in-a-day lady team just starting the standard first pitch. I love when ladies are out, and this sighting helped fuel the excitement of the start of our mission. It was my first time on that pitch, but even though I had to climb it by headlamp, it didn't lower our stoke or change the pace too much. Notable moments included sticking my hand in fresh urine from some Italians who planted their portaledge in the middle of the Stovelegs, and Josie cruising the upper pitches and passing a few more parties who were all incredibly gracious. Eight hours and 50 minutes after starting, we were on top. One route down, six to go.

Day two. We started early again to slog up to Lost Arrow Spire. We knew some friends (the editor of this book, in fact!) were doing *Lost Arrow Direct* wall-style, and it increased our stoke to know that we would have a break in the pace to chat with friends wherever they might be. This wall is notorious for howling winds due to its location in the Yosemite Falls amphitheater, and they were indeed blowing when we arrived at the base of the route. I bundled up and started up the chimney system, but about two pitches in I was sweating a ridiculous amount. I shed some layers, and onward we went. I led the first block to the major ledge system where Lauren and Phil were just beginning their day, having slept on the ledge. Josie swapped into lead mode. My favorite moment from this day was when she hollered down to me, "Cam hook, heel hook, mantel, no problem!" Climb time was 7 hours and 20 minutes, thought to be an overall speed record. About 10 hours camp to camp.

Day three. A shortish approach and a shorter wall. Both of us had climbed the *West Face* on Leaning Tower before, and since it was day three, I was hoping we could squeeze out the last drop of "try hard" from both of us. I had attempted a speed ascent on Leaning Tower previously with Jes Meiris after we broke the female speed record on the *Nose* in 2012, but the morale had been low. I was hoping Josie and I could establish a better time, as it had been ten years since anyone had come close to the speed record held by Heidi Wirtz and Vera Schulte-Pelkum. Josie led us off on the steep and intimidating first block. We transitioned at Ahwahnee Ledge and swam to the top of the wall in good style and good spirits, with a new female record of 4 hours and 6 minutes; we were back to beer at the car in just 6 hours. Since this was a relatively shorter day, we headed over to friend and Yosemite climbing ranger Bud Miller's house to stretch, shower, and relax. It really helped give us a little reset.

Day four. I was hoping the reset would fuel us for the grueling hike/manzanita bash-about to Mount Watkins. I had climbed this wall once before in 2014 with Jens Holsten and Josh Lavigne, but Josie had not been on it. The hike isn't too bad, but in the dark it didn't feel familiar. As we approached the arching first pitches, we noticed a party of four on the wall in front of us. Luckily, our timing was perfect: they finished the pendulum pitches just as we started. We swung through them and up onto the dihedrals. I lost a little time wandering in the blocky terrain before our transition point. We were thrilled to find jugs of water on the Sheraton-Watkins ledges, and we slugged the warm water down, as the sun was out in full force. Josie started up the harder, grassier, more technically demanding pitches. Anyone who saw us would have seen how mentally exhausted we were this day. She fixed the line after the long, leaning 5.6 pitch, and I decided to lower out and jug instead of following the pitch behind her—not our best choice. I ran out of rope lowering myself out and made the awful decision to just swing. I jumped hard into a neighboring dihedral and smacked my ass on the wall. It could have been worse, but the painful slap reminded us both to reel in the decision-making with our fatigue. Josie continued up through the splitter last pitches, and we topped out as the sun was setting. A long day with just under 10 hours of climbing time, likely another female speed record. From the top of Mount Watkins, it's a short, flat walk out to Tuolumne Meadows or a long, steep slog back down to the Valley. Knowing that we'd be exhausted, we had planned for friends to come swoop us up from the Meadows. We piled in their car, shoved food in our faces, and semi-slept on the hour-long drive back to our campsite.

Day five. Sleep! Gloriously, we slept in, ate a great breakfast, and around ten o'clock biked over to Washington Column. We were both notably tired but also aware that this should be a short day on a familiar and straightforward route. I led up through Lunch Ledge and over the Kor Roof, and trended left. We passed a party of two here. The man was leading, and he kindly stepped down and lowered a little way for me to do a shallow cam move over a smaller roof. I placed a cam and climbed on. The man placed that same cam following in my footsteps, except his cam blew and he took a small whipper. His female partner asked if we were training for something. I responded, "We're in it!" When she pondered why my cam held and his didn't, I said something about eating hamburgers. Josie swung through and free climbed up the gravely chimney and dihedral systems to the top. We had climbed for 4 hours and 1 minute, and were back at our campsite an hour later. River time to soak the legs, wash the body, and sip a cold beer occupied the rest of our day until the sun set. Two more days left.

Day six. We were a little uncertain about how we were going to handle days six and seven until the time came. We had asked around among ranger friends regarding staying at the cabin up near Half Dome or rallying someone to stash gear at the base of Liberty Cap. These two walls are right next to each other, but each has a steep approach, so we wanted to find a creative way to lessen our workload. By the morning of day six, we had a plan. We biked from the Pines up to Mirror Lake and wandered back and forth a few times in the dark in our search for the trail leading to the Death Slabs approach to Half Dome. Thankfully, Josie and I had climbed the *Regular Northwest Face* in June, when I flew out for a five-day climbing stint. The route had been impacted by serious rockfall in July 2015, which had significantly changed the climbing. A pitch or two had completely fallen off, meaning a new path to connect the established pitches needed to be sorted. We were not the first to attempt this new terrain, but what would be required was still a bit uncertain. Our June attempt had had us throwing a lasso loop of rope 10 feet to the right from one dihedral to another in hopes of wrangling a jutting boulder. Once Josie had successfully caught her boulder, she was able to pull herself over to that portion of the cliff.

Returning in October during the seven in seven, we knew what to expect. We simul-climbed the first half of the route with me leading the way through the bolt ladder into the new, scarred terrain. Josie then led up the curving, left-facing dihedral and fixed me below her pendulum point. I jugged up and got her on belay just in time for her to throw the rope and work her way over. I followed the rest of the way to the top. We summited with a climb time of 7 hours and 40 minutes, a new female record given the altered terrain. We descended via the cables route and down the trail in the last light of the day.

Our last objective, Liberty Cap, is on that same trail. It's a fairly long hike, and without many water sources in the autumn months, we wanted to refuel wherever possible. Thankfully, our good friend Max Barlerin had agreed to hike a giant backpack up from camp with two sleeping bags, a small stove, a jug of water, and freeze-dried food for us. We arrived at the Liberty Cap climbing trail after dark and searched for a short while for the bag Max had left for us hanging in a tree. Having food and water and being able to sleep directly at the base of our final wall made us feel very lucky. We were very tired.

Day seven. We woke up to the sounds of a person, or two, hammering pitons and working a route on Liberty Cap's face. Fortunately, the sounds weren't coming from our intended route, the *Southwest Face*. Logistically, the order of our walls worked out perfectly. Neither Josie nor I had climbed this wall, and it had a C3 section right off the deck; although the section was short, aiding sketchy gear for breakfast after a long week was definitely trying. I took my time while Josie patiently encouraged and supported. We swapped somewhere in the middle, with Josie leading the last of the last with some challenging C2 moves and run-out slabs. She kept it together, and we topped out in 6 hours and 13 minutes, possibly setting an overall speed record. Most important, we were two ladies pushing ourselves and each other as friends and climbing partners in a style we were proud of. We were safe, despite my stupid move on Watkins.

We hiked out the rest of the way to the valley floor, hitting the river just below the bridge and bus stop. We both soaked, washing away all the dirt but none of the joy or exhaustion. I was stoked to have followed through with this random compilation of climbs I had been pondering for years. We made it back to our campsite in daylight to find friends waiting with warm dinner and cold beers. What an incredible adventure with one of the most solid and pleasant humans in a spectacular place! Where else in the world can you climb that many vertical feet of world-class granite with less than twenty miles of hiking?

Quinn Brett's parents were committed to taking their children to national parks during summer vacations, gradually traveling farther and farther west from their home in Minnesota. When she first saw El Capitan, Quinn knew that she'd climb it someday; ten years later, she did. After that first climb in 2010, Quinn amassed an impressive list of big-wall ascents, speed records, and difficult free climbs, first in places like Yosemite and Zion, and then on larger mountains in Patagonia, Greenland, and India.

But everything changed in 2017, when Quinn took a 120-foot fall while climbing the *Nose* of El Cap, leaving her paralyzed from the waist down. Today, Quinn lives in Estes Park, Colorado, where she works for the National Park Service, using her background as an environmental advocate to speak up for increased accessibility on public lands.

MAGIC MUSHROOM

Babsi Zangerl

Forty meters below the summit, what had seemed impossible at first has finally become reality. It's day nine on the wall and we are both tired from the previous days of climbing, but we are more motivated than ever. We are hanging out in our portaledge, and the weather is on our side. Although it is too warm to try the next hard pitch in the sunshine, we keep getting perfect conditions at night. Waiting impatiently for sunset, our eyes keep wandering up the last big challenge of *Magic Mushroom*, the 5.14a Seven Seas pitch shortly before the top.

Trying to memorize the movements, I always get to a point where I doubt it will work out. Never before have I felt such a strong desire to climb a route. Thoughts about failure and having to return next year seem absurd, yet it's likely. Having to start it all over again, with 900 meters of climbing, thirteen pitches harder than 8a, and hardly any fixed pro, seems unthinkable. In light of this, the chance to climb it now feels like a gift. Jacopo is in high spirits. He has checked everything out and found a perfect solution for the crux shortly before the belay. But I am doubtful and feel anxious that pitch twenty-seven could mean the end of my journey.

When we arrived in Yosemite on October 10, we weren't sure which route we would finally end up on. We knew we wanted to be on El Cap, though, because no matter which of its many routes you choose, it never disappoints. My big dream was to climb the *Nose*, while Jacopo had cast an eye on *Magic Mushroom*, which leads up a steep wall a bit farther to the left.

Of course I was psyched to try that as well, but when I saw the topo map for the first time, my heart nearly stopped. So many hard pitches, most of them on the upper part of El Cap—that sounded more like an interesting long-term project. I quickly realized that this would be a really hard task, maybe way beyond my climbing skills, but at the same time I was keen to give it a go and see what happened. Looking up at El Cap for the first time quickly made us dump our *Nose* plans. It was naive to think that it would not be overcrowded at the best time of the year.

After a well-deserved rest day, a pleasant stroll took us to the bottom of *Magic Mushroom*. The first pitch, called *Moby Dick*, blew our socks off. Perfect splitters and beautiful, varied climbing up perfect Yosemite granite. This continued better than we ever could have imagined until we reached the first hard pitch, number six. We immediately knew we would not be able to just climb that pitch, not even with the occasional rest. There was one rivet missing a hangar at the crux, and getting there was the first big challenge. We tried our luck, taking turns, and finally got up, although this way of moving had little in common with climbing. We then spent hours cleaning the crack after the crux before we were able to redpoint the pitch. The same applied to the next pitches, which required days of cleaning before we considered them to be climbable.

Our chosen style of climbing was ground up, without checking out pitches from above. This took a lot of time, as there is hardly any fixed protection on the route, and on the hard pitches it is often impossible to place gear. We were forced to aid some pitches to place a few beaks we could use as protection for the free ascent. With our lack of aid-climbing practice, this was adventurous and thrilling, and we had to fight hard for every pitch. After another eight days on the wall, we finally made it to the top, our first milestone, but we were still far away from any serious bid to free climb the whole route.

After that we invested some more days working on the crux pitches (there are plenty of them) and spent quite a lot of time on the Seven Seas, that last hard 5.14a pitch before the top, which turned out to be the most difficult for me. I was able to climb all the sequences of the Seven Seas pitch, but linking it all up in one go seemed impossible. My feet kept slipping off the greasy rock in overstretched positions, and I could not keep up my body tension. I kept trying, finding three potential solutions, but each one felt way too hard to be climbed coming from the bottom. My optimism quickly dwindled.

On top of that, time was running out. We had already changed our flights, but we had only two weeks left, meaning one single chance would be all we would get. We both decided to lead all pitches harder than 5.12. This would take additional time, but since we had stashed food and water on our previous attempts, we would be able to stay on the wall for twelve days.

ON NOVEMBER 30, THE ALARM CLOCK RANG AT FOUR IN THE MORNING and off we went, free climbing the first pitches in darkness. Our objective for the first day was to get up ten pitches to Mammoth Terraces, the only place on the wall where you can sleep without a portaledge. The second pitch revealed that this would be harder than expected, as many of the lower pitches were wet. It was mainly luck that kept us from slipping off the wet holds of the first 5.13b pitch, but the climbing got better, and when we finally arrived at the Terraces, we were exhausted. After some quick binge eating, there was silence, and we fell asleep under a clear sky.

The next morning, I felt as if I had been run over by a train. It took a lot of effort to get out of the sleeping bag and put on my climbing shoes. We grabbed two pairs of new climbing shoes each, all the food, six gallons of water, and the sleeping bags, stuffed the lot into two additional haul bags, and off we went. Hauling turned into an enormous feat, costing us half an hour per pitch. We stopped for a long pause on the Grey Ledges. Feeling drained and tired, I could hardly imagine leading the next pitch.

My stomach was hurting, but my motivation to climb was strong. It was a battle, but I finally made it to our portaledge on pitch twenty at midnight. I felt really ill, and after just two spoonfuls of rice and a cup of tea, it got worse. It seemed like an eternity until sunrise, and it was quickly clear that this would be a rest day. We spent the day sleeping, playing cards, drinking tea, and eating, which at the time was more agony than pleasure. In the evening I felt better, but again I spent most of the night sleepless.

The next morning was completely different from what I had expected. I was still weak, but as I climbed the first few feet, I realized that my head felt free. No matter how this day would end, I felt relieved to be climbing at all, and this feeling took away all the pressure. This was the key to success for my go on pitch twenty. I could hardly believe I had made it when I reached the belay.

I went to sleep very pleased, but a storm woke us up the next morning. It was snowing and the wind was howling; the portaledge felt like it was ready for takeoff. At noon the wind calmed down, and the first sunbeams made their way through the clouds. With another 5.13b pitch ahead of us, Jacopo was ready long before the rock had dried off. He bouldered through the hard sequences and studied the moves while I belayed from my sleeping bag. After his first go, he was full of confidence, and he hardly managed to sit still while I was sanding the loose rubber off his climbing shoes. The next attempt ran like clockwork, and a few minutes later I heard him scream for joy from the belay. The second big hurdle was behind us.

The next day, the first 5.14a pitch waited for us. I felt recovered and fresh, and my stomach problems were a thing of the past. Everything went smoothly, and on day eight we arrived at pitch twenty-six without falling. After a challenging night in which we moved our portaledge to the last bivy, we were looking forward to a long-awaited rest.

Day nine saw us fully engaged with the next pitch. We had been waiting for it in joyful anticipation: finally, a really easy pitch we could savor. But we found it soaking wet, and it kept us busy for hours. We brushed silly amounts of chalk onto dripping wet holds and removed big soggy patches of moss—a typical rest day! The next morning it was still completely wet. We fought our way up the dihedral, jamming wet hands and feet, slipping off the moist footholds, relieved to get it behind us. After that, the atmosphere became tense as we approached my personal nightmare, the Seven Seas pitch. When we arrived, it was still too hot to try this overhanging endurance monster, so we waited for the evening. Unusual for December, conditions became perfect at night. My first try immediately confirmed my concerns: I still was not able to maintain my body tension. I kept trying and trying, hoping it would start to feel easier at some point, but it didn't. I kept slipping off.

Jacopo saved the evening and fought his way to the belay totally pumped. I felt very happy for him, but at the same time disappointed about my own failure. It was hard to accept, and giving in was not yet an option. Half an hour later, the same story again. I could not manage to hold back my emotions and went off cursing and swearing for at least ten minutes before I regained my composure. I knew I was too tired for another attempt, but my head would not let me give in without looking for yet another possibility. And it was my head, indeed, that finally became the key to climbing the crux. Pressing it against the left protruding side of the crack, under my elbow, enabled me to keep my foot on the crucial smeary foothold.

After another rest day I managed to complete the Seven Seas pitch, and our cries of joy echoed from El Capitan in the first light of the morning. It was the end of the line and a big dream come true.

Babsi Zangerl is a native of Austria whose passion for climbing started as a teenager in the gym. She soon became immersed in the world of bouldering, but a herniated disc redirected her path toward more endurance-focused roped climbing. As with everything she does, Babsi faced adversity head-on, and in the ten years since her injury, she has completed five free ascents of El Capitan in Yosemite, more than any other woman in history. Babsi and her partner, Jacopo, made the second free ascent of *Magic Mushroom*, recounted in this story; hers was the first free female ascent.

She is widely respected in the climbing community for her kind spirit and well-rounded approach to the sport, which she pursues on top of a career as a radiology assistant.

LIKE MOTHER, LIKE DAUGHTER

Jane Jackson and Catherine Cullinane

What does it mean to have a mother who climbs? The familiarity I felt when I led my first few easy crack climbs, was it in my blood? Or is that a total cliché? When I began climbing on my own, really climbing, I felt like I was molting. As though I had discarded my awkward and rebellious teenage self like a snakeskin and had become a climber—strong, capable, and self-assured. With climbing, my young life gained clarity and direction. With this newfound focus, my parents became interesting to me—full of stories and inspiration. Though climbing has given me all sorts of gifts, it's shown me how to meet my parents again as people, as partners.

Out of high school and in my early twenties, I was convinced I was on my own path. I was doing *my* thing. How funny that must have looked to my mom, watching me follow her steps, almost to a T. One summer, I scheduled my college classes so that I could take a monthlong trip to Yosemite Valley. That spring semester, I obsessively trained for this trip by taking weekend trips to Indian Creek, determined to get my crack-climbing skills dialed in so that I could take on the towering granite walls of the Valley. At the time and so narrowly focused on my own plan, I hardly realized my mom had followed the same pull.

It was 1973 and I had just graduated from high school. Rather than heading off to college, I did what is now called a gap year and moved to Yosemite Valley, where I got a job at the cafeteria. I chose Yosemite because I wanted to be close to the mountains and be in a place I could get around without a car. I had done a little bit of climbing in high school and had gone on a number of backpacking trips with my family and later with the Sierra Club. I enjoyed how I felt after those trips—strong and fit from days in the backcountry, hiking and being outside.

In the Valley, I quickly met lots of climbers, big names now, but then they were just my new friends doing amazing things on rock. They started taking me climbing, and I was really quite good and a bit of a natural. I received tons of positive support and encouragement. I didn't lead much those first few months climbing in Yosemite.

On my first trip to the Valley, I struggled to find similarly motivated climbing partners. I was determined to go big. I was so excited to climb, I could hardly sleep. I lay in the dirt in Camp 4 reading Roper's climbing history and analyzing tick lists given to me by my more experienced friends. I was overwhelmed with the potential of the place and what I dreamed I could accomplish there. At some point, one of my partnerships dissolved into chaos. After an extremely long, hot day on Higher Cathedral Rock, my friend Joey was over it. I had pushed too hard and he had had enough. Around the same time, my mom had a few days in between visiting family and decided to come through Yosemite to see the place where she had spent so much time as a youth.

We rode bikes around and wandered through Camp 4. She pointed out boulders where she used to climb and offered advice as I navigated my climbing-partnership woes. The next day, we decided to climb the *East Buttress* on Middle Cathedral, a moderate classic that's on most first-timers' tick lists. My mom let me lead the whole route, and she followed pitch after pitch effortlessly. When we got to the bolt-ladder pitch, now rated 5.10c, I tried to free climb but fell, unable to imagine standing on such small holds. I stood on a bolt and grabbed a draw. My mom followed up behind me and casually said, "I remember coming up here with my friend KB because we wanted to try and do that pitch." More than thirty years before, my mom had freed the pitch I couldn't do. We carried on to the top of the formation and scurried through the manzanita, making our way down the descent gully and back to the base. My mom, fifty-eight years old, had styled the route and bought us beers, which we shared by the Merced River as she reminisced.

> *I remember climbing some routes on Middle Cathedral with Bachar and Ron. This was early on, probably 1975, because I remember I had just started using a chalk bag. I either had one and didn't bring it, or I didn't have one yet. But the whole time on the route, Ron and Bachar were like, "Catherine! You have to use chalk on this stuff! Take a dip out of ours before you follow this pitch." That was a pretty memorable day for me. I think it might have been* Stoner's Highway.

MY NEXT TRIP TO YOSEMITE, I FELT READY FOR BIGGER OBJECTIVES. AFTER college, as my friends and classmates thought about where to move and what to do for work, I had one vision in my mind—Yosemite. I didn't care what else happened. I had no five-year plan. I just knew I was going back to the Valley. I wanted to climb El Capitan. Again, I wrangled two friends into my endeavor. We arrived in the Valley, and I pushed for Half Dome. I wagered that we weren't going to learn how to wall climb unless we started doing it, so why not?

We spent a few hours packing before we started up the Death Slabs with extremely heavy packs, full of water and way too much gear. We got to the base, fixed a pitch, and fell into a restless sleep as tiny rocks whizzed to the ground from the wall high above.

The next morning, laden with extremely heavy bags and poorly thought-out tactics, the three of us cast off up the wall. After three pitches of learning to jug with a thirty-pound pack and trying to understand how a seemingly overhung hand crack could be rated 5.9, our team turned around, shattered from exhaustion and complete failure. I was humbled. Years later, my mom casually mentioned the time *she* had climbed the *Regular Northwest Face* in 1976.

> *All I remember is we were psyched! I mean, I think it was the easier of the routes on Half Dome, the* Regular Northwest Face? *Anyway, we were psyched. I think it was late summer 1976. I climbed it with*

my friend Jill Lawrence. She was from the UK and just so damn funny. And so fun to climb with. She and I climbed a lot that summer. And then we decided to go for the Regular *route on Half Dome. We hiked up there and fixed a couple pitches and bivied at the bottom. The next day, I think we climbed way up somewhere and bivied again. The next day, we climbed to the top and walked down. We were psyched on that for sure. Super psyched! I don't remember if we jugged or not. I feel like we followed free climbing, but I'm not sure. Either way, we felt like we made pretty good time—a day and a half! We got down and the guys were kinda like, "Huh, wow!" Impressed, you know.*

MY NEXT SEASON IN YOSEMITE, I LANDED A VOLUNTEER POSITION AS A climber steward. I got a campsite and a reason to be there for six months. I flailed on Tuolumne slabs until I was told to get stiffer shoes. I met my favorite and most consistent climbing partner, who wanted to climb walls as much as I did. She and I spent weeks in Tuolumne Meadows climbing route after route, working our way through every classic 5.8, 5.9, and 5.10 we could find. I learned how to stand on my feet and edge and take a deep breath and keep moving when I felt scared and run out.

My mom was turning sixty that summer. She'd made a goal for herself to climb Matthes Crest on her birthday, right in the middle of the summer. Similarly, when she was in her twenties she'd made a goal to climb El Capitan by the time she was thirty. So far, she'd stuck with her goals.

So a week before her sixtieth birthday, my mom arrived in Tuolumne and relaxed seamlessly into the long-term campground that was the stewards' home for the summer. Tarps were strung up in the trees above picnic tables covered in stoves, spices, and recently picked bolete mushrooms.

We headed out on her birthday past Cathedral Peak and Budd Lake, out through glacier polish and forest and glacial erratics that sit like white pearls among the pine and granite slabs. We started up the first pitch of the Crest, me in the lead and my mom following. It was a blustery, cold day for summer in the Sierra, the wind whipping on the exposed portions of the traverse. I stepped across an airy section and looked back to see my mom hesitating. "Breathe, Mama. You got it! Just breathe and step across," I said. She made the move and we carried on along the ridge. The rest of the climb was uneventful, and my mom got her feet under her again. On the way back to camp, she thanked me for encouraging her, and we felt a shift for a moment as we wavered between climbing partners and family.

> *In the middle of summer, we'd go up to the high country to escape the valley heat, so I spent a lot of time hanging in the Meadows, bouldering, swimming in the lake, and climbing domes. One summer, my friend KB and I did this route on Pywiack Dome. We wanted to climb* Golden Bars *because it was kind of a face-climbing testpiece of the time and we wanted to give it a go. So we got our tiny little rack together, probably just a couple of slings and carabiners and a few nuts, and headed out.*
>
> *I remember I backed off one pitch and KB led it, and then we ended up swinging leads from there. She did the 5.11 pitch, totally run out. And when we got down, we went back over to the Tuolumne Store, and Claude Fiddler and everyone were giving us total shit: "You women went and did that route. None of the guys would even go try it! We were all blown away."*
>
> *The route was pretty run out and it was face climbing—we were into face climbing. KB was really good. And it was a beautiful face! Anyway, I had moments of wanting to be the best climber out there, but I never fully committed to it or had the time. I had moments of brilliance as a climber and a lot of mediocrity. At the time, though, I think what I was doing was actually pretty unusual.*

There's still a few more routes left on my list as I attempt to follow in my mom's footsteps all these years later. Pawing through bins of old photos, I unearth images of her that look so much like me. I'm mesmerized by this young version of my mom. Standing in the boulders in Camp 4, climbing at Arch Rock, racking up at the base of the *Nose*. Slowly, my mom has revealed more of her story—tiny details coming out here and there, filling in gaps in my imagination. I'm hungry for more. These images and stories, entwined with my own experiences, anchor me to a history and place me on my feet in time.

Jane Jackson grew up in the Tetons in Wyoming, surrounded by the world of climbing. For the first eighteen years of her life, she thought climbing was the most boring activity adults could possibly spend their time doing. She begrudgingly spent her childhood scrambling peaks, hanging out at crags, and learning to climb cracks in Indian Creek. In her early twenties she had an epiphany, rediscovered climbing for herself, and moved to Yosemite Valley. There, she made many ascents of El Cap, including the first all-female one-day ascent of *Zodiac*.

For the past ten years, Jane has pursued ideal climbing conditions in inspiring locations from Yosemite to Patagonia to the Verdon Gorge. She lives in Bishop, California, which has ideal climbing conditions nearly all the time.

Catherine Cullinane, Jane's mother, was captivated by mountains from a young age. She grew up in the Bay Area but frequently went on family backpacking trips into the Sierra Nevada as a child. In her teens, she worked on various Sierra Club trail crew projects in the Sierra and other ranges. Those projects ultimately led her to Yosemite Valley, where she found climbing. Her time in Yosemite led to adventures in the greater ranges, including an attempt on Mount Everest from the Tibetan side in 1986. After her time in the Valley, she moved to the Tetons in Wyoming, where she became the first female guide at Exum Mountain Guides.

In addition to climbing, Catherine has had a long career as a nurse and diabetes educator. She splits her time between Jackson, Wyoming, and Castle Valley, Utah, with her husband, Renny Jackson.

LETTER FROM A MOTHER TO HER VILLAGE

Eliza Kerr

This story originally appeared in a 2018 Patagonia catalog.

May 14, 2017, Mother's Day. Dear friends, yesterday I topped out on *Zodiac* on El Capitan. Some of you have loyally and patiently supported me for almost six months while I prepared for and fretted about this adventure. Some of you have no idea what *Zodiac* is. No matter. Thanks for being part of the journey now.

I've probably said this before, and if I'm lucky I'll say it again: This was one of the biggest challenges of my life. You'd think it wouldn't have been that big of a deal considering that I climbed *Zodiac* in 1995, but this go around felt entirely different.

Because this time, I did it with my precious thirteen-year-old daughter, Calliope.

It was also different because I am old now and know better, physically and mentally. I know about death on big walls. And because there was no strong, knowledgeable dude who could bail me out. The spark of the idea ignited well over two years ago when Calliope and I agreed we should try and do El Cap before she went to high school. It started coming together when our friend Miranda said she'd join us. Miranda is a graceful, easygoing woman, the kind of person you trust and want to spend time with. She also happens to be a badass free climber with a lot of experience.

MY TRAINING BEGAN IN EARNEST IN JANUARY: RELEARNING HOW TO AID climb, asking every experienced wall-climber friend I have about the details of seamless hauling, portaledge setup, pitch-by-pitch pitfalls. These friends generously and patiently talked me through detail after detail. My husband, Nate, began helping me prepare gear and soothed me during anxious moments, gracefully finding the balance between being there when I needed him and knowing I really wanted to do this on my own. Most important, he believed in me.

Fast-forward to this past Tuesday. We had six pitches fixed and prehauled. We were as prepared as any wall climbers in the course of history have ever been. (How did I do it on the fly while living out of my VW twenty-plus years ago?) And still, I was feeling afraid and anxious—and not in a good way.

On Tuesday afternoon, my friend and wall mentor Erik Sloan stopped by. He had been patiently easing me through each question and concern since January. How do I pass a knot while hauling? What's the difference between a sky hook and a grappling hook? Which bivies are best in a storm? But on Tuesday, he shared his most important wisdom: he told me he knew I was as ready as I ever would be. It was time to put all worry aside and move into a place of appreciation, trust, faith, and gratitude.

In the course of that conversation, my energy shifted completely. I got totally excited, in a good and grounded way, for the climb. And I fell into a place of surrender, knowing that everything would be alright, no matter what—life or death included. As we reached the base of the climb early Wednesday morning, I saw Yosemite and El Cap with fresh eyes and an open heart, yet again. God, it's a beautiful world we live in. The gifts are so abundant. Calliope rigged herself and started jugging up the 700 feet of free-hanging fixed line. I watched in awe, with complete confidence in my little girl, knowing she had the calm mind and technical skills to do this. And so did I.

Day one was long. So much work. Miranda and I each took proud lead falls. We all arrived at the top of pitch nine just before dark, grappling with portaledges and enjoying cold Tasty Bites under a bright full moon. Exhausted. God, was it fun though. We were doing it!

Day two. We woke up to sore muscles, but we were in the flow. It was a beautiful sunny day with the flooded Merced River reflecting boundless waterfalls and granite below. After a full second day, we were grateful that our bivy that night had the tiniest little ledge. It felt so good to have our feet rest on something solid.

Day three. We woke to dramatic swirling clouds, dropped temperatures, and a 40 percent chance of rain. It felt like Patagonia. We had only three pitches to the top, but that sounds quicker than it actually is. Calliope was so stoic and positive, it was hard for Miranda and me to complain too much about our freezing hands as we led the pitches. As we finished the last pitch, Nate popped his head over the top, there to greet us with a strong back and a warm thermos of tea. I was the last to jug up the final pitch, and I had a moment to myself as my emotions began to seep out, knowing we had made it safely.

You could say that it would have been a good day to die, but it was not our day. I was overwhelmed with gratitude for the people in my life, for the stone and river and sun and beauty we live with, and for the mystery of creation that I could so tangibly feel—right then, right there.

A climber on a quest for sustenance and connection, Eliza Kerr moved to Yosemite after graduating from college. Her studies in Nepal forged her deep passion for yoga and Ayurvedic medicine, leading her to found Balanced Rock, an organization offering yoga and wilderness retreats in the Yosemite wilderness.

Now, thirty years later, Eliza's journey as a climber has taken her through the full spectrum of human emotions, from deep losses to soaring joys. She lives in El Portal, a tiny hamlet on the western border of Yosemite, with her husband and two daughters, where she continues to climb, play, and enjoy the beautiful community around her.

ALONE ON THE NOSE

Miranda Oakley

At times I find myself despising the comfort of my own bed. Deep in the night, my warm body lay between smooth sheets under down comforters. But then my alarm went off at 3:30 a.m., just a couple of hours after I fell asleep. I had lain awake for most of the night, unable to calm my mind and stop thinking obsessively about the climb I was about to start.

I wondered if I was crazy. If I should roll over and go back to sleep. No one would have to know what I had been planning to do. They wouldn't find out that I had set my alarm for the middle of the night to have an epic but then bailed before getting out of bed. I could just close my eyes and pretend it had never happened. The beauty of solo climbing is that the plans never have to leave the head of the soloist. No discussing strategies or meeting times with partners. No disappointing anyone if you decide to bail. I lay in my sweet cocoon, turning the idea over in my head. But then I got up, leaving warmth, comfort, and security to throw myself at a wall with no one to keep me company.

I would never have thought that I'd attempt to do a climb by myself in one day that had once taken me three and a half days with two partners. I first climbed the *Nose* of El Capitan in 2011 with my ex-boyfriend from high school and his friend. It was a tumultuous ascent, but we battled our way to the top. I realized then that the *Nose* really is the best rock climb in the world. It's a vertical obstacle course that follows a natural line straight up one of the proudest seas of granite. It's got splitter cracks that literally go on for days, a 100-foot pendulum, a massive flake shaped like Texas, a great roof that makes you feel like an ant.

I've always enjoyed long days. I like having epics on big routes, climbing through the night and getting passed by swifts and bats as they dive in and out of the cracks during twilight hours. Soon I started climbing long routes in single-day pushes and linking routes together. My objectives kept getting bigger in order to satisfy my urge to suffer. Just like all my favorite climbs in Yosemite, I climbed the *Nose* many times. What was once a multi-day epic turned into a ten-and-a-half-hour burn. To move quickly, my partners and I would short-fix, forcing the leader to self-belay. Before long I realized that a belay from a partner is not a necessity but a luxury.

I had heard of people soloing the *Nose* in a push, and some suggested I try it. I brushed them off, figuring they were crazy. But the idea still lingered in the back of my mind. In the fall of 2015, I decided to try it. It was my first solo ascent of any wall. I made it to the top in just under twenty-seven hours. I got to try a lot of new things. Some went well and some failed miserably. I learned a lot about solo climbing. Not long after, I had forgotten how painful it was, so I decided I should try it again someday.

By the following spring my thoughts had begun to drift back to soloing the *Nose*. I started to obsess over ways to move faster. On my first solo ascent I had kept my plans a secret, not wanting to commit to anything, let anyone down, or feel any external pressure. I hadn't asked for advice or solicited beta. The following year I asked a few people for tips. Hearing other people's strategies and comparing their methods was incredibly helpful. Some climbers used rope tricks, running it out with almost no protection, and they free soloed many sections. This strategy scared me. Others said they roped up and belayed themselves the whole way. Roping up for every pitch using the typical aid soloist strategy is by far the safest option but also the slowest. It requires climbing, rappelling, and jumaring all thirty pitches. I decided to rely on my quick-climbing abilities and rope up for every pitch. The security of having a rope and protection would make it less scary and allow me to climb faster. It also made it easier for me to get out of bed that morning before starting the climb.

I CHOSE TO DO THE CLIMB ON AUGUST 5, THE MIDDLE OF A HOT AND sweaty Yosemite summer. Tourists waddled around in bathing suits as the temperature climbed toward the triple digits. Every climber in her right mind knew to stay away from Yosemite Valley for fear of heatstroke and traffic jams. I was surprised to see headlamps above when I got to the base of the route. *Who is crazy enough to climb this route in this heat?* I wondered. The giant monolith loomed above me like a tidal wave, and I wondered if I, too, was crazy. At 5:30 I started climbing. I convinced myself that the wall would seem smaller as the day went on.

I quickly caught up to the party ahead of me, a team of three Koreans spread out between Sickle Ledge and the pitch above. They hit on me shamelessly in very broken English. "Prettiest girl in Yosemite," they said. I laughed and told them I was the prettiest girl on El Cap, knowing I was probably the only girl on El Cap, the only person on El Cap besides them. They stopped to let me pass, making me pose for a dozen or so photos with them. I complied, trying to smile for pictures as I restacked the rope and racked the gear. Before long, the Korean team became a distant memory as I kept chugging along through the Stoveleg Cracks up toward Dolt Tower.

The only way I can commit to such a long climb by myself is by not committing. My first goal of the day was to make it to Dolt Tower. From there I would decide if I wanted to keep going to the top. I got to Dolt in under five hours and found almost a dozen bottles full of water. I did a little dance knowing that things were going too well to bail. The early morning sun was already hot. I took the abandoned water as a sign to keep going. I emptied one bottle into my bladder, crunched it up, and threw it into the bottom of my backpack. I drank as much as I could from another bottle until I almost needed to vomit. On I went.

Soon I realized there was yet another party up ahead. What were people doing up here? Didn't they know it would probably get to 100 degrees today? The sun blazed in the sky, and the wind failed to blow. I tried to ignore the mild pain in the back of my head. Behind the Texas Flake I was relieved to find cool air untouched by sunlight. More than 1,000 feet up on a wall, this sliver of shade was as refreshing as jumping into the Merced River. The other party was just above me now. They saw me advancing quickly and told me they would stop at the top of the Boot Flake and wait for me to pass. Great!

The dull ache in my head was turning into a pounding throb. I was dehydrated despite all the water I had drunk on Dolt. The team waited patiently on top of the Boot Flake. I could tell that the sun was taking a toll on them as well. They politely asked if I could take their rope and fix it to Eagle Ledge. "You don't want to do the King Swing?" I asked. I was very confused. They had been so nice to wait for me to pass, I figured it was the least I could do. There seemed to be some confusion on their end about how they would get over to Eagle Ledge once their rope was fixed. I tried to explain that they could use a jumar. My explanation was met with blank stares on sunburnt faces. Our brains were frying in our helmets under the scalding sun, our thoughts swimming in stagnant air. I decided to let them figure it out on their own. I rapped down below the giant boot and started swinging around 2,000 feet above the ground. The breeze I generated from swinging back and forth felt amazing. I pulled over the lip to Eagle Ledge and heard hoots and monkey calls from the meadow.

I was concerned about water. It was so hot that I needed to drink much more than usual. One week earlier I had climbed the route with a friend. On that day there was a bottle of water at Camp V and a half gallon at Camp VI. It didn't seem like anyone had been up there since then, so I assumed it was safe for me to drink up.

The Great Roof marks the halfway point of the route. I was amazed to get there in just over ten hours. After the Great Roof, the sun ducked behind the west end of the wall. The shade was a huge relief. I was worn out by the sun but pushed on, telling myself I could chug water and eat a sandwich at Camp V. But when I arrived at Camp V, there was no water. I rapped back down to my bag and found a few sips left in my bladder. I wanted to cry. Just when I thought I would be suffering less, I realized I would be suffering much more.

I had seven more pitches to the top. I decided to ration one sip of water per pitch and not eat any food (the salami and cheese sandwiches I had brought would only make me thirstier). I prayed to the monkey gods that there was still that old stinky water at Camp VI. The past couple of times I was on the route, there had been the same two water jugs, each a quarter full. Both times I had smelled the water and put it back in the crack it was stashed in, deciding to risk running out of my own water over drinking someone else's abandoned funky water stash. I was thankful for my past decisions, cursing my decision this morning to bring up only three liters.

It got dark, the wall steepened, and I embraced the aid climbing. My hands and feet were swollen but felt good compared to how they had felt the year before. I was glad to have invested in comfortable free-climbing shoes two sizes too big and to have worn tape gloves. Despite my thirst and fatigue,

I was feeling pretty good. I arrived at Camp VI and was overjoyed to find the same water still stashed there. I literally danced and sang. I chugged water and ate a sandwich. It turns out that even funky, backwash-infested water that's been steeping in a plastic jug in the sun for weeks (maybe months) is better than no water at all. I felt like a new woman. I finished off the water and clipped the empty jugs to the outside of my backpack.

Like an inchworm, I continued up the last fourth of the climb: extending and retracting, two steps up, one step back, until I reached the last 100 feet of scrambling to the top. I was too tired to trust myself without a rope, so I threaded one end through the last anchor and clipped it back to myself. This rope trick, often referred to as the Pakistani Death Loop (or the American Hero Loop), gave me just enough protection to get to the top. As the climbing turned into walking, I untied the rope and attempted to pull it through. Of course, the rope got stuck. I pulled as hard as I could, but it wouldn't budge. I knew I wasn't done until I *and* all my gear were at the top, so I fixed the rope to the summit tree and rappelled down to get the rest of the rope. I retrieved the rope and made it back to the tree. The time: 3:17 a.m., 21 hours and 47 minutes after I started. I managed to take one selfie after checking the time before my phone battery died. I had used up so much of my phone battery on the climb trying to text my coworkers to see if they could take my shift for me the next day that I almost didn't get to see what time it was when I topped out. It turned out that I would have made it to work on time anyway.

I was so happy and satisfied that I curled up and slept for a couple of hours by the summit tree. At first light I made my way down to the valley floor, and before I knew it, I found myself back in my cozy cocoon, between soft sheets under down comforters.

Miranda Oakley is a true climbers' climber, and her down-to-earth nature often belies the stream of accomplishments she has piled up in recent years. Originally from Maryland, Miranda packed up the car and headed for Yosemite days after graduating from St. Mary's College of Maryland. She worked and lived all over the park before settling in, more than ten years on, as one of Yosemite Mountaineering School's only female guides.

In 2016, Miranda became the first woman to climb the *Nose* of El Capitan alone in less than twenty-four hours, making use of her competence on

Yosemite's big walls and her prowess at climbing difficult traditional routes. She's since taken her climbing skills to the far corners of the earth, establishing first ascents and sharing her love for the sport with a global community, but she always returns home to Yosemite.

YIELD POINT

Alexa Flower

This story first appeared in *Alpinist* in 2017.

It's 1:00 a.m. in Yosemite. Darkness floods the valley floor, so I look up to find some light. A crescent moon hides behind the clouds that drift through the night sky like ghostly travelers. Even the giant granite walls seem to lose their incandescent pallor and blend into a curtain of gray. I sit with Dave and Nick at the search and rescue site near Camp 4, beneath ponderosa pines and black oaks. Dave sets a bottle of whisky on the picnic table, and the dull thud draws me back from my thoughts: recollections from earlier this evening, of brown shoes and a tangled blue rope. The three of us click our headlamps off. Nick picks up the bottle and takes a long swig before passing it to me. I hold my breath and let the whisky burn my throat.

Hours earlier, an earsplitting alarm yanks me awake. My hand finds the small dial on a lantern hanging from my tent cabin. I turn it on and wait for the beeping to stop. "Three Valley SAR siters needed as a hasty team to the base of El Capitan," announces the small black pager next to my bed. What an odd call, I think. At night, I typically receive pages about lost hikers or sprained ankles; requests for climbing-related rescues wait until dawn for safety. I put pants on in the dark and wrap myself in the warmth of my puffy to step outside. Lights click on in other cabins nearby. My family.

Six members of the search and rescue team meet at the center of the site. Some perch on a picnic table in their boxers, others huddle on the ground, their eyes half open. No one speaks. This is our fourth night call in a week, and the team is exhausted. The faint rumble of a car engine echoes in the distance.

"OK, I'll go," Dave says finally. I watch his chest fall as he exhales. His auburn hair and beard run wild in all directions. Nick joins, too, even though he returned only a few hours ago from a four-day ascent of El Cap. My headlamp flickers on his dirt-streaked face while he clumsily laces his shoes with swollen hands. I volunteer as the third. The others head back to their beds. The three of us stuff our packs with gear, and then we bike to the search and rescue cache for a briefing. The incident commander informs us that there has been a rappelling accident at some fixed ropes on the East Ledges—the typical descent route on El Cap. One climber fell, perhaps hundreds of feet. His partner rappelled to him and found his friend unconscious with no signs of life. We will be the first rescuers on scene.

I fall in step behind Nick, in front of Dave, as we trudge up the trail. Two park rangers follow behind. The five of us hike in silence, listening to the chatter of leaves in the breeze, to the crunch of gravel beneath each footfall. I know this trail well: I was here with two friends less than a week ago, after we climbed El Cap.

Black millipedes and beetles scuttle across the light from my headlamp. The grade steepens as we enter a loose gully, littered with large boulders, dead branches, and jagged trees: the aftermath of a major rockfall last winter. Images from past rescues flit across my mind. This is mental preparation, perhaps, as I walk toward another reminder of our finite existence on this planet. Disjointed memories—the touch of cold skin as I check for a pulse, tufts of hair speckled with blood—wake me at night with an anxious mind; they linger in the growing shadows at my belay stance when I haven't climbed quickly enough to beat the darkness. I make a promise to shield myself from haunting details I don't need to see in order to do my job well. After forty-five minutes of hiking, we reach the base of the fixed lines. A cry stops me in my tracks.

"We hear you and we're coming!" Nick yells.

Nick reaches the shouting climber first. "It's going to be OK, man. Are you hurt?"

I scramble up to them, and my headlamp beam pauses upon an inert heap. Slotted into a shallow corner, a tattered blue rope lies next to another climber, his body contorted and covered with branches and leaves. His shoes are blown off. I remember my promise to myself and look away, as if it's not too late.

I join Nick and the other climber, who I guess is in his early twenties. He sits with his gaze fixated on a patch of dirt between his legs. I struggle to find an appropriate response to someone who just watched his friend fall hundreds of feet. In desperation, I want to say, *It will be OK*, to tell him how sorry I am, but these shallow expressions hold no gravity. Nothing I say will change what happened or make it bearable. I feel helpless and look down at the dirt. I imagine a team's final embrace on the summit; the sun fading between monoliths into a deep blue; one overlooked detail as a climber weights the rope; and the sudden confusion of everything plunging downward.

"We are here to think for you," one of the park rangers says to the young climber, and together they walk away down the trail.

With the young climber gone, I reach into my backpack to find a pair of medical gloves. I grab a biohazard bag and kneel upon the soft earth, carefully picking up pieces of gear: plastic from exploded water bottles and the remnants of a helmet, splattered with blood. The motions keep me focused on the task at hand and distracted from a faint pain in my gut. There's an eerie silence to the night as we place the other climber into a black bag and move him off the trail. Trees and granite obscure a dark, clouded sky. We wrap the brush near the bag with yellow caution tape. I do this all with shaky hands, then walk back down the trail.

OVER THE NEXT FEW DAYS, I BATTLE A FAMILIAR FATIGUE: MY LIMBS FEEL heavy, like snow-laden trees after a storm. Nevertheless, I find myself racking up and carrying heavy loads to the base of the *Salathé Wall* on El Cap with Jane, my friend and fellow YOSAR member. During our short hike, I remember past climbs together: the times we navigated broken seams over the smooth headwall of the *Shield* or summited the *Nose*-in-a-day under a black velvet sky. We had grown into big-wall climbing together, our partnership tempered and solidified by the hardships of climbing El Cap.

This time, as we arrive under the wall's shadow, I drop my pack, and my shoulders hunch. Jane looks at me with a concerned and knowing stare.

"I'm fine," I say. I force myself to act unaffected by what I'd seen. My mind feels chaotic, fragmented, incomplete, and I find it hard to breathe. I sit on some rocky steps to drink from my water bottle, gasping between gulps.

The next day, I belay Jane on the Hollow Flake, a long, gaping offwidth, too wide for any of our gear. She gets to the anchors within minutes. "Off belay!" she shouts. I begin jugging the line to join her, but I pause after a few feet. Beneath me, ravens are landing in El Cap Meadow. I feel an urge to join them among the tall grasses, to play in the dirt with my feet, to let the ground cradle every contour of my body. Instead I am a thousand feet above, tethered to the rock by a thin line. Fear snakes into my mind. Granite slabs stretch out below me like pallid claws. The valley floor appears as a distant green blanket, where visitors wander about like tiny black ants.

My jugging quickens to a sprint. I reach the belay and shove nuts and cams into Jane's arms for her to continue her block as fast as possible. She throws the sling of unorganized gear over her shoulder and rushes upward. Silently, I plead for her to go even faster. We feed off each other's distraught energy, fleeing up the wall in a disarray of ropes and equipment. Jane and I make it to a ledge two pitches below El Cap Spire by midafternoon. Two climbers rappel from above, and soon the four of us, our gear, ropes, and haul bags, sling together into a tiny, sloping belay. I pass Jane gear, elbowing one of the climbers in his side, and our ropes tangle together.

"Do you need more water?" one of them asks. I stop fiddling with cams and look up to see amber eyes and a sideways smile. The climbers introduce themselves as Alan and Mike. We shake hands, an odd gesture since we're already piled on top of one another.

Mike—the experienced big-wall climber of the two—waits patiently for Alan to get situated at the belay before pulling their rope from above. "This is my first time on El Cap!" Alan exclaims. He gazes about from behind thick, black-framed glasses. Alan and Mike cackle when their rope cracks Alan in the face. I smile. My tension dissolves as my mood melds with theirs—unfazed and unhurried. It's as if we are lounging in El Cap Meadow, enjoying a subtle breeze and cold beer. When I mention that Jane and I work on YOSAR, the mood seems to change, and Mike looks away. The climber who fell last week was a friend of theirs. I close my eyes, and I am back at the base of the rappels with Nick and Dave, looking down at the fragments left behind.

At the bivy ledge that night, I dream: *I am back in a classroom with other YOSAR members. I sit on the floor, fixated on a SAR coordinator standing in the front of the room. He raises his long index finger, pointing at the white board, titled ADVANCED ROPE RESCUE COURSE, where a graph has been jotted down in blue marker. "The yield point," he begins, brushing his finger over a curved line. "When a material—let's say a carabiner or a rope—under stress reaches its yield point, it is permanently damaged and can no longer return to its original strength or shape." His finger lands on the apex of the graph, where the line clearly starts to plummet. "Like a chocolate bar. As you bend it apart, the chocolate breaks and turns that milky color. It can never go back to its original state."*

A few days later, we are back on the valley floor. Dave, Jane, and I walk through the search and rescue site. It's a cloudy morning and we stroll over to a get-together at Camp 4, where climbers are invited to grab a warm cup of coffee, socialize, and exchange news of upcoming events and recent happenings in the park. We form a circle and share a moment of silence for the climber we lost on the East Ledges. The wind gusts around us, bending the cedar boughs above. About our feet lie broken remnants of dry needles and soft, evergreen leaves. After a moment, I open my eyes. Barely perceptible, shafts of light stream through the clouds. Above the gray, beyond my sight, I know, the light remains.

Alexa Flower hails from the mountains of Colorado, where her love of the natural world first propelled her into rodeo. She competed in barrel racing at Colorado State University before being introduced to rock climbing in Fort Collins. She was instantly hooked and soon followed her newfound passion to Yosemite, where in 2016 she joined the Yosemite Valley search and rescue team (YOSAR). As a rescuer, Alexa participated in hundreds of incidents: searching for missing hikers, pulling injured climbers off big walls, fighting wildfires, and saving drowning swimmers. Her climbing highlights span more than a dozen ascents of El Cap, including the first all-female one-day ascent of *Zodiac*.

EPICO

Lola Delnevo

Epic—no other words are needed to describe my latest trip. We arrived in Yosemite Valley on a scorching Wednesday afternoon, with unwelcome news of a storm heading our way the following week. We had planned our climbing trip thinking we would have about ten days to see our project through, but we now had less than a week! As soon as we arrived at our destination, we barely had time to settle into Camp 4, our temporary home in Yosemite. We decided that we had to start arranging everything in order to be at the base of *Zodiac* before the weekend.

Yosemite would have been quite a new adventure for me even before my accident. I had been climbing in the Alps, where approaches are really difficult, especially at high altitude, but the style of rock is so different from the rock on El Capitan. I had never seen a wall so steep, so huge, so vertical and smooth.

I met Timmy O'Neill the day we arrived, during one of the Yosemite Facelift presentations. Timmy has explosive energy, and in a short amount of time he turned Yosemite around for us, giving us support and taking on all the responsibility of getting me both to the base of *Zodiac* and, if all went well, down from the top of El Capitan.

It really felt like the whole Yosemite community came alive together to support my dream. Timmy announced our project and looked for volunteers, both through his personal contacts and as the presenter for Yosemite

Facelift. He reached out to his incredible network of local climbers, rangers, and the amazing Yosemite Search and Rescue (YOSAR) team.

Our date with Timmy was set for the next day at noon at El Cap Meadow. Within fifteen minutes of parking our car, we witnessed an army of volunteers arrive, with YOSAR and the climbing rangers leading the way. Timmy quickly shifted our perspective to a powerful positive mindset, changing the way we spoke about the support we were receiving, reminding us that we were at the center of the greatest party in Yosemite. Where else would you want to be on a Friday afternoon if not here?

The thirty-person party turned out to be an international gathering of the kindest humans and mountain lovers, calling upon volunteers from the Yosemite Facelift project, local climbers, and even weekend tourists who just wanted to be part of something truly unique and special, if only for a few hours.

As with my first attempt two years earlier, the crew arrived with a litter, or stretcher, for me to lie on as we made our way up the trail. This time, though, there was an extra piece of equipment: a giant version of a wheelbarrow's wheel. After securing me to the litter, they lifted it and attached the wheel underneath it, and off we went! Their sixty legs marched to the top.

Never in my life would I have thought that this level of support was possible. It was incredible to see how the crew's knowledge, coordination, and strategy were fundamental in getting us up in no time: finding the right pathways, directing a group of strangers with clear instructions, foreseeing where pullers and pushers would need to be positioned in the formation.

Meanwhile, Antonio and Diego worked relentlessly, reaching the sixth pitch by sunset. By late afternoon, we were all together at the base of *Zodiac.* We spent the night under *Zodiac* and a wonderful starry sky.

WAKING UP AT THE BASE OF THE ROUTE, WE STARTED OUR DAY BEFORE sunrise. But once we realized what a truly strong climber Antonio is, our new strategy to climb *Zodiac* became clear: Antonio, "The Machine," would lead all the way to the top. Diego and Mauro would follow to help with the hauling, allowing Antonio to climb as fast and clean as possible. I would have to pull myself up the whole 550-meter-high granite wall on fixed ropes.

I had practiced at home, trying to find a way to climb again; even though I could no longer lead, I could at least ascend the ropes. We stole some tricks from aid climbing, paragliding, and biking. As a matter of fact, on the advice of some friends, we asked a large climbing gear manufacturer to help us weld a traction device to an old bike handlebar so that I wouldn't have to use jumars but instead could pull on the bar to move up. Another trick we devised was the use of a pulley system to create a mechanical advance. With this, I would not pull up all my weight but just half of it. Finally, I decided to use an ultralight paragliding harness, because without support to hold my legs, I felt too much pain in the lower part of my back where I had had my surgery. With this new harness, I was seated comfortably.

Everybody in the Valley seemed to be keeping an eye on our team of Italians who were attempting something epic. The team was climbing. Yosemite was watching. The Yosemite spirits were alive and kicking.

The following day, we climbed through the sixth pitch: a lot of pull-ups! My mind switched gears the moment I started to pull myself up. My mood sparkled with happiness, joy, freedom, and great memories. I was ready and eager for the days to come.

We worked hard, all four of us, everyone with their own tasks. Our strategy worked like clockwork. It worked so well that we did not need to change anything in our tactics, from our first day until the very end. Antonio was always tirelessly and quickly leading. Gibe climbed second, hauling the bags. Then it was my turn, climbing up the fixed rope while the guys set up the portaledge at the next belay. Last but not least, Diego climbed and cleaned all the pitches.

I was on the wall again, two years after my previous climb there, but this time with my best climbing mates and dear friends. I can never have enough time, nor words, to thank these awesome guys for what they have done. Being there with them was truly special. They made me feel like nothing had changed since before my accident more than three years earlier. We climbed, we talked, we laughed. We lived with great intensity. We made decisions together to find the most convenient way to get to the top as fast as we possibly could.

We spent three and a half days up there, always worried that on Tuesday, the weather would turn on us—and it did. Our days on the wall were quite long: we would usually climb from sunrise to after sunset, until around eight o'clock. During our last night on the wall, with a lot of effort, we decided to just not stop.

This was my favorite moment of the climb. But really, I was scared to death. We climbed in the dark, and we lowered out in the dark. We were challenged, tired, and not exactly fresh at this point. We moved relentlessly. Our physical condition and the storm heading toward us made this tactic even more epic and memorable. On the last pitch, I nearly collapsed with fatigue.

On Tuesday, just before dawn, I was at the top of *Zodiac* with Diego and Antonio. Just Mauro had yet to arrive, and—at the very last moment—the haul bags decided to get stuck in a crack, making it impossible to haul them. I, in the meantime, was trying to start breathing again after my enormous pull-up effort.

BY THE TIME FIRST LIGHT APPEARED ON THAT GREAT TUESDAY MORNING, we were all at the top together. But we had no time to romanticize the moment or celebrate our climb, as the storm was already upon us. The rain arrived fast and strong—so strong that we decided to open one of the portaledges to give us some shelter. Water started to run down the slabs, and soon a small waterfall had formed just behind us. This blocked us in, and our rappelling plan was not an option anymore.

Our bad luck continued when we learned that the YOSAR team had been diverted to a major rescue at the top of Half Dome the previous evening and had not yet returned. We were really counting on a few strong extra arms and legs to help with my descent. Good luck arrived soon, though, when we saw two other climbers descending from the *Nose*. We got their attention, and together they helped move me far from the dangerous spot we found ourselves in. Surprisingly, we had to move upward, to the top of El Capitan and, eventually, Tuolumne Meadows. Since we didn't have the YOSAR tools at hand, we made our own makeshift stretcher with the raw materials at our disposal.

And then we saw them. During our very long way down, we spotted silhouettes in the distance and heard voices. Soon we just could not believe our eyes: a dozen young guys and gals from Camp 4 were coming to our rescue with the litter. We would be back in the Valley in no time.

Born and raised in Bergamo, Italy, Eleonora (Lola) Delnevo was introduced to climbing while attending university. She instantly fell in love with the mountains and quickly excelled in the long traditional routes that surrounded her home. Traveling all around Europe, she grew as an alpinist and climber, but in 2015, an ice-climbing accident left her paralyzed from the waist down.

Today, Lola has a newfound passion for kayaking and has embraced the teamwork required to get her into her beloved mountains, which made possible her paraplegic ascent of *Zodiac* on El Capitan. Lola works as an environmental consultant and still calls Bergamo home.

IS IT WORTH IT?

Josie McKee

This, here and now, is where I'm supposed to be. It wasn't so much a thought as the sense that every part of my being was perfectly connected, focused on my movement through this space. My lungs burned, but I kept my breathing calm. Heart rate down. Movement controlled, precise. Each foot perfectly placed, hands settling into the undulations of stone, each move executed as choreographed: the dance up the stone.

I put my hand into the last perfect jam of the hundreds of feet of perfect hand crack that make up the Stovelegs on the *Nose* of El Capitan. I moved left, my next hold a thinner crack. Then I reached and grabbed the cam. *Perfect,* I thought briefly, this being my tenth time climbing the route. The cam was right where I had asked her to leave it to make that move just a little easier, more fluid, so I didn't have to stop moving.

Somewhere above, Quinn continued swiftly, just a little less than the full 200 feet of our rope between us. I kept pace with her (barely!), moving up as she moved. The extra loop of rope was a buffer for moments when I needed to pause while she was moving. Everything was done with that same level of precision. She was not leaving much gear to protect a fall. Any mistake could be catastrophic. I could not risk slipping or accidentally pulling on her.

Farther up, I paused. She was moving more slowly, somewhere in the chimney, beyond several ledges. I had a moment to think: *If I remove this cam now, there won't be any gear between us. But no matter, there are ledges. Surely a fall wouldn't pull us completely off the side of El Cap.*

I suppose it wasn't about being *where* I was meant to be. It was about the fact that in that moment, I could not be anywhere else, because if my mind strayed, it could cause the whole system to fail. It wasn't that we were being reckless; it was just that our values had shaped our decisions. We put more value on experiencing these moments of fluid, continuous movement, more value on the speed of our ascent, than on our safety.

We wanted to know: How fast can we climb the *Nose*? Right then and there, about one-third of the way up a 3,000-foot face of granite, my choices were fueled by this curiosity. Decisively, I pulled the last cam out and kept moving. The best I've ever moved. Fingers in the familiar crack, in just the right position, toe on *this* crystal, core tight, reach to the next hold, sensing each grain of rock. Focused, present, in flow. Perfect. *Fast.*

I WONDER WHAT IT'S ACTUALLY LIKE TO BE UP THERE. I WAS EIGHTEEN. MY climbing partner and I were on our way from my home on the central coast of California to go sport climbing in the Eastern Sierra. We drove into the Valley, stopping in El Cap Meadow to take in the view. The last light faded from the sky, and headlamps were beginning to wink on, high up the face—big-wall climbers making their beds for the evening. The top of the giant monolith shone white in the light of the rising full moon.

I imagined sitting on a portaledge, legs dangling over 2,000 feet of air, 1,000 feet of silver-white granite still rising above me. My stomach flip-flopped. Someday, I vowed to myself. Someday, I would be one of those tiny lights up there on the wall. I will climb El Capitan. I really had to go *be* there, to experience it for myself.

At that time, I really had no idea what skills it would take or what equipment would be needed for such an endeavor. I had probably climbed three routes that were over 100 feet, but 3,000 feet? Pretty much unfathomable, the idea was merely a bucket list dream.

A couple of years later, I was beginning to learn to trad climb. A friend showed me photos of his recent climbing on El Cap. Seeing the look in my eyes and fueling my questions, he said, "Just go," and told me what gear I would need for big-wall climbing.

So I showed up. I got beat down more than ever before. Tired, hungry, thirsty. I tested the limits of my body and mind. I lived in the tension of exposure, day and night. I epic-ed. I climbed a "small" wall. I bailed from a "small" wall. I learned. It was hard. The climbing was hard, finding wall partners, being in the heat... so I followed the summer season to Tuolumne Meadows.

THERE IS A LONG RIDGE OF GRANITE THAT RUNS LIKE A RIBBON ACROSS the alpine sky. Hiking below it, we traversed nearly a mile along its base. At the southern end, we put on our climbing shoes and moved upward to reverse the mile, this time climbing along the knife-edge of Matthes Crest. I followed behind, unsure, questioning my capacity to move across so much exposed terrain without a rope. My hands slotted precisely in the crack, feeling each grain of rock, a toe pressing on a crystal of quartz. Move up, reach, connect with the crack. One move more. One perfectly executed move at a time, the ground began to fall away. Fifty feet, 100, 300... Reaching the crest, we moved northward, hundreds of feet of air below to the east and west. Blue sky and the seemingly endless, sprawling alpine peaks, lakes, meadows in all directions. My breath was the only sound to be heard.

Moving this way demanded attention; it taught me awareness. Moving my body through this space created stillness in my mind. I was no longer concerned with the insecurity of wondering *if* I could do it. The question was laid out across the ridge, behind and in front of me. The answer was each move.

I felt the buzz of being fully awake for thousands of feet along this ridge. The next climb was planned by the time we walked into camp that evening. The summer strung together miles of granite, endless movement, scrambles and handjams across the Range of Light. Absolute freedom.

The possibilities were limitless. I began to explore with friends, then alone. I gained a deep understanding of my body's movements and capabilities, an awareness of precision. I got scared, got into places I wished I hadn't. And got out of those places, because I knew how. The Sierra alpine was my playground, and I felt that I could do anything.

But what could I do on the Valley's big walls? Fueled by curiosity about what was possible, I set out again, this time with that bucket list goal: to climb El Cap. Wall climbing was still hard, but it got easier. And after a couple of routes on El Cap, the goal became to climb it in a day. Then, climb harder routes in a day. And, can I climb it solo? Solo in a day? How fast can I actually climb it?

THEN QUINN FELL ON THE *NOSE*. AT THIS POINT THERE WAS A BOLT between us, but it didn't matter. She fell past me, hitting ledges and coming to a stop in the jumbled boulders at the bottom of the chimney. The rope never came tight. Perfection turned to catastrophe. I thought she was gone.

I moved to her to stabilize her and initiate the rescue. She survived something that most thought was unsurvivable. But her back was broken. Her spinal cord no longer communicates signals below her midback.

What is it actually like to be up there? Gorgeous. Awe-inspiring. Incredibly fun! Terrifying. Awful. Stupid.

As the weeks passed, I tried to climb again. I suffered from visions of falling. A body (her body, my body?) falling through the air. I cried while top-roping and could find zero motivation for climbing. What is the point of doing something so dangerous? I began to ask: Is it worth it? How could any of it be worth what happened to Quinn? I had never stopped to question if I should do these things or why I wanted to do these things. I just wanted to know what I was capable of. And I still wanted to know what I was capable of. The goals were still there, but the value was not. Somewhere along the way my values had become muddled with my goals and it was no longer obvious which stemmed from which. The chicken or the egg?

Several of our friends decided that it was not worth it for themselves. I found myself morally grappling. I had to climb. Didn't I? But I felt like I could not say, "Yes, it is worth it," because it wasn't fair. What happened to Quinn did not happen to me. What happened to me was different. I felt only emptiness. Questioning if it is worth it was like pulling on bare threads. My sense of self was beginning to unravel. It felt like an impossible question.

"HAVE YOU MOURNED THE LOSS OF THAT PERSON?" MADALEINE WAS referring to my former self: the carefree, playful human who loved scrambling through the mountains. It was an interesting question. I became curious about that person. I couldn't be so carefree. I couldn't unlive what I had been through, from Quinn's accident to the loss of other friends in climbing accidents. But parts of my former self are still there. Which parts? And which parts did I need to let go of?

I stood on the small ledge looking up at the Teflon Corner, the crux, the hardest pitch of climbing that I would have to do to climb El Capitan free. It is an aptly named, nearly featureless corner about 2,000 feet above the valley floor. Each move requires perfect body positioning, intense core tension, and a whole lot of belief in the improbability of fighting gravity with merely friction for holds.

I was scared, not because it was dangerous but because of the intensity of the exposure. And because it was hard. I always had fallen on this pitch. And falling means failure.

Taking two deep breaths, I began up the familiar sequence. My palms pressed against the rock. Powering through my shoulders, I lifted my hips a little higher, slowly bringing my foot up, just under my hand. The exposure no longer existed; it was just me and the minuscule details of the wall in front of me. A slight shift in the angle of my hips. Shuffle my palm to the next dimple in the smooth rock. Breathe but don't release core tension. The fear of challenge no longer existed; I was in it. Another subtle shift. Foot up, palm up, repeat. I reached toward the first real hold on the pitch, the final hard move. Felt my fingers connect, lock in. Heart pounding, muscles shaking. I could still fall. *This is it. Breathe. Collect yourself!* my inner voice yelled.

It meant so much not to fall, because free climbing El Cap seemed like the ultimate test. I thought it could show me what I am truly capable of. To succeed on this pitch would prove that I could do it. It would prove that after everything I'd been through, I still have what it takes. I couldn't think about falling. I couldn't think about failing. I willed myself to focus, to stay with the climbing.

As I finished the pitch, a quivering tension grew from deep in my core. There is a fine line between excitement and anxiety. The physical manifestations of the emotions are the same. The subtle difference is in the mind.

In that moment, the goal of climbing El Cap, free, became a real possibility. But this was just a practice run to work on the crux section. In order to accomplish the goal of free climbing El Cap, I would still have to climb every move for 2,000 feet up to this point perfectly, without grabbing a cam or hanging on the rope. *Then* climb the Teflon Corner. *And* another 1,000 feet, with several additional cruxes.

The intensity of understanding the whole thing, the enormous effort involved, pushed the sensation toward anxiety, then doubt. I knew what it's like up there: how hard it is, how scary. I knew it was physically possible. And I knew the emotional tax of the desire to succeed.

FROM THE SAFETY OF THE MEADOW BELOW, I LOOK UP IN AWE AT WHAT I like to call the vertical sea of granite: El Capitan. My mind drifts through past experiences. It is more like a sea than I ever realized. The memories pass in waves, ups and downs, vast exposure, a distant horizon that is certainly not the end of anything, with still so much unknown. *Is it worth the effort?* I wonder, pondering a free attempt.

Curiosity is the fire of inspiration. But this question threatens to snuff the flames. It holds me back as I wrestle with the doubt. The impossible question, again. The question that attempts to weigh the value of one experience against another experience that *could* occur instead. As if any experience in life can be isolated from the course of our existence and placed on a scale. *Is it worth it?* is the wrong question.

I cannot quantify the experience of a journey up El Cap. The experience has no specific value. It is an experience that cannot be isolated and made separate from who I am.

What's it like up there? What part of me is still intact? What am I capable of? These questions pull me together instead of tearing me apart. They light the fire, bringing excitement rather than anxiety. These questions make me want to go. They don't require a yes or no answer. Or any answer at all. Because it's never about finding the answer. It's about asking the right question, then decisively following the curiosity wherever it leads.

Curiosity is Josie McKee's inspiration. The intrigue of wild places and exploration of personal limits has drawn her on adventures around the globe. Her drive for climbing large routes began in Yosemite and led her from Patagonian peaks and Himalayan expeditions to first ascents and speed records. She worked on the Yosemite Search and Rescue team, conducting many rescues before being involved in one herself. As a wilderness EMT and technical rescue specialist, she has taught dozens of courses to help others prepare for the worst.

After spending time in Wyoming off and on for years, she moved to Lander in 2020 to challenge herself on steep limestone, explore the peaks of the Wind River Range, and work as executive director of the Central Wyoming Climbers' Alliance. She holds a flow diploma from the Flow Center and coaches others to find their personal potential.

ACKNOWLEDGMENTS

To Tim Noakes and Josh Schneider at the Stanford Special Collections and University Archives, who were instrumental in finding key archival materials and providing patient guidance. To Dougald MacDonald and Katie Sauter at the American Alpine Club, whose creativity and expertise helped bring old photos and archival materials to life. To John Rawlings, Steve Roper, Irene Beardsley, Glen Denny, Ken Yager, Dean Fidelman, John Dill, Werner and Merry Braun, Ed Hartouni, Don Harder, and John Long, whose deep knowledge of Yosemite climbing history pointed me in the direction of lesser-known climbers, stories now brought to light.

To Emily White and the entire team at Mountaineers Books, who took a leap of faith and signed an unknown author living in a tent in Camp 4. To Steven Tata, for sending magazine clips and book excerpts that fueled the initial stoke well before I ever thought I could do this. To Alexa Flower and Jane Jackson, whose encouragement of my Yosemite ambitions brought me the closest friends and best community I've ever known. To everyone with whom I've worked a Yosemite rescue, for teaching me what it means to be bold, brave, dedicated, and compassionate. To all the women with whom I've shared a rope, for demonstrating brilliance and strength and for proving time and time again that we are here, and always have been.

To my husband, Bud, whose support and acceptance of me, and whose dedication to playfulness and growth, have been the greatest gifts of my life.

To all those who entrusted in me the legacies of loved ones who are no longer on this earth, who demonstrated vulnerability and courage. To the indigenous communities for whom Ahwahnee is home, we climb on your land with grateful hearts. To the talented photographers who helped brighten these pages, so that the next generation can see more climbers who look like them.

And to this book's contributors, who opened up their hearts, who inspire us to push ourselves and never back down from our dreams, you trusted me and helped make this book happen—for that, I am eternally grateful. It has been a tremendous honor to share your stories.

GLOSSARY

In mountaineering, routes receive grades based on the type of terrain: class 3 is moderate scrambling, class 4 is more difficult scrambling, and class 5 is technical rock climbing. In the United States, rock climbs are graded using the Yosemite Decimal System, which assigns a difficulty along with the class 5 denotation. The difficulty rating can range from 0 to 15; 10 to 15 ratings are often expanded for specificity with the letters *a* through *d*. Routes rated 0 through 8 are considered moderate; 9 through 11 are intermediate; 12 and 13 routes are difficult; 14 and 15 are for experts. For instance, a 5.5 is a beginner rock climb, a 5.10a is easier than a 5.10d, and a 5.12c is easier than a 5.13a.

Large climbing routes are sometimes also given a grade to indicate their length and seriousness. These Roman numeral grades range from grade I to grade VI, though I and II are rarely used. Aid climbing has two classes, denoted with either a *C* or an *A*. *C* stands for *clean aid*, a route that does not require pitons. *A* stands for *aid* and typically requires pitons. Both types are also rated 1 to 5 for difficulty.

aid climb To climb by standing or pulling on pieces of protection placed in the rock to make upward progress.

beak A piton with a thin, tapered head used for aid climbing thin seams.

belay To protect a roped climber from falling by controlling the movement of the rope, usually involving the use of a belay device; the end of a section of climbing where a climber establishes an anchor to belay.

beta Information shared by climbers about a climbing route or area.

bivouac Often referred to as bivying; a temporary camp, usually with little cover; to camp with little cover, without a tent.

bong piton A large, angular piton.

builder To climb buildings.

boulder To climb on large boulders close to the ground without ropes.

cam A spring-loaded device used for protection in cracks.

chimney A crack large enough to fit a climber's entire body.

chockstone A rock wedged tightly into a crack.

clean To remove all the protection on a route placed by the leader.

copperhead Also aluma-head, circlehead; a small nut with a head made of soft metal on a loop of wire used in difficult aid climbing.

crimp A small handhold; to grip this type of handhold.

crux The most difficult move on or section of a climbing route or bouldering problem.

deadpoint A controlled, dynamic motion in which a climber grabs a hold overhead while maintaining contact with one or both feet.

EBs A brand of climbing shoes popular in the 1960s and 1970s.

etrier A webbing ladder for aid climbing.

free climb To climb without aid other than a rope used for protection.

free solo climb To climb without aid and without the use of a rope.

gobies Wounds incurred from crack climbing, often on the backs of hands.

handjam To put your hand in a crack and squeeze your thumb toward your palm to secure your hand in the feature.

haul bag A large bag for carrying supplies on big walls. Also called a pig.

hexentric Often referred to as a hex; a protective device consisting of an eccentric hexagonal nut attached to a wire loop.

hip belay A method of belaying in which the belayer increases friction by passing the rope around their hip or waist.

hook Equipment used to hang on small edges; to use a hook.

jam To wedge parts of or your entire body into a crack.

jug To use a mechanical ascender. Also referred to as jumaring.

jumar A mechanical ascender. *See also* jug.

kneebar A move in which a climber cams their thigh or knee against a protruding section of rock, usually with their foot pushing in an opposing direction; to use a kneebar.

layback Also lieback; to press your feet against the rock while pulling on a vertical edge; a route that requires this technique.

mantel To push down with your hands on a ledge to lift your body up onto it.

offwidth A crack that is too wide for effective handjams or footjams but is narrower than a chimney.

onsight To lead a difficult climb on the first attempt without knowing the route or moves beforehand.

pitch The portion of a climb between two belay points, typically the length of a standard rope.

piton A blade of metal used in aid climbing; common types include Lost Arrow, knifeblade, pecker or beak, and angle; also known as a pin.

prusik A hitch tied to apply friction to the rope; to use a prusik hitch to ascend a rope.

pumped A state where an accumulation of metabolic waste products in a forearm prevents the climber from gripping anything with their hand.

quickdraw Also 'draw; equipment featuring a piece of sewn material connecting two carabiners used to secure the rope to pieces of protection.

rack The set of equipment used on a climb.

redpoint To free climb a route after practicing it.

runner A loop of webbing used to attach the rope to protection.

runout The distance between a climber and the last piece of protection along a rope while leading; a route with large gaps between rock features where climbers can place protection or clip bolts.

RURP Realized Ultimate Reality Piton; a miniature piton.

sandbag A climb graded lower than many climbers believe it should be; to describe a route as easier than it is.

send To successfully climb a route.

sharp end The end of the rope attached to the lead climber.

short-fix To attach the rope to an anchor, establish a self-belay system, and continue climbing while the second follows the previous pitch.

simul-climb To climb with both climbers moving upward simultaneously.

sling A loop used to attach the rope to pieces of protection.

splitter A parallel-sided crack.

stem To press your hands and feet outward on widely spaced holds on opposing rock faces; common in corners or dihedrals.

Sticht plate A friction belaying device consisting of a flat plate with holes.

stopper A wedge-shaped nut used for protection.

swami belt An early harness consisting of a long length of webbing wrapped around the climber's body and secured with a knot.

TCU Three-cam unit; a small camming device manufactured by Metolius.

top rope To climb with the rope running through an anchor fixed above.

whipper A long lead fall above the last piece of protection.

zipper A lead fall in which pieces of protection pop out in sequence.

SOURCES

The editor has made every effort to track down and credit the copyright holders of the previously published stories. Stories without an attribution were written for this collection or previously unpublished, and all the stories, both new and previously published, are printed with permission.

Cohen, Valerie Mendenhall, ed. *Woman on the Rocks: The Mountaineering Letters of Ruth Dyar Mendenhall.* Bishop, CA: Spotted Dog Press, 2007.

Cranor, Maria. "Sandbagged by the Stonemasters." Patagonia catalog, 2010.

Davis, Steph. *High Infatuation: A Climber's Guide to Love and Gravity*. Seattle: Mountaineers Books, 2007.

Farquhar, Marjory Bridge. "Pioneer Woman Rock Climber and Sierra Club Director." Interview by Ann Lage, February 9, 1977. Sierra Club Oral History Project, Sierra Club Women Series. San Francisco, CA.

Flower, Alexa. "Yield Point." *Alpinist* 60 (Winter 2017).

Hechtel, Sibylle. "Walls Without Balls." In *Ordeal by Piton: Writings from the Golden Age of Yosemite Climbing*, edited by Steve Roper, 262–266. Stanford, CA: Stanford University Libraries, 2003. Previously published as "Untitled," *American Alpine Journal*, 1974.

Higgins, Molly. "My First Time." In *Yosemite Climber*, edited by George Meyers, 54–81. Newcastle upon Tyne, UK: Diadem Books, 1979.

Hill, Lynn, with Greg Child. *Climbing Free: My Life in the Vertical World.* New York: W. W. Norton, 2003.

Kerr, Eliza. "Letter from a Mother to Her Village." Patagonia catalog, 2018.

Little, Meredith. "Crackdown in Camp 4." Little family private collection.

Meek, Hope Morehouse. "We Were the Jewels." Meek family private collection.

prAna. "Sarah Watson: Humbled by Yosemite." Produced by James Q Martin, July 17, 2012. Video, 4:26. www.youtube.com/watch?v=gtlBt1jR2NU.

Robbins, Liz. "First Ascent." *Alpinist* 23 (Spring 2008).

Roper, Steve. *Camp 4: Recollections of a Yosemite Rockclimber.* Seattle: Mountaineers Books, 2004.

Vogel, Bea. Interview by John Rawlings, August 20, 1997. Stanford Alpine Club Oral History Interviews. Department of Special Collections and University Archives, Stanford University Libraries, Stanford, CA.

IN GRATITUDE

Thank you to the many donors whose generosity supports transforming lives through books like *Valley of Giants*. Our giving levels were inspired by the names of these stories. To learn more about how you can support the publication of powerful stories and outdoor adventure by Mountaineers Books, please visit mountaineersbooks.org/donate.

Pioneering Peaks ($1,000)

Marci and Don Heck
Mark Kroese and Lisa Tillman
Anonymous, In Honor of Dick Hayek

Walls Without Balls ($500)

Regan Chewning
Art Freeman
Donald Immerwahr
Michael Riley
Anne Smart and Frank McCord
Christine Spang
Vera and Jon Wellner

Leading Ladies ($250)

John Andresen
John Cashin
Virginia Felton
Carla Firey
Monica W. Gerber
Donald Goodman, In Memory of Diana Dailey

Linda Lewis and Polly Powledge
Gin and Ed Lucas
Doug McCall
Steve and Colleen McClure
John Ohlson
Matthew Ray
Tom Shimko
Seitz-Subramanian Family
Mary Stout
Carol Thomas
LaVerne Woods

Girls Can Be Dirtbags ($100)

Gianna Cannataro and Gabe Aeschliman
Molly Bauer
Alexa Jane Cantwell
Helen and Arnie Cherullo
Piera Damonte
Donna DeShazo
Danielle Graham and Lelia Pedersen
Lillian M. Harris
Colleen Hinton
Homestretch Foundation
Raymond B. Huey
Alyssa Kuraishi
Ger Potze
Manisha Powar and Vineeth Madhusudanan
Maura Rendes and David Johnson
Mindy Roberts
Hanke Roos
Siula Hendrickson Sperry
Terence Stanuch
Gail Storey
Una Toledo
Elizabeth Watson

INDEX

ABOUT THE EDITOR

ALEXA FLOWER

Lauren DeLaunay Miller was raised on the East Coast, hating dirt and sweat and never having had a single thought about mountains, ever—until she picked up a copy of *National Geographic* in a doctor's office and discovered the world of Yosemite big-wall climbing. Since then, Lauren has dedicated much of her life to climbing and exploring the mountains of the world, focusing on the granite walls that originally enticed her. She has climbed dozens of big walls, including the first one-day all-female ascent of the *Triple Direct* on El Capitan, the same route that saw the first all-female ascent of El Cap forty-three years prior. Lauren's love for Yosemite climbing brought her to the Yosemite Search and Rescue team, where the longing to document the stories of her climbing foremothers took hold.

She is deeply involved in her beloved climbing community, serving as the vice president of the Bishop Area Climbers Coalition and as an event coordinator for the American Alpine Club (AAC). Her creative work has been featured in the *Climbing Zine*, and she is a regional editor for the AAC's publications, the *American Alpine Journal*, *Accidents in North American Climbing*, and the Cutting Edge podcast. As a journalist, Lauren is dedicated to righting the wrongs of underrepresentation. She craves stories that capture the spirit of our natural world and emphasize marginalized communities. Lauren is currently pursuing a master's in journalism at the University of California, Berkeley. When not in school, she lives in Bishop, California, with her husband, Bud, and their rescue dog, Bodie.

recreation • lifestyle • conservation

MOUNTAINEERS BOOKS is a leading publisher of mountaineering literature and guides—including our flagship title, *Mountaineering: The Freedom of the Hills*—as well as adventure narratives, natural history, and general outdoor recreation. Through our two imprints, Skipstone and Braided River, we also publish titles on sustainability and conservation. We are committed to supporting the environmental and educational goals of our organization by providing expert information on human-powered adventure, sustainable practices at home and on the trail, and preservation of wilderness.

The Mountaineers, founded in 1906, is a 501(c)(3) nonprofit outdoor recreation and conservation organization whose mission is to enrich lives and communities by helping people "explore, conserve, learn about, and enjoy the lands and waters of the Pacific Northwest and beyond." One of the largest such organizations in the United States, it sponsors classes and year-round outdoor activities throughout the Pacific Northwest, including climbing, hiking, backcountry skiing, snowshoeing, camping, kayaking, sailing, and more. The Mountaineers also supports its mission through its publishing division, Mountaineers Books, and promotes environmental education and citizen engagement. For more information, visit The Mountaineers Program Center, 7700 Sand Point Way NE, Seattle, WA 98115-3996; phone 206-521-6001; www.mountaineers.org; or email info@mountaineers.org.

Our publications are made possible through the generosity of donors and through sales of 700 titles on outdoor recreation, sustainable lifestyle, and conservation. To donate, purchase books, or learn more, visit us online:

MOUNTAINEERS BOOKS

1001 SW Klickitat Way, Suite 201 • Seattle, WA 98134

800-553-4453 • mbooks@mountaineersbooks.org • www.mountaineersbooks.org

An independent nonprofit publisher since 1960

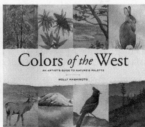